WHEN ROOSEVELT PL

TO GOVERN FRANCE

WHEN ROOSEVELT PLANNED TO GOVERN FRANCE

Charles L. Robertson

University of Massachusetts Press

Amherst and Boston

LC 2011021550
ISBN 978-1-55849-881-5 (paper); 880-8 (library cloth)

Designed by Steve Dyer
Set in New Caledonia and Linotype Didot
by House of Equations, Inc.
Printed and bound by Thomson-Shore, Inc.

Library of Congress Cataloging-in-Publication Data
Robertson, Charles L., 1927–
When Roosevelt planned to govern France / Charles L. Robertson.
    p. cm.
Includes bibliographical references and index.
ISBN 978-1-55849-881-5 (pbk. : alk. paper) —
ISBN 978-1-55849-880-8 (library cloth : alk. paper)
1. World War, 1939–1945 — Diplomatic history. 2. France — History —
German occupation, 1940–1945. 3. Allied Military Government.
4. United States — Foreign relations — France. 5. France — Foreign relations —
United States. 6. Roosevelt, Franklin D. (Franklin Delano), 1882–1945.
7. Gaulle, Charles de, 1890–1970. I. Title.
D752.R58 2011
940.53'44—dc23   2011021550

British Library Cataloguing in Publication
data are available.

Contents

PREFACE

SITTING AT A DINNER TABLE IN A PARIS APARTMENT IN 1979 I listened while an aged former member of General de Gaulle's wartime entourage told me how, at the time of liberation in 1944, he and several others had turned back a ship crammed with American military government personnel and bales of documents, all destined to establish an American-run military government in liberated France, one that would last for up to a year until elections could take place to determine a genuinely legitimate government for the country. My dinner partner boasted that, standing on the quay with the others, he had sent the Americans packing with all their equipment and elaborate documentation. Behind the lines, French sovereignty would be preserved; only Frenchmen would administer France, and only those Frenchmen approved by de Gaulle's Provisional Government of France, which the Americans had so far stubbornly refused to recognize as such. General de Gaulle, my new acquaintance went on, had prevented a second and inevitably unpopular occupation of France, this time by the Americans. The whole absurd and regrettable incident was the result of Franklin D. Roosevelt's irrational dislike and distrust of de Gaulle, whom the American president was determined not to impose on the French. Roosevelt, he said, was convinced that de Gaulle would find he had no support in France once the Allied armies drove out the Germans. "You Americans," he scoffed, "knew nothing about France!"

I was amused and somewhat skeptical. Being in no position to argue with him, however, I laughed weakly and put the matter aside. But twenty-five years later, during the sixtieth-anniversary celebrations of the August 1944 liberation of the city, I was to hear several panelists on television shows assert that de Gaulle had blocked an American military government for France, including one declaration to that effect by Larry Collins and Dominique LaPierre, authors of the 1965 best-seller *Is Paris Burning?* No

American that I knew remembered the incident, but it obviously lingered in the memory of French historians, journalists, and public figures.

In the respected *Monde Diplomatique* of May 2003, I read a front-page article by the prominent Sorbonne historian Annie Lacroix-Riz, who wrote: "In 1941–42 the United States intended that France, together with soon-to-be defeated Italy, Germany, and Japan, was to be part of a protectorate run by the Allied Military Government of the Occupied Territories (AMGOT). According to the agreement of November 1942 between Admiral Jean-François Darlan and U.S. General Mark Clark, which secured France's commitment to the Allied cause, AMGOT would have abolished its national sovereignty, including its right to issue currency." This seemed to me ridiculous on the face of it, and made me more skeptical, but by now I was also curious, particularly when I discovered that other French historians—in addition to Lacroix-Riz—appeared to believe that the United States had supported an effort launched late in the war by Vichy France's hated prime minister Pierre Laval to re-create a Third Republic government headed by the old Radical-Socialist leader, Édouard Herriot, which would be in place to greet American liberators when they reached Paris, thereby forestalling the installation of de Gaulle's Provisional Government.

This book is the result of my determination to find out—to the extent possible—the truth of the matter. I knew that the United States government had created military governments in Sicily and Italy, and would ultimately follow suit in Germany and Austria. An American Military Government for Occupied Territories was a reality. (I was myself in the American army of occupation in Germany.) But was AMGOT really envisaged for a liberated country, France, as so many French still seemed to think? Since no such military government was ever established, what, in the event, happened?

Luckily I was able to find ample documentation in the library of the Fondation Charles de Gaulle on the rue Solférino in Paris, and in its publication, *Espoir*, where many former members of the Gaullist World War II movement published their recollection of the events of the time, with their views on Allied policy. Charles de Gaulle, of course, told his side of the story, accompanied by a wide collection of documents, in his three-volume *Mémoires de guerre*. The extraordinary Archives nationales contained exhaustive files of telegrams, memos, and letters of members of the Gaullist movement, and in particular, once de Gaulle had shifted his headquarters from London to Algiers in mid-1943, the thousands of messages that flowed between the offices and the embassy he still maintained in London and his new base of operations in Algiers. There were also numerous messages between these two headquarters and emissaries who had been sent into occupied France. The library of Documentation française provided further information.

For the American side of the story, the State Department's extensive collection of documents in the volumes on relations with Europe during the war years, *Foreign Relations of the United States: Diplomatic Papers,* provided much of the story, while the Department of the Army's series of histories of the U.S. Army in World War II included in its "Special Studies" a volume edited by Harry L. Coles and Albert K. Weinberg titled *Civil Affairs: Soldiers Become Governors.* It constitutes an exhaustive collection of relevant documents on the planning, the infighting, and the diplomacy of the whole issue of what to do behind the battle lines as the armies moved forward. The "History of the Second World War" series provides the British equivalent of Coles and Weinberg in two volumes by F. S. V. Donnison, *Civil Affairs and Military Government.* In addition I relied heavily on numerous memoirs of participants on all sides of the story and many of the hundreds of French, British, and American secondary sources on the period, all of which are listed in the notes. On the French side these included, in particular, works by Jean-Louis Crémieux-Brilhac, André Kaspi, François Kersaudy, and Jean-Paul Cointet, and on the American side, Julian G. Hurstfield, Arthur Layton Funk, Robert O. Paxton and Nicholas Wahl, Milton Viorst, Mario Rossi, and Hal Vaughan.

I am grateful for the help of many people: my wife, Denise Rochat, who read and reread the book in manuscript and made numerous useful suggestions; Hal Vaughan, who shared my interest in the era and provided constant comment and encouragement; Guillaume Papazoglou, the librarian of the Fondation Charles de Gaulle, who guided me to sources in *Espoir;* the friendly and accommodating staff at the Archives nationales; and the staff of the University of Massachusetts Press.

I have, in many cases where quotations were in French, provided my own translations and occasionally included the original French to give a better idea of the flavor of the quotation. Errors and omissions are, of course, my own. I must add that my admiration for the great protagonists of this story—Charles de Gaulle, Franklin D. Roosevelt, and Winston Churchill, with all their faults, mistakes, and prejudices—knows no bounds.

WHEN ROOSEVELT PLANNED
TO GOVERN FRANCE

Introduction

Roosevelt's and French Views on AMGOT

I N A MAY 8, 1943, MEMORANDUM TO WINSTON CHURCHILL, Franklin D. Roosevelt wrote: "I am inclined to think that when we get into France itself we will have to regard it as a military occupation run by British and American generals. . . . [T]he top line, or national administration must be kept in the hands of the British or American Commander-in-Chief. I think that this may be necessary for six months or even a year after we get into France, thus giving time to build up for an election and a new form of government."[1]

This memorandum makes it clear: a year before the liberation of France, Franklin D. Roosevelt was convinced that the Anglo-Americans should create a temporary military government for France under the Allied commander in chief, who in the event turned out to be General Dwight D. Eisenhower. That government would work with whatever local civilian authorities it found in power, apart from those who had clearly collaborated with the Germans. Moreover, in England and in the United States, schools created by the British and American administrations were training military government and civil affairs personnel to take over the governments not only of occupied territories such as Germany and Austria but also of France, a liberated country. The English schools prepared information handbooks for all French communities, and American editions were issued with a preface by Brigadier General Walter Bedell Smith, who would become General

Eisenhower's chief of staff. The British and American armies, it seemed, would be prepared to carry out President Roosevelt's wishes.

As late as November 1943, Roosevelt wrote in the same vein to Secretary of State Cordell Hull and significantly, as far as the French were concerned, continued to use the term "occupation." The president's memo to Hull read, "The thought that the occupation when it occurs should be wholly military is one to which I am increasingly inclined."[2] But six months were to pass before D-Day.

D-Day, June 6, 1944: the scene is familiar from hundreds of newsreels, books, and movies. With a fleet of six thousand ships behind them and hundreds of Allied planes filling the skies, Allied paratroopers landed behind German lines in Normandy, while at five separate beaches Allied troops—British, Canadian, Polish, and American—struggled through the surf to gain a foothold on Normandy shores that were littered with German mines and traps of all kind, all of this under deadly crossfire from hundreds of German strong points. Early in the day General Dwight D. Eisenhower had broadcast a proclamation to the soldiers, sailors, and airmen of the Allied Expeditionary Forces: "You are about to embark on the great crusade toward which we have striven these many months. The eyes of the world are upon you. The hopes and prayers of liberty-loving peoples march with you." He ended: "I have full confidence in your courage, devotion to duty and skill in battle. We will accept nothing less than full victory! Good luck! And let us all beseech the blessing of Almighty God upon this great and noble undertaking."[3] Despite meticulous preparation and successful deception—Hitler was convinced that the Allies would land to the north, at the Pas de Calais, and kept crack German units there—their success was no foregone conclusion: poor weather made it a close thing, and Eisenhower, in command of the whole gigantic, complicated, bloody project, had tucked a handwritten note into his shirt pocket, just in case. It read: "Our landings in the Cherbourg-Havre area have failed to gain a satisfactory foothold and I have withdrawn the troops. My decision to attack at this time and place was based upon the best information available. The troops, the air and the navy did all that bravery and devotion to duty could do. If any blame or fault attaches to the attempt it is mine alone."[4]

Winston Churchill, harking back to the difficulties of previous amphibious landings and wary of the strength of the German forces now facing the Allies, was dubious about the success of the landings. As we all know, however, Eisenhower never had to broadcast his brief note. Despite heavy losses, the landings succeeded, and by the end of the day, 155,000 Allied soldiers were ashore, along with their equipment, never to be dislodged. Owing in part to German hesitation and confusion, and in part to concerted action by the French Resistance, German reinforcements were slow in reaching the area; and owing in part to the horrific Allied bombing of German cities and production facilities, the Luftwaffe was kept busy elsewhere, so the Allies had clear command of the skies. Still, it took considerably longer than planned for Allied troops to break out of the beachhead, and for several days success still remained in doubt.

Less well known is that in the midst of this enormous and incredibly complicated project, a meeting between Eisenhower and General Charles de Gaulle resulted in a fracas involving Churchill and de Gaulle that would last almost the whole night before the D-Day landings. In Eisenhower's proposed broadcast to the French people, edited by the State Department, the French population was told to obey his orders as Supreme Commander. The State Department, a bulwark of anti-Gaullism in the American administration, had taken out of the original draft any mention of either de Gaulle or his recently renamed Provisional Government of the French Republic. De Gaulle was supposed to follow Eisenhower's speech with his own proclamation but now refused angrily: he would appear to be endorsing what he called an imposition of "Allied Military Government of Occupied Territories" upon France. Since 40 million copies of the proclamation had already been printed and the speech recorded, there was no opportunity to revise it.

De Gaulle's refusal to broadcast at the time allotted him, and then his decision to allow only a handful of his liaison officers to accompany the landings, infuriated Prime Minister Winston Churchill, already on edge about the landings, and resulted in bitter exchanges between Churchill's headquarters and de Gaulle's lodgings in London. De Gaulle finally broadcast to the people of France that night (but restricted the number of his liaison officers who were to accompany the Allied forces): "The supreme battle is under way. . . . It is, of course, the battle of France and France's battle. . . . France, submerged for four years, but not diminished, nor vanquished, France is standing upright to take part. . . . For the sons of France, wherever they are, whoever they are, the simple and sacred duty is to fight by all the means they have. . . . For the nation[,] . . . instructions given by the French government and French leaders who have been authorized to give them must be exactly followed." Then came the magnificent finish: "Behind the cloud so heavy with our blood and our tears, the sunshine of our grandeur reappears!"[5]

One sentence in the speech, "instructions given by the French government and French leaders who have been authorized to give them must be exactly followed," conflicted directly with Eisenhower's instructions to the French to follow his own orders, and indirectly with his declaration that only after France was liberated would the French choose their own leaders and form of government. In the event, as Allied armies eventually moved forward, French Provisional Government administrators quickly moved in to reestablish a republican order, and there were basically only minor conflicts between the French administrators and the British and American civil affairs officers who accompanied the armies. De Gaulle's administrators were by and large accepted by the French as the older Vichy administration faded away. No AMGOT or its equivalent ever appeared.

Yet among French officials attached to de Gaulle who wrote their memoirs and to historians who followed, the threat of AMGOT appears to have been a real one, blocked only by the action of de Gaulle's lieutenants and his own stubbornness. De Gaulle himself would write in 1956: "Roosevelt persisted in denying us the quality of being the French authority at the time of liberation. . . . [T]he refusal . . . covered, in reality, the *idée fixe* of the president of the United States to institute in France his arbitration. . . . In the United States an allied military government (AMGOT) was being created, destined to take in hand the administration of France."[6] He also apparently believed that the United States supported a failed last-minute effort by Vichy prime minister Pierre Laval to create an acceptable new government in Paris that would be there to greet the Allied armies, thus forestalling a Gaullist takeover. For de Gaulle, Eisenhower's hesitation in ordering troops to enter Paris was clear evidence that Roosevelt had held him back to see whether Laval's maneuvers might succeed.[7]

According to André Gros, who was a member of the negotiating team for a civil affairs agreement at the time of the Normandy landings, a former jurist at the French Foreign Office, and later a judge of the International Court of Justice,

an AMGOT plan was prepared by the United State and the United Kingdom to establish in France alone and not in the other liberated

Allied countries an Anglo-American system of military government from the moment of landing and until the constitution of a new French authority, a military government that would have assumed administration of the territory and the population of France. . . . De Gaulle, between the fourth and fourteenth of June 1944, settled the sinister issue of AMGOT[,] . . . *précis* of a reconquered France which would have to carry out the orders of the commander in chief, General Eisenhower.[8]

In a publication of the Fondation Charles de Gaulle, Diane de Bellescize of Le Havre University wrote that the gradual creation of a French provisional government beginning in 1943 had a double objective: that of preventing an anarchy that would favor the communists and of blocking Allied plans: "The Allies had foreseen putting in place their AMGOT, based on the example of Italy, with well-trained English or American administrative officers who had taken courses at schools in Wimbledon and Charlottesville and were ready to assume power. Equally plausible was the menace of a Vichy government more or less purged of its most radical elements, supported by the Americans."[9]

In his memoirs Claude Hettier de Boislambert, a trusted aide of de Gaulle's, goes the furthest. He writes that on May 15, 1944—three weeks before D-Day—his swift perusal of the ultra-secret Allied "Civil Affairs Handbook" revealed the exorbitant character of Allied pretensions as "not merely an interference in our affairs but a total taking in hand of the administration of France down to the smallest detail." In particular, "there would be Allied money, officers acting as mayors, municipal finance run by our liberators, our railroads, our post office, our networks of distribution, all the infrastructure of the country would be in the hands of those who would not fail to be quickly called 'our new occupiers.'"[10] In yet another article referring to the "Civil Affairs Handbook," Charles-Louis Foulon, a historian previously in charge of preparing the administrative apparatus in France at the time of liberation, added that "the legislative chapter foresees that French nationals would be judged by Allied military tribunals."[11]

The Gaullist writings would have their lasting influence both in France and elsewhere. As late as October 14, 2003, the website of Miquelon.org, a French-Canadian-based watchdog group "dedicated to documenting French-bashing and anti-French activity," stated simply:

When the Allies liberated France from German occupation, their intention was not to give France back to the French. Instead, they planned to install an Allied Military Government of Occupied Territory, or Amgot. This scheme for postwar transition would give the Allies control over currency, transport, the appointment of civil servants[,] and war tribunals in formerly occupied countries. They assumed that the French would accept Amgot, given the shape the country was in. When the liberators landed, the paper money had already been printed.

Was President Roosevelt really ready to install a military government in France at the time of liberation? Did the Gaullist officials really expect an AMGOT to be established in France? Did de Gaulle—as André Gros writes—really block it only in the days between the June 4 and 14, 1944? Or is there evidence for a rather different story?

To answer these questions, this book reexamines the growth of the meager Free French movement created by General Charles de Gaulle in 1940 into a full-fledged government-in-exile, during which time President Roosevelt, partly under the influence of his closest advisers, partly as a result of a series of wartime developments, grew to distrust de Gaulle as a self-important irritant with dictatorial ambitions, to the point where he tried any number of ways to prevent de Gaulle from coming to power. It demonstrates that de Gaulle had one basic aim: to overcome the consequences of the defeat of France in 1940 by turning his ad hoc military movement into a vigorous, revived French government-in-exile that could define and defend French interests at the end of the war, a task he could not depend on the Allies to carry out. This revived government would also be able to participate in the international conferences that would draft the peace treaties and shape the postwar world. France would rejoin the powers. All of this clashed directly with Roosevelt's conclusion after the fall of France in 1940 that it was largely finished as a world power, that no new legitimate French government could be established until the French people had a chance to assert themselves through free elections, and that events would show that de Gaulle simply did not have the support within France that he claimed to have. Throughout the war years Roosevelt—with an almost flippant arrogance—meddled in French affairs, trying to dictate the course of events.

What this book also shows is how the interplay of complex events and personalities eventually led to a situation in which a frustrated Roosevelt was unable to block a highly popular de Gaulle from establishing his administrators throughout liberated France and entering a newly liberated Paris, where he was greeted rapturously, and to which he soon moved his government from Algiers. It was all contrary to Roosevelt's explicit view that de Gaulle had little real support and would fade into obscurity.

For some reason unknown to anyone but himself, perhaps because he found it difficult to admit he had been wrong, Roosevelt still hesitated to recognize de Gaulle's Provisional Government. Not until six weeks after de Gaulle entered Paris and put his government to work did he do so. When de Gaulle was informed of the move and asked for his reaction, the French president said dryly, "I am satisfied that the government is to be called by its own name."[12] Roosevelt's long opposition to de Gaulle, and his hesitation at the end, gave enough ammunition for French authors to insist that up to the time of the D-Day landings, the Allies were still ready to install a military government in France or else support the last-minute moves by Vichy leaders Marshal Henri-Philippe Pétain and Pierre Laval to create a French government acceptable to the Allies. What is true is that across the years, the contentious General de Gaulle, who had started as an unknown on June 18, 1940, with nothing—almost no money, and almost no one at his side—outmaneuvered the man who headed one of the two most powerful nations in the world. As one Frenchman put it, "FDR's knowledge of the general never went beyond the caricature that his entourage traced for him."[13] He did apparently envision having Americans govern France for six months to a year and to reach out to other Frenchmen besides those who supported de Gaulle. But even though no one on the spot was really ready to install an AMGOT or anything like it, the belief still exists among many of the French that it was a close thing. There were, it will be shown, political reasons for maintaining and perpetuating this view.

CHAPTER I

America and the Fall of France

WHY DID GENERAL CHARLES DE GAULLE BECOME anathema to President Franklin D. Roosevelt? Why did the American president do all he could to keep the Frenchman from assuming power, including proposing an American military government in France at the time of liberation? What lay behind the American view that General de Gaulle had no support in France?

The events of 1940 had much to do with Americans' wartime attitudes toward France, and in particular those of leading American officials, including the president. In the spring of that year, in the space of six weeks, the unbelievable happened: the French Third Republic suffered a crushing defeat at the hands of Nazi Germany. It was unbelievable because at the time, almost nobody thought that such a collapse could take place. The worst that could happen would be a stalemate that would lead to peace negotiations.

Moreover, in retrospect, it should never have happened. It was true that France had lost 1.3 million soldiers in World War I, with as many soldiers wounded, and 400,000 civilians. It had suffered bitter internal political divisions all through the 1930s. But in 1940 France still appeared to be a great power, if a reluctant one. It had the second-largest empire in the world, on whose manpower and resources it could draw. Its modern navy was four times the size of the German navy, twice the size of the Italian, and equal to that of the Japanese. Its army had been characterized in 1938 by Winston Churchill as "the most perfectly trained and mobile force in Europe."[1] For years the French government had spent millions on constructing along its German frontier the impregnable Maginot Line—which Churchill, after visiting it, declared was a guarantee of "absolute security against the horrors of invasion"—and French troops and tanks were ready to move forward across the adjacent Belgian frontier to take up defensive positions in Holland and Belgium if the Germans attempted to circumvent the Maginot fortifications.[2] Despite what many have written, the French had more and better tanks than the Germans; their air force was at least equal in numbers and would be supplemented in time of war by squadrons of superb British Spitfire and Hurricane fighters, and several hundred new American fighters were in the pipeline.[3] The Allies could field more divisions than the Germans. In March 1938, when Hitler invaded Czechoslovakia, American ambassador William C. Bullitt had wired President Roosevelt that in the face of the new inevitability of war, the spirit of the French people was "incomparably better than in 1914," and he wrote of their "quiet courage."[4]

The Allies were buoyed by the resistance tiny Finland put up against the far more numerous Soviet attackers in the Winter War of 1939–40: the defense, it appeared, could hold out.[5] In light of all this, even German military leaders, who had told Hitler they would not be ready for war before 1942, were convinced that the gamble they were taking in launching their attack in May 1940 wouldn't pay off; the German chief of staff suggested that the odds were ten to one against success, and his field commanders expressed doubts that they would succeed.[6] But their unexpected attack through the supposedly impenetrable Ardennes forest and across the deep gorge of the Meuse River, bypassing the Maginot Line, worked. Allied forces were cut in two as the Germans rushed across northern France to the sea, severing Allied communications to the armies that had moved north, to defensive positions in Holland and Belgium.

Panic ensued in France, which was unprepared for anything of this sort. Ambassador Bullitt wired President Roosevelt: "It seems obvious that . . . the French army will be crushed utterly. . . . [I]n order to escape from the ultimate consequences of absolute defeat, the British may install a government of Oswald Mosley and the union of British fascists which would cooperate fully with Hitler. That would mean the British navy would be against us."[7] Later he reported what French prime minister Paul

Reynaud had told him: within two months the war would end with a total defeat of France and England. With France conquered, German submarines and bombers operating from French bases would strangle England, Hitler would establish Nazi governments in South America, and the United States would face the same situation France now faced.[8] All of this was accompanied by frantic and useless pleas for immediate aid, for a declaration of war by the United States, for a flood of airplanes and American pilots. The Germans, Reynaud claimed hysterically, had a ten-to-one superiority in planes. Unreality dominated.[9]

German intelligence had accurately predicted that the French High Command would be too slow to react to the German attack through the Ardennes, and the Allies were never able to regroup and mount a serious counterattack. On June 14 the Germans entered an undefended Paris. On June 18 the new French government, headed by World War I hero Marshal Pétain, temporarily quartered in the southwest of France in Bordeaux, asked for an armistice. It was signed four days later in Compiègne, where the armistice that ended World War I had been signed by a defeated Germany. Flushed with their almost inconceivable success, the Germans—like Ambassador Bullitt—now expected Britain either to sue for peace or to fall within six weeks. Knowing that British soldiers had left most of their equipment in France on the beaches of Dunkirk at the time of their escape from the continent, French general Maxime Weygand declared, "Three weeks after we sign an armistice, the English will be on their knees!"[10] To young General de Gaulle, Weygand said, "When I'm beaten here, England won't wait a week to negotiate with the Reich."[11] Admiral Jean-François Darlan, head of the French navy, told Bullitt he "felt absolutely certain that Great Britain would be completely conquered by Germany within five weeks unless Great Britain should surrender sooner."[12] And Reynaud, who had just resigned as prime minister, told the American chargé, Anthony Biddle, that he should explain to Washington that without an American intervention, England was lost; Lord Halifax would replace Winston Churchill, and he would become the English Pétain.[13] Earlier, when Winston Churchill informed a Franco-British meeting on June 11 that Britain would fight on if France fell, Anthony Eden recorded that General Weygand tried politely to conceal his skepticism, while Marshal Pétain, soon to become France's prime minister, was "mockingly incredulous. . . . [H]is attitude was obviously *'c'est de la blague!'* [what a joke!]."[14]

· · · ·

The rapid defeat of the mighty French army was an astounding event: it bolstered Hitler's still shaky hold over the German High Command, shattered the traditional French enemy, and greatly boosted the morale of the German public, which had been depressed at the thought of a new war so soon after the disastrous one of 1914–1918. But even more, as many people failed to realize, it overturned the entire structure of world power. Nazi Germany now dominated continental Europe and had access to all the resources of Europe and French North Africa. It received a steady flow of raw materials from Soviet Russia, and the armies of its ally Italy, attacking across Egypt from their colony Libya, threatened to take the Suez Canal. Control of the oil-rich Middle East seemed to lie within Hitler's grasp. General Francisco Franco, Spain's leader, owed much of his success in the Spanish civil war of 1936–1940 to material support from Germany and Italy. If he now acceded to Hitler's request that German armies be allowed to cross Spain, the great British base at Gibraltar might well fall, making the Mediterranean a closed Axis sea and allowing the Germans to use the French naval base in Dakar, on the bulge of West Africa. German submarines using Dakar would have far greater leeway in the Atlantic and closer access to the major German-influenced governments of Brazil and Argentina. With ports in Norway, Germany, France, and Dakar, and with the Mediterranean closed, German submarines could indeed cut off any attempt to supply England from either the United States or the British Empire.

Many in England understood this and feared the worst. Churchill had to convince cabinet members, including his foreign secretary, the wavering Lord Halifax, that his government should not explore what Hitler's terms for peace would be. Duff Cooper, Churchill's minister of information, later wrote: "We were very near to defeat that summer. There were many who never knew it, there are as many, perhaps more, who prefer not to remember it."[15] According to Harold Macmillan, then in the Ministry of Supply, "it needed stout hearts to resist some degree of alarm and despondency."[16] The chief of the Imperial General Staff told Anthony Eden, Churchill's secretary of war, that he did not believe "we could hold out alone for more than a few months" and added, "This is the end of the British Empire." Under Churchill's leadership, however, Britain did hold out. Six months later, after the fall of France and after England and its Royal Air Force had thwarted Hitler's invasion plans by a hair's breadth, Eden's diary entry for December 19, 1940, reads: "Winston was tired but cheerful. We spoke of the dark days of summer. I told him that [Air Marshal Charles] Portal and I had confessed to each other that in our hearts we had both despaired at one time. Winston said 'yes, normally I wake up buoyant to face the new day. Then I awoke with dread in my heart.'"[17]

Among other consequences of the fall of France, in the Far East the French defeat gave the Japanese the chance to obtain a toehold in French Indochina, bringing them closer to the coveted oil, rubber, and minerals of Southeast Asia and to Australia and provided them with a new jumping-off point. As a consequence, everywhere the Axis seemed triumphant, its worldwide influence growing. With the Soviet Union neutral but cooperating with Germany, the only hope that existed among those determined to reverse the Axis hegemony lay in the far-off United States of America. Britain, alone and still undefeated, could certainly not do it.

In those United States, however, isolationism reigned. President Franklin D. Roosevelt had warned the French government earlier that his hands were tied. He faced a third-term election in the fall of 1940, the year that France collapsed. Knowing that a majority of Americans hoped that England would win but 85 percent were against becoming involved in the war, knowing also the extent of isolationist sentiment in key states and in the Congress, he had only sent messages of encouragement to the frantic pleas for help that had come from the French in their desperate hour of need. There was no way he could get a declaration of war. Even materially, there was no way he could have sent the "clouds of airplanes" for which Prime Minister Reynaud had pleaded on the night of June 3. Like many European leaders, Roosevelt wondered when the fog would fall upon Britain, what forces the British had left to repel a German attack.[18]

As a result, support for Britain would have to be carefully managed. Little else could be expected. It was even uncertain whether the airplanes ordered by the French before the defeat could now be shifted to the British. Few among American voters understood how far the balance of world politics had shifted in six weeks, and those who did were divided on what to do: aid England to resist the Nazis or concentrate on strengthening America's defenses at home. Many, including the chief of the Army Air Force, General Henry "Hap" Arnold, thought that military materiel sent to a soon-to-be-defeated England would simply be lost when England went down and could better be used in preparation for defense of the United States against the Nazis, which would then become necessary. General Arnold, in the midst of frantic and disparate efforts to increase the relatively diminutive American air power, had long resisted giving the French and English the planes they wanted—in 1939 they had ordered 1,500, and by March 1940 their orders totaled 5,500—at a time when American productive and training facilities were minimal and expansion was haphazard.[19] Outside of government, the two currents of thought were represented by two organizations, the Committee to Defend America by Aiding the Allies and, on the opposite side, America First, for which the all-American hero Charles A. Lindbergh was a prime spokesman.

To a great many Americans, and certainly for Franklin D. Roosevelt, the incredible collapse of France showed that it was finished as a power of any kind in any future world. How to explain the disintegration of what had been and was supposed to be such a great military power? If the efficacy of the so-called fifth column—that is, internal traitors who sabotaged the war effort—was one popular explanation in both France and the United States, the view that the whole French social and political structure must have been rotten was far more widespread.[20] This view led directly to the idea that for any foreseeable future, France no longer really counted as a player on the world scene. The disillusion that had followed American participation in the Great War of 1914–1918 was only reinforced. "The Last Time I Saw Paris," the nostalgic Jerome Kern–Oscar Hammerstein song, popular among expatriates who had returned to the United States, was simply a requiem.

The reaction does much to explain Roosevelt's subsequent relations with France and its potential leader, Charles de Gaulle. Roosevelt had learned French and visited France both in his youth and during the Great War, when he came close to the front lines and admired the valor and courage of French soldiers, and he attended the Versailles peace conference in 1919. As a result he had a sentimental attachment to France typical of his class, but was disappointed at British and French reactions to the rise of the fascist states in the 1930s. He was also convinced at the outbreak of the war that Hitler's Germany was a threat to the United States as well as to Europe, that the Allies must win, and that although he would like to help, he was hobbled by American isolationism. But in strong contrast to Winston Churchill and his cabinet members, who looked to a resurrected France after the war, as far as Roosevelt was concerned, the unexpected and stunning military, political, and moral collapse of France in

1940 showed that France was finished. No postwar French government should be allowed in world councils. What is even more startling is that, in line with the utter disappointment he felt, he went so far as to consider, in an offhand manner, an actual dismemberment of France: he suggested to British foreign secretary Anthony Eden that a new state named "Wallonia" be created out of parts of Belgium, Alsace-Lorraine, Luxemburg, and the north of France, an idea that he had broached earlier to another British diplomat, Oliver Lyttleton.[21] The French colonial empire should be dissolved. Poor old Pétain, Roosevelt thought, with his government in Vichy instead of Paris, was an admirable man doing what he could for his ruined country, and the obscure General de Gaulle and his growing pretensions to representing all of France and its empire was merely an irritant. Clearly, President Roosevelt no longer had much use for the French.

Who was this annoying General de Gaulle, anyway, and where did he come from? Why was his name in the news now, in 1940, and how and on what basis could he claim to represent France when a legitimate French government under the venerable and respected Marshal Pétain still existed in Vichy? France may have been defeated, but it still had a government with which the Americans and numerous other countries maintained diplomatic relations. Marshal Pétain, to Americans, was the victor of the battle of Verdun in the First World War, the man who was wined and dined when he visited the United States in 1931, where he was given a tickertape parade in New York. Roosevelt was said to have for Pétain an "old and deep affection."[22] Tellingly, there is no mention of de Gaulle in correspondence between Franklin D. Roosevelt and Winston Churchill during the year 1940. For Roosevelt, in contrast to Pétain, de Gaulle was in effect a nobody.

It is hard to remember now that the unknown Charles de Gaulle virtually emerged from out of nowhere. In France itself hardly anyone had heard of this undistinguished minor military officer, apart from a few other French army officers and a few political leaders, many of whom considered him a typically reactionary army officer. A product of a conservative, Catholic military family, he was known in some European military circles before World War II for his writings on armored warfare and on the need for a professional army, but he was known also to officers of the French High Command as an irritating heretic to whom they would not pay much attention. General Maurice Gamelin, who dismissed de Gaulle's notions of tank warfare as meaningless and who would be in command of the French army at the time of the debacle in 1940, had blocked the annoying de Gaulle's promotion to colonel in 1936 until he was overruled by the minister of defense.

Then, in May 1940, as one among thousands of colonels, de Gaulle distinguished himself with an armored division he had thrown together in successful tank action against the Germans near the Somme, where, however, he had had to withdraw for lack of reinforcements, artillery, or air cover. He was promoted to the temporary rank of brigadier general, making him one of the youngest generals in the French army, but a hasty change in government in the face of imminent disaster brought to power as the new prime minister the vigorous if erratic Paul Reynaud. He knew de Gaulle and his views, and made him undersecretary of state for defense and of the army on June 5. It was de Gaulle's one and only government office during those waning days of the Third Republic. From this position he observed the growing defeatism of a government that fled Paris in disorder on June 10, and he fought hard to have the government move either to a redoubt in Brittany or to North Africa to continue the fight.[23] On June 17, convinced that the proponents of surrender in a new government had vanquished those who wanted to withdraw to North Africa, and informed that he might be arrested now that he was no longer a minister, de Gaulle abandoned his post and, with the connivance of General Edward Spears, the chief British liaison officer to the French government, flew to England on the general's plane, accompanied only by his aide-de-camp Geoffroy de Courcel.

Once he disobeyed orders to return from London, the new French government in Vichy first stripped him of his rank as a deserter in July, and then condemned him to death for treason a month later. On August 15 the Vichy government made the law against deserters applicable to the colonies, rendering anyone who joined de Gaulle a traitor, whose goods would be subject to confiscation. As a result, many men, especially those who still had families in France, were hesitant to join him.[24] It was only with the decisive personal support of Winston Churchill, who immediately saw in him a man of destiny, that Charles de Gaulle could begin the perilous journey that would transform him into a towering political figure in the mid-twentieth century.

His story has been told by many: by himself, in his eloquent *Mémoires de guerre;* in the memoirs of those who surrounded him as he built his movement; and by innumerable historians. Tellingly, René Cassin, an eminent jurist who was among the first to join de Gaulle, titled his own memoirs *Les Hommes partis de rien* (The Men Who Started from Nothing). The unknown de Gaulle in his first weeks in England had the derisory sum of 100,000 francs ($20,000), given him by Reynaud, and a mere handful of supporters. He had arrived with only the one French officer, his aide Geoffroy de Courcel. A second arrived a few days later, Lieutenant Claude Hettier de Boislambert, who, after escaping from France, had difficulty finding anyone in London who could even tell him where de Gaulle had his office. Officials at the French embassy, where the atmosphere was "unbreathable," were not about to help him find a rebel general.[25] Many British officials, still hoping that the French empire would continue the fight, were unwilling to place any bets on an obscure Frenchman who had not even been a general a few weeks earlier and who had a reputation, reported in the *Times,* as an aggressive right-winger with few followers.[26] To many in the British military he was a lowly officer who had disobeyed orders, and therefore was not to be trusted. Others still hoped to persuade the new French government of Marshal Pétain to resist German demands, and they persisted in enrolling stranded French soldiers into British units or sending them back to France instead of allowing them to join de Gaulle.

In fact, all through 1940 and 1941 the British government maintained discreet contact with the Vichy authorities, hoping to persuade Pétain to resist the pressures of those French who wanted a deeper collaboration with the Germans, and pressuring his government in Vichy to keep the powerful French fleet and French North Africa and West Africa out of German hands. De Gaulle's broadcast appeal to the French nation on June 18 to resist and continue the war, later to become famous, was heard by only a few at the time. In describing the reaction of those who did hear of it, French historian Henri Michel wrote: "What use resisting? With what? Sustained with what hope, given that the French army, judged invincible, was crushed? In this climate of lack of will the appeal of June 18 is totally ignored; few heard it."[27]

Numerous French writers note the relief with which the demoralized French, in the midst of unforeseen chaos, largely accepted not only the armistice but also Pétain's leadership as that of the revered victor of the battle of Verdun, the strong man who would bring peace with Germany and restore order out of indescribable disorder. A second appeal that de Gaulle wanted to make the next day was judged premature by the

English authorities, calling as it did upon Frenchmen to join him when it was not yet clear whether a dissident French government might still move to North Africa. Three days later, however, when the German armistice terms became known, he did broadcast an invitation to Frenchmen wherever they might be in the world to join him. What was crucial in his thinking at this time was that the great French fleet was still intact, and so was the French empire, with its resources and manpower. France, therefore, with proper leadership, could still continue the fight.

On June 22, 1940, informed that the Pétain government in Bordeaux had signed an armistice with Germany, Churchill published a declaration to the effect that the French government had lost its liberty, independence, and constitutional authority, and he secured cabinet authority to recognize a French national committee to be established by de Gaulle. On June 23, having assured Churchill that prominent Frenchmen would join, de Gaulle broadcast a declaration of intent to form a French national authority, and of British approval and support.

This was de Gaulle's earliest attempt at forming a French political authority. It misfired. De Gaulle had sent a message to each of the great proconsuls of the far-flung French empire asking them to join him in rejecting Pétain's call to cease the fight, and letting them know he was ready to subordinate himself to one of them if they would continue the battle. But disastrously for de Gaulle, out of respect for Pétain and in line with their oath of loyalty, only one—General Georges Catroux in Indochina—accepted. The rest all rejected the call of an unknown French officer in London and accepted Pétain's leadership and the government the elderly marshal had established in Vichy.[28] General Charles Noguès in North Africa, whom de Gaulle had hoped might head a movement of resistance, and General Pierre Boisson in French West Africa had both originally condemned the armistice. But neither responded to de Gaulle's call: so long as the armistice kept North and West Africa out of German hands, they would respect it. Both would subsequently play an important role in opposing de Gaulle and hampering the Allies. Heartbreakingly, Admiral Darlan, whose enormous modern fleet was relatively intact, also rejected the call. If the French fleet joined the British, Germany could not hope to defeat them; if the Germans seized it, it would probably mean the end of Great Britain.

Geoffroy de Courcel, who had left France with de Gaulle, would write later of these leaders who had rejected de Gaulle, "None of these men, who had in their hands considerable means to keep France in the war, had the sense of moral responsibility incumbent upon them to dare everything to uphold the honor and the independence of France." De Gaulle, de Courcel noted, had hoped until the last moment that someone whose authority and stature was greater than his own would head up the resistance. But, he wrote, "de Gaulle alone, without an army, without money, without support, decided that, whatever the circumstances, he would carry on the battle in the name of France."[29]

Others, however, thought that de Gaulle had acted too precipitously. Jean Monnet, an eminent French economist in government service who did much to mobilize the British and American arms effort, was in London at the time. His own view was that de Gaulle's call to the proconsuls conflicted with his attempt to set himself up as head of a committee in London supposedly representing France. The leaders in the far-flung empire would see de Gaulle either as a creature of the English government or as taking upon himself a leadership position none of them would see any reason to accept. After all, who was an obscure low-ranking general who had deserted his post compared to a distinguished marshal of France?[30] Other French figures who had escaped to London shared his opinion: the former permanent secretary of the French Foreign Office, Alexis Saint-Léger (known to many by his pen name as the poet Saint-John Perse); writer André Maurois; Charles Corbin, the French ambassador to London; and conservative politician Henri de Kerillis (who nevertheless would for a while support de Gaulle in the United States).[31] In those early days no prominent French political leader emerged to join de Gaulle in London. A few who might have supported him tried to flee from France to North Africa when they knew the defeatists had won out in Bordeaux. There they hoped to establish a government-in-exile to carry on the fight. But in Algiers Governor-General Noguès, who had by now opted for Pétain, kept them in seclusion. Churchill sent British envoys to meet with them, but the British were not allowed to land and speak to them, and they were returned to face imprisonment in France. They included several able and prominent leaders who might well have given enough luster to de Gaulle's enterprise to make it succeed.

Most of the French intellectuals who fled to Britain following the armistice moved on to the United States, convinced that Britain might well fall, and seeing in de Gaulle simply another unknown, stubborn, reactionary general, haughty, or timid, depending on who was judging, who was certainly in no position or did not have the capacity to represent France. The cold reception some received who presented themselves to him turned them off completely.[32] Others, such as André Labarthe, the brilliant scientist and military adviser to the former French government, at first joined de Gaulle, then later separated themselves and turned against him.[33] One de Gaulle supporter, Hervé Alphand, later told Labarthe that "to parade around London insulting the single man who saved our honor and can coordinate our action is to do great damage to the cause of our country and to your espousal of a second front and guerrilla action."[34]

In London most French embassy officials refused to join de Gaulle; some who opposed Vichy nevertheless rejected de Gaulle as their leader; and French military contingents back from the disastrous earlier campaign in Norway and from the Allied evacuation of Dunkirk chose largely to return to France. Many British military officers, resisting political pressures to act otherwise, did all they could to hasten the departure of French soldiers with whom they didn't want to deal. Three weeks after his first call, when de Gaulle formed his first military contingent, it consisted of fewer than two thousand men. In mid-August, out of what had been a French army of 3 million men, he could muster only 4,500.[35] François Coulet, a French diplomat who did join de Gaulle early on, was dismayed and surprised that so many of his fellow diplomats failed to follow him into de Gaulle's camp; it would so have eased de Gaulle's task. He writes in his memoirs that if it horrified him to see how supine many of his fellow Frenchmen were in accepting utter defeat, he could recognize the effect this must have had on General de Gaulle, how much it contributed to how hypersensitive the general could be.[36]

Yet to decide to join de Gaulle was no easy task. For a military man it meant losing his rank, his military decorations, his civil status. As one Gaullist writer put it, to choose de Gaulle was "to break openly with the victor of Verdun, to turn against people whose patriotism was not in doubt, to put a distance between themselves and those who, remaining in place, would have to support the rigors and misery of the occupation—all this required a firmness of spirit. The first victory that the first dissidents won was often a victory over themselves."[37]

The British bombardment of units of the French fleet moored at Mers-el-Kébir in Algeria was one of the saddest chapters in a long history of Anglo-French conflict. It also shattered any hopes that de Gaulle might have had of gaining support among French naval personnel and in North Africa. The Germans knew that the French would not sign an armistice if Germany insisted on surrender of the French fleet, so they had allowed it to remain under nominal French control, but it was to move to French ports under German and Italian supervision. Despite numerous assurances by the French that they would never let the Germans get their hands on the French vessels, Churchill was not reassured: promises from the Nazis to leave the fleet under French control were no better than any of their earlier promises, and he did not trust French assurances that the ships would be scuttled if the Germans tried to seize them.

On May 26 Secretary of State Cordell Hull had asked the French government to move the fleet out of the Mediterranean. A month later President Roosevelt told the French that if they failed to keep the fleet out of German hands, there would be fatal consequences for the eventual restoration of French independence and autonomy. The American appeals, however, had had no effect, and Ambassador Joseph Kennedy in London wired the president that the British Foreign Office had told the French that the armistice terms put the fleet entirely under German command.[38]

As a result, on July 3, ten days after the armistice, the commander of the British fleet off Mers-el-Kébir gave the French four alternatives to a fight: join the British, move the ships to British ports with diminished crews, move them to Western Hemisphere ports and decommission them, or scuttle the fleet. Abortive negotiations with the Anglophobe French admiral who was in charge led to the British decision to attack the French. It was Churchill's decision. The action was taken to make sure the ships would not fall into German hands, to reduce a naval threat in the Mediterranean, and to show the world Churchill's determination to continue the fight. The French suffered heavy casualties: 1,297 men killed, 351 wounded. "The consternation, bitterness . . . the fury of the sailors, of the military and civilians of the area reflected the number of casualties. . . . Anglophobia was the order of the day." The English consuls in North Africa were immediately expelled.[39] Said one sailor bitterly: "The English! To think that we wanted to continue the war with them! And they come to assassinate us!"[40]

De Gaulle agonized, considered dropping out and retiring to Canada, but eventually publicly supported Churchill's decision, on the basis that only if Britain continued to resist Germany could France eventually be liberated. His stand earned him the enmity of much of the French naval, military, and political leadership in North Africa, as well as many in England.

A typical reaction was that of one sailor: "the bastard, the traitor . . . a dozen bullets in his hide!"[41] A few, on the other hand, understood de Gaulle. The day after the assault one French officer wrote of the English: "I cursed them, hated them! . . . Yes, it's horrible! The English are bastards, assassins, but the enemy is Germany and not the English. . . . [T]he tragedy of last night has not made me change my mind. The English must win the war, and we with them. It's atrocious but there's nothing we can do. Either the English win the war and we win it with them, or we are lost."[42] French writer Antoine de Saint Éxupery was in Algiers at the time, however, and de Gaulle's defense of the British action along with his criticisms of Marshal Pétain, which Saint-Éxupery viewed as divisive when the French should be united, set him on a trail of growing opposition to de Gaulle.[43]

Whatever the reaction of French naval personnel, de Gaulle won Churchill's admiration for what the English leader realized was a painful but courageous stand. But one thing was clear: in the first year or so following de Gaulle's appeal of June 18, 1940, he would have little support in North Africa or in the French navy.

The attack on the French fleet at Mers-el-Kébir had the one desired result: it proved to the Americans and others that Britain would fight on. It also had one other result: a decisive break in official Franco-British relations, already strained by France's decision to seek an armistice, in violation of an earlier agreement with the British government. Ambassador Bullitt, still in Vichy, cabled Roosevelt that after Mers-el-Kébir the Pétain government came close to aligning itself with Germany by declaring war on Britain, and that many French people had become bitterly anti-English.[44]

If General de Gaulle was unknown at the start, with almost no cards in his hand, he did have one major one: the unqualified support of Prime Minister Winston Churchill. "With any other British prime minister," said Geoffroy de Courcel much later, "it is clear that de Gaulle would never have spoken over the BBC and would have had to pack up his bag."[45] Despite the earlier failure of the attempt to establish a French national committee, late in June 1940, ten days after de Gaulle's radio appeal, Churchill had his cabinet "recognize" de Gaulle as leader of Free French Forces, while a month later, in a complicated agreement, it spelled out the nature of British relations with the Free French and began financial support for the movement that would continue through most of the war years. A honeymoon period ensued, during which the two leaders saw each other almost every day; de

Gaulle spent a weekend at Churchill's country house, Chequers, and when de Gaulle moved to his new headquarters, Carlton Gardens, in late July, Mrs. Churchill walked up the three flights to de Gaulle's office to bring him a basket of flowers.

In the years that followed, de Gaulle and Churchill would engage in bitter disputes. De Gaulle would accuse the British of trying to take over parts of the French empire, and Churchill would try to have de Gaulle replaced. But almost from the start, following Churchill's lead and a deliberate propaganda campaign to build up de Gaulle as a Free French leader, the British press and public, the House of Commons, and key members of Churchill's cabinet all chose to support the stubborn Frenchman. Churchill ordered the BBC to give the general broadcast time which he should be able to consider his own. While many in the British military had little use for de Gaulle (they certainly did not feel they could spare any of the weapons he sought for his few troops), Churchill pressed the minister of war to hasten the issue of weapons to the French forces. The press and many political leaders saw de Gaulle as the sole member of the French government who had honored the earlier Franco-British agreement of March 1940 that neither government would independently seek an armistice, the only French leader determined to fight on against the Nazis. He had quickly become, in other words, the symbol of continued, *legitimate* French resistance.

Apart from a period following the Dakar fiasco (see chapter 2), most would continue to provide him with an almost fervent support throughout his time of troubles, even as they found him very, very difficult. English officialdom had a hard time coming to terms with a Frenchman who was unlike any other they had known, and who, in his isolation and bitterness over what had happened to his country and to his people, most of whom supported Pétain's armistice and failed to rally to him, seemed to many officials cold, distant, and ungenerous in his response to Allied support. Some reacted very strongly against him when first meeting him, and many continued to deplore his conduct. But according to one writer, when de Gaulle visited English factories, workers who knew he hadn't abandoned the alliance cried out, "Good old de Gaulle!" or "Bless you!"[46] General Edward Louis Spears, Britain's official liaison to the Free French, a friend of Churchill's, and former liaison to the French government in World War I, did all he could in this period to ease matters for de Gaulle.

The press and many parliamentarians who supported de Gaulle found themselves occasionally in conflict with Prime Minister Churchill but even more so with their future ally, President Franklin D. Roosevelt, author of America's Vichy policy, and with the U.S. Department of State.

From the moment when the Americans began to take cognizance of de Gaulle's existence and movement, British and American policies toward him diverged. In March 1943 Anthony Eden, now British foreign secretary, visited the United States and talked about the French future at the time of liberation. He later recalled:

> I found our policies at odds with those of the United States. The Americans did not want to see a sole French authority established, even if it were not recognized as a government. They preferred to deal with individuals and . . . wanted to act separately with the local French. . . . This dispersion of authority was contrary to my doctrine and I explained in all our conversations that the British Government would much prefer to deal with a single French authority. . . . Nor could I agree to another American project, that Allied forces landing in France should administer liberated French territory. It seemed to me that Roosevelt wanted to hold the strings of France's future in his own hands so that he could decide that country's fate. I did not like this and preferred a French civil authority to work with the Allied forces from an early stage.[47]

One reason for the divergence was that for two and a half years, Washington had never broken relations with Marshal Pétain's government in Vichy. (Churchill found it useful to have the American listening post in Vichy and encouraged Roosevelt to maintain American representation there.)[48] In August 1940 the Vichy government sent a new ambassador to Washington, Gaston Henry-Haye, and after a period during which the United States was represented only by chargé d'affaires H. Freeman Matthews, in December of that year Roosevelt sent an old friend, the politically inexperienced Admiral William Leahy, as ambassador to Vichy, where he would stay until mid-1942. Matthews and Leahy, both of whom observed Pétain and the French scene at first hand during the early years of the Vichy government and admired the aged marshal, would be among those who would have a strong influence on Roosevelt's negative view of de Gaulle. Following his stint in Vichy, Matthews, from London, bombarded Washington with negative information about the de Gaulle headquarters there, reporting on all the infighting.[49] Matthews was also contemptuous of Gaullist claims.

On March 22, 1943, he wrote, "Whatever the facts of feeling in France, de Gaulle and his entourage sitting in the relative isolation of London and listening only to their own representatives paid by their funds (advanced from the British Treasury!) and brought from France at their instigation have at least partly convinced themselves that suffering France demands the leadership of de Gaulle the man, not merely de Gaulle the symbol."[50] He went on to note, with some satisfaction, that the Gaullists knew that the chief obstacle to their recognition as the de facto government of France was American policy.

Admiral Leahy, for two years ambassador to Vichy France, came to take a realistic view of how little America could influence the Vichy regime in any meaningful way, but he retained a great affection for Marshal Pétain and remained persuaded that Gaullists in France were both more radical and fewer in number than outside observers thought. In his memoirs he wrote, remarkably, "There was no indication in occupied France that the self-styled 'leader of French resistance' had any important numerical following."[51] Though Leahy had never met de Gaulle, he could not abide him, and when the admiral later became Roosevelt's personal military aide, he had a great influence on the president's view of France. Typically, in July 1941 he told Roosevelt, "Frenchmen with whom I can talk, even those completely desirous of a British victory, have little regard for General de Gaulle." They looked upon de Gaulle as a paid British agent.[52] In contrast, a year later Vichy prime minister Pierre Laval, perhaps better informed than Leahy, would declare to another member of his government that de Gaulle had 80 to 90 percent of the French population behind him.[53] More important, a flow of messages from within France in 1942 testified to de Gaulle's increased standing in French public opinion.[54] Diplomat Charles Bohlen, who served as liaison between the secretary of state and the president and saw Admiral Leahy every day, wrote: "My conversations with Leahy followed a definite pattern. In his snapping turtle manner, he usually had some crack to make about General de Gaulle."[55] In February 1944—only three months before D-Day—a startled British ambassador learned that Admiral Leahy had told the president that only the aging Marshal Pétain would be able to rally the French people at the time of liberation.[56] In his memoirs Leahy would write that in April 1944, two months before D-Day, it was his "personal opinion that we, the Americans, would have constant friction with General de Gaulle until he should be eliminated from the problem of French participation in the war."[57]

When, on October 23, 1944, the United States finally gave de facto recognition to de Gaulle's government and the British were able to follow suit, Sir Alexander Cadogan, head of the Foreign Office, gave vent to widespread British feelings, noting in his diary: "At last! What a fuss about nothing! Due to that spiteful old great-aunt Leahy. Hope he's feeling pretty sick!"[58] Roosevelt's military aide so despised the French leader that even at the war's end he was quoted as resenting having to meet the "dirty frog."[59]

Two other consequences flowed from the continuation of diplomatic relations between Washington and Vichy. The first was that President Roosevelt and the highest State Department leaders—like some, earlier, in Britain—still hoped to use American influence with Pétain to get him to hold out against German demands. They therefore avoided any open support for de Gaulle that might alienate Pétain. The issue of "legitimacy" also loomed large. In contrast to Churchill's early declaration to the effect that the Vichy regime had forfeited any claim to legitimacy, Pétain, they argued, was the legitimate leader of France, having been invested with full powers by a large majority of the last freely elected French Assembly. The United States should therefore do what it could to help Pétain resist Laval and others who wanted France to collaborate more closely with the Nazis.

De Gaulle, on the other hand, had no claim to legitimacy. State Department officials ignored a declaration made by him on November 16, 1940, that the Vichy regime had lost any such claim, given its declaration that it would follow the path of "collaboration," and that it had been established by an illegitimate delegation of power by the remnants of the Third Republic.[60] Obviously the United States government could not entertain official relations with two separate French governments. Any recognition accorded to de Gaulle, whom American leaders mistrusted anyway, would mean a break in relations with Vichy.

The Department of State's top officials were vehement in support of this view. Assistant Secretary of State Breckinridge Long, in January 1942, asserted, rather wildly, that any indication of recognition of the de Gaulle movement would mean "we would be at war with Vichy." He was also convinced that the British supported de Gaulle so that in the postwar period they could use him to help them in their control of western Europe, from which they would exclude the United States. Later he would write, "The radical press here is enthusiastic for him [de Gaulle] and hypercritical of us [the Department of State]."[61] Presumably the "radical press" included the influential Republican *New York Herald Tribune* and the widely read Henry Luce publications *Time* and *Life* magazines.

In July 1943 Assistant Secretary of State Adolf Berle wrote in his diary that he had received a tragic call from the son of Pastor Marc Boegner, the prominent French Protestant leader. Young Boegner was in Washington with the conservative General Henri Giraud, whom the Americans had hoped might replace de Gaulle. Boegner, who had been ousted from a position in the Free French movement, told Berle that de Gaulle was running a dictatorial movement: "I am persuaded that de Gaulle, despite his protestations, is the promoter of a French Nazi movement of which he is the Fuhrer. . . . If we let him he will seize the army and with American cannons will impose his dictatorship on France."[62] It all stuck: as late as July 28, 1944, well after D-Day and a month before the liberation of Paris, Berle wrote, "The British have been backing de Gaulle to the limit, and there is no question in my mind that he will attempt to establish himself as virtual dictator of France and that if he ever gets into the saddle he will be dislodged only by force."[63] De Gaulle would, he continued, use his powers under martial law to control press freedom and move toward reliance on Russia. He wrote this despite all the concrete moves de Gaulle and his Provisional Government had already made in reestablishing French democracy (see chapter 4). In this he was echoing an earlier statement made by Undersecretary of State Sumner Welles to a British official in September 1942 that if de Gaulle came in with the occupying armies and established a provisional government, he could never be removed.[64] A year earlier, following Pearl Harbor, Welles had told the British ambassador Lord Halifax, who pleaded for more sympathy for the Free French, that "unfortunately there were not outstanding men with qualities of leadership and initiative directing the Free French movement and providing that kind of inspiration to free men . . . to join in a movement against their German oppressors. . . . I could not see that either General de Gaulle or his associates provided any rallying point for French patriotism."[65]

In 1940 de Gaulle had nominated a diplomat, a wounded veteran named Jacques de Sieyès, to Washington, but he had not been received, though he did have contact with and was a member of a growing pro–de Gaulle organization, "France Forever," founded by a wealthy Philadelphian, Eugene Houdry, who would establish chapters throughout the United States. When de Gaulle reorganized his office in Washington in 1941, naming René Pléven to head it, and including several prominent Frenchmen (including

Boegner), Welles initially refused to see Pleven, on the grounds that he was "reluctant to jeopardize the delicate rapport with Vichy by extending anything in the nature of official recognition to the Free French."[66]

State Department personnel stuck to their guns: late in 1944 a State Department French Desk official named James Bonbright drafted an eighteen-page memorandum titled "Reasons Underlying This Government's Lack of Confidence in General de Gaulle."[67]

Secretary of State Cordell Hull, throughout his voluminous memoirs of the war years, remains consistent: no one really knew how much support de Gaulle had in France (like Admiral Leahy, he was sure he had very little), and whatever the information coming out of France, no one could possibly know until after liberation. In 1942 he wrote to British ambassador Lord Halifax: "One of the tragedies of the De Gaulle situation . . . was that De Gaulle had attracted to himself not a single eminent Frenchman. The very few who had gotten away from France distrusted him and could not work with him." In another memo in May 1942 he wrote, "It is clearly evident that the French people who have rallied to De Gaulle as the head of a military movement are not prepared to regard him as the future leader of France."[68] A premature break with Vichy in the early years, occasioned by giving in to pressure from the British and from the many pro–Free French groups in the United States to recognize de Gaulle's movement in some way, would vitiate all the advantages the United States secured by its Vichy policy.[69]

Moreover, Hull wrote, de Gaulle "showed few signs of political acumen, being more likely than not to go off on tangents." He was also "desperately temperamental. . . . The President and I," continued Hull, "early adopted the view that we should do nothing that would impose de Gaulle upon the French. . . . According to our Embassy in Vichy at the time, there was more popular support . . . for Marshal Pétain than for de Gaulle." Hull had actually been much more vehement during the war years than his memoirs indicate. In a December 1941 letter to Roosevelt he wrote, "According to all my information and that of my associates, some 95 percent of the French people are anti-Hitler whereas more than 95 percent of this latter number are not de Gaullists and would not follow him."[70] In his memoirs he observed, "The pressure and propaganda on the part of de Gaulle's friends continued in waves of intensity as such pressure usually does, throughout the war, but the President and I were able to hew consistently to the line we early adopted."[71] The highest virtue, apparently, lay in consistency, however harmful it might be, rather than in adapting policy to changing circumstances and the mounting evidence from all sources of growing support for the general. According to Admiral Leahy, Hull referred to de Gaulle's supporters in the American press as the de Gaulle "Polecats."[72] When Lord Halifax learned that Hull "thought it was better for the United States to walk down one side of the street while we walked on the other," a British Foreign Office official derisively called this "the sheerest balderdash, meaningless, unreal, and evasive. The State Department can perfectly well find a way of walking on both sides if they really try."[73]

It should be noted that at the time René Pléven came to Washington as de Gaulle's representative in 1941, when Undersecretary of State Welles refused to see him, numerous other top administrators all held cordial conversations with him—Secretaries Henry Morgenthau (Treasury), Henry Stimson (War), and Frank Knox (Navy), Vice President Henry Wallace, and members of the Senate Foreign Relations Committee. Their cordiality unintentionally highlighted the State Department leaders' particular attitude of wariness and thoroughgoing animosity. In fact, all through the war years numerous officials in other departments tried to get Hull and Roosevelt to support de Gaulle, to no avail. Pléven, in addition to finding encouragement elsewhere in the administration, found it in another important source: he spent time at the summer home of the most influential and widely read American columnist on foreign affairs, Walter Lippmann, whose support for de Gaulle in the *New York Herald Tribune* began early.

The second consequence of continued relations with Vichy France was that Vichy could use its official presence in the United States to attempt to cultivate backing for Pétain in government circles and at the same time indulge in anti–de Gaulle propaganda, among both Americans and French residing in the United States. In late 1940 Bullitt apparently wired Washington that the new ambassador, Gaston Henry-Haye, was an intimate friend, of whose grandson he, Bullitt, was the godparent, and that he trusted Henry-Haye completely as one who did not fully support Pétain. Another dispatch from Vichy, however, claimed that Henry-Haye was a traitor, a corrupt politician who would sell his soul, and who hated the United States.[74] *Time* magazine of March 10, 1941, which featured him on the cover, recounted that he had been a member of the German-subsidized France-Germany Committee while mayor of Versailles, where he had become friends with John D.

Rockefeller Jr., who had helped rebuild Versailles, and with General John J. Pershing, the commander of the American Expeditionary Forces in World War I. Subsequently Raoul Aglion, one of the first Free French officials in New York, wrote that Ambassador Henry-Haye was "the most aggressive and devoted agent of Vichy's pro-German policy."[75]

Despite resignations among Henry-Haye's staff, particularly after the return to power of the collaborationist Pierre Laval, "he succeeded in maintaining all of the consulates, the large majority of the French colony [85 percent, according to a State Department survey] and the majority of French activities—the Alliance Française, the Society of the Legion of Honor, the Chamber of Commerce, the Veterans' Association, and others—under the aegis of Pétain."[76] Many French veterans residing in the United States depended for payment of their pensions on the Vichy French consulates. Fortunately for de Gaulle, however, Henry-Haye was not popular among high administration officials and stumbled in his task of creating American public opinion favorable to Pétain. For one thing, he was associated with the Laval wing in Vichy at a time when American officials were partial to Pétain and had come to distrust Laval thoroughly as an archcollaborationist who was known to have declared that he "hoped ardently that the English would be defeated."[77] Moreover, stories circulated widely in the press to the effect that the French embassy and the consulates were spreading subversive propaganda and actually carrying on espionage activities on behalf of the Germans. Some of the stories were false, planted by a British agent in New York; others emerged from anti-Vichy émigrés. But close government surveillance and surreptitious monitoring of Henry-Haye's communications with Vichy revealed that he discounted American mobilization efforts and was sending greatly inflated stories about strikes and production delays. His idea was to bolster the view in Vichy that America would never contribute much to the Allied war effort, so collaboration by Vichy with a Nazi Germany that would emerge victorious was fully warranted. In an effort to drive a wedge between the British and the Americans, he made speeches attacking American policy for failing to understand and sufficiently support the Vichy regime, and criticizing British bombings that killed civilians.

Despite all his attempts, in the end Henry-Haye probably did little to improve relations between the United States and the Vichy regime and, as one chronicler noted, may well have served to strengthen the popular appeal of Gaullism.[78]

. . .

As far as the American press was concerned, René Cassin notes in his memoir, *Les Hommes partis de rien,* that the *New York Herald Tribune,* as well as two less prestigious New York newspapers, *PM* and the *New York Post,* came to support de Gaulle and his movement. So did the widely read magazines *Time* and *Life:* an early firsthand report on conditions in France published in *Life* in the spring of 1941, "Vichy vs. France," by an American, Richard de Rochemont, who had just returned to the United States, brought "the first real movement of opinion in the United States in support of Free France." The *New York Times,* he wrote, remained "systematically" anti–Free French, calling de Gaulle, in early 1944, a "liability."[79]

Some 135,000 persons born in France resided in the United States, along with many more of French descent. By and large they took no stance on the issue of relations with France, many of them evincing confusion over whether to support Pétain in Vichy or the unknown de Gaulle in London. Members of the older, largely Catholic and conservative communities in Louisiana, California, and New England seem to have had primarily local concerns and more or less followed the lead of the American government and the Vichy French embassy. (In Canada, the conservative French Catholic community of Quebec for a long time remained attached to Pétain's Vichy regime but changed over time.)[80]

A large, new, different group of several thousand French refugees arrived in the United States between the fall of France in the summer of 1940 and American entry into the war at the end of 1941. They included prominent political figures, journalists, writers, diplomats, academics, film actors and directors, artists, and businessmen and industrialists.[81] Unfortunately for de Gaulle, they brought with them all the ideological, religious, and partisan divisions that had plagued France in the prewar period. One sympathetic observer, Henri de Kerillis, wrote to de Gaulle: "Wherever there are twenty Frenchmen they fight among themselves. There are those for de Gaulle and those against him, those for him and against the British, those for the British and against him, those for Pétain, those for Weygand, and those for Laval. There are also the fools, the cowards and those who are afraid. There is all and everything. The terrible tragedy has taught them nothing and has changed nothing."[82]

If some in the French refugee colony sided with de Gaulle and others opposed him, the majority refused to take sides. People such as the well-known author and pilot Antoine de Saint-Exupéry, whose books were wildly popular in the United States, never rallied to de Gaulle. In fact his early distrust of de Gaulle, fanned by friends who found the general "impossible," hardened into almost virulent anti-Gaullism: he referred to Gaullism as "Fascism without a doctrine."[83] Saint-Exupéry's biographer Curtis Cate writes vividly of what he sees as the wrongheadedness of the Gaullists in the United States in attacking their opponents when they should have been seeking to unite the French in the war against Germany; they deemed any who were not openly Gaullist to be enemies. Saint-Exupéry's friend Raul de Roussy de Sales, another writer popular in the United States who was anti-Vichy and for a while worked for the Gaullist cause, nevertheless told Gaullist envoy René Pléven, "I am not a Gaullist and I will probably never be one."[84] Jacques Maritain, the eminent Catholic philosopher who taught part-time at both Notre Dame and the University of Chicago, was in the United States when the war broke out. Like so many others, he accepted the legitimacy of the Vichy government only up to a point, sympathized with de Gaulle, but when asked, refused to serve in the Gaullist delegation in the United States. Apparently "his position as a philosopher compelled him not to take sides, to remain totally independent."[85]

There were many others, all distrustful enough of de Gaulle to stay on the sidelines or to oppose him. Hervé Alphand, sent by de Gaulle to the United States in January 1943 to deal with the Treasury and Commerce departments on matters of finance, wrote that he found among the French in Washington "horrible and dishonoring calumnies, an unleashing of hatreds, personal ambition, mindless confusion . . . spread out in public before our friends and enemies." It could be explained by the misery and humiliation the French had suffered, the nerves so on edge that people let themselves go, but it was "an atrocious spectacle."[86] The quarrels and factionalism among émigrés served to further public disenchantment with *all* the French and convinced the anti-Gaullists in Washington that the general did not command broad French support.

Unfortunately, those who backed de Gaulle also quarreled, and de Gaulle, from London, tried to mend matters by various maneuvers, with little success. Moreover, as he moved from being merely a military leader of Fighting French forces to a position of political leadership in which he claimed to be the only legitimate representative of France, some who had originally supported him as a purely military leader moved into opposition, and they had considerable influence on Roosevelt.

One such was Henri de Kerillis, a conservative newspaperman and former deputy from Brittany, mentioned earlier, whose convictions about Nazi Germany's ambitions made him the sole representative on the right to vote against the disastrous Munich agreement of 1938 that sold out Czechoslovakia. He had talked to de Gaulle in London in 1940 and then moved on to New York, to be de Gaulle's ardent supporter in both Canada and the United States, where he published a book titled *Français, voici la vérité!* (Frenchmen, Here Is the Truth!).[87] In it he proclaimed his confidence in the general and his faith in the resurrection of France. In short order he became chief editorial writer of the French-language New York newspaper *Pour la Victoire*, established by another refugee, the frail but energetic Geneviève Tabouis, a world-renowned editor, bitter anti-Nazi, and friend of Eleanor and Franklin Roosevelt. When the newspaper first appeared in January 1942, it received letters of congratulation from de Gaulle, from former American ambassador to France William Bullitt, from Eleanor Roosevelt, New York mayor Fiorello LaGuardia, and many others. De Kérillis was able to attract a brilliant staff of French writers—people like Jacques Maritain, Eve Curie, Claude Lévi-Strauss, André Breton, and Henri Peyre, and occasional contributors such as Julien Green and even Antoine de Saint-Exupéry.

But when de Gaulle moved to eliminate his political rival General Giraud, who had escaped from a German prison camp and come to North Africa in 1942 at the request of the Americans when they landed there, de Kerillis, like many others, moved into active opposition. He and Geneviève Tabouis had at first called for unity of the de Gaulle faction in London and the emerging Giraud faction in North Africa. When de Gaulle rid himself of his rival and assumed sole leadership of the external and internal resistance to German rule and began to create a government-in-exile under his control, de Kerillis's view hardened: to him de Gaulle, by his political actions, now represented an old anti-republicanism known in France as "Bonapartism"—the combining of military and political leadership. The conservative de Kerillis had always hated the communists, and his anti-Gaullism became strident when de Gaulle took communists into his fledgling exile government. The communists, de Kerillis argued, had betrayed France at the time when the Nazi-Soviet pact had enabled Hitler to make war in the west and defeat France. To take these traitors into the de Gaulle shadow government was unconscionable. Then, charging wildly that men in de Gaulle's entourage had delivered his son to the Gestapo, along with Jean Moulin, the man whom de Gaulle had sent to unify the disparate French resistance groups in France, de Kerillis ended up publishing a book in Canada called *De Gaulle dictateur,* a violent diatribe encapsulating all the charges ever made against the French leader. Among them was that many of those surrounding de Gaulle were former Cagoulards, members of a secretive, authoritarian and anti-republican organization that had carried out terrorist acts in the 1930s. The charge that Cagoulards were prominent in the Gaullist intelligence service run by Colonel Passy (the nom de guerre of André Dewavrin) was widely circulated in London and Washington.[88]

In time Geneviève Tabouis also took her distance. She too had called for unity between de Gaulle and Giraud. *Pour la Victoire* had an agreement to print editorials from a Gaullist newspaper in London, *La Marseillaise.* When some of these became strongly anti-American in the face of the U.S. refusal to recognize the Gaullist movement, she declined to print them. One result was that when de Gaulle finally visited the United States in 1944, her name was on the list of French refugees de Gaulle said he would not meet. Another result was that on May 23, 1943, a new, frankly Gaullist newspaper appeared in New York, *France-Amérique.* Its tone was more strident: an editorial called the 1940 armistice the greatest act of treason in history; it published passionate attacks on the Pétain regime, printed lists of hostages shot by the Germans which were posted on walls in France, reproduced much of what appeared in the underground press in France, and called for swift punishment by postwar tribunals of all those who collaborated. When the editorial writer of *Pour la Victoire* observed that this attitude could lead to a terrible civil war at the time of liberation, the editor of *France-Amérique* replied that there would be no civil war but rather a "civic cleansing."[89] (Both newspapers, whatever their differences, rejoiced in the eventual Normandy landings, the liberation of Paris, and the final victory over Nazi Germany. After the war, in 1946, they merged under the title *France-Amérique.* By this time Geneviève Tabouis had returned to France. The bitter De Kerillis never did and died on Long Island in 1958.)

Gaullists and de Gaulle himself tried to persuade some of the distinguished refugees in America to join his movement. One such was the diplomat and poet Alexis Saint-Léger. He had been the permanent secretary of the French Foreign Office but was removed by Prime Minister Reynaud in 1940, at the time Reynaud took de Gaulle into his cabinet. The incident apparently rankled; he seems to have linked the promotion of de Gaulle to his own dismissal. Despite several offers of an official position from de Gaulle and pleas from Winston Churchill, Saint-Léger, like de Kerillis, eventually moved into an active opposition which, through his close friendship with Sumner Welles, certainly influenced President Roosevelt.

The president trusted Welles more than anyone else in the Department of State. Welles, among other things, passed on to Roosevelt a memo of a conversation he had had with Saint-Léger in August 1942 in which the poet-diplomat explained all the reasons for his opposition to de Gaulle, including de Gaulle's dictatorial tendencies, his hostility to the "Anglo-Saxons," which would lead him to base his authority on Soviet support, and the fact that there were plenty of anti-Nazi resistants who were not Gaullist. The United States, Saint-Léger told Welles, should therefore go no further in its support than it had done so far. Any formal recognition, in other words, was out of the question, and the American government should maintain its contacts in both occupied and unoccupied France so as not to have to rely on the obviously biased pro–de Gaulle information coming from Free French and British sources. Later, Saint-Léger wrote directly to the president to argue that any seizing of power by the Gaullists would be strictly illegal.[90] In February 1943 he apparently told Gaullist diplomat Hervé Alphand that de Gaulle, in an interview with former American ambassador Bullitt, had said that he, de Gaulle, hoped for a communist France after the war. Saint-Léger was himself somewhat skeptical but insisted that he was deeply worried by the current alliance of communism and Gaullism. (Bullitt would later tell Alphand that he had never said such a thing.)[91]

Historian Jean-Louis Crémieux-Brilhac argues that the evident divisions among French expatriates and refugees, and the evident opposition of men like Saint-Léger, Saint-Éxupery, and de Kerillis, strongly reinforced Roosevelt's conviction that there was more to French resistance than de Gaulle, and that it was legitimate to depend on others and not just him, echoing all of Saint-Léger's arguments, and refusing to accept some of his close advisers' recommendations.[92]

All of this—the consistently hostile view about the upstart de Gaulle that emanated from Foggy Bottom, the views of the president's close advisers Admiral Leahy and Sumner Welles, the admonitions of the many and vocal anti-Gaullist Frenchmen, and bitter divisions among the French refugees—served to confirm Roosevelt in his view that in the interest of democracy he could not allow de Gaulle to assume power in France; he would not impose an unpopular de Gaulle upon the French and would have to block him somehow. The imposition of a temporary Allied military government on France that could organize free elections seemed an obvious solution. A series of wartime events to be considered in the next two chapters were probably even more crucial in hardening the president's opinion, one that he would maintain throughout the wartime years.

CHAPTER 2

Positions Defined

E GAULLE'S SELF-PROMOTION AS THE LEADER OF A resurrected free France, along with numerous wartime events, hardened President Roosevelt in his determination to rid the Allies of this obstreperous man who kept getting in the way of prosecuting the war effectively.

In June 1940 few people understood General de Gaulle's intention to reconstitute and maintain a French political power that would be, in his words, "for free men and in the eyes of its allies, the legitimate authority of France" and that would participate, alongside its allies, in the reconquest and liberation of France.[1] His goal was first revealed in the failed, premature attempt to create a French national committee in June 1940, and it remained the theme of his actions during the next four years. By his own refusal to submit at the time of the armistice with Nazi Germany, and when no other leaders emerged to continue the fight, he considered that he had put himself in a position to head not merely armed contingents fighting alongside the Allies but such a new French political power. He would bring together all Frenchmen who would accept his position as legitimate.

This meant creating a military force under his command, securing a territorial base for a governmental authority—one that would not be situated within the sovereign territory of another country and therefore subject to limits imposed by that country but would be specifically French—and obtaining recognition from foreign powers. France would again have an international role to play as the war came to an end. It would be able to defend its crucial interests in the fate of Germany, of central Europe, of Italy, and of the empire, interests that de Gaulle knew he could not depend on the other Allies to defend. Only if France participated in the defeat of the enemy—as a nation with a recognized government—would France become, once again, a real power able to protect those interests, join in shaping the postwar world order, and help its people regain the civic pride necessary to the revival of the real French nation. It would not be until January 2, 1943, however, that he would openly publish his intention to create a provisional government, which, as he repeated, was indispensable in giving inspiration and direction to French participation in the war.[2]

The French empire, it must be realized, would play a key role in his ultimate success. It was there, after initial rejection, that he would establish his government-in-exile. It was the empire that provided most of the military strength he could bring to the fray: three quarters of the French army at the time of liberation would be recruited from the empire, and half of that was composed of native troops. If the empire was key to his success, however, its continued existence was anathema to President Roosevelt, who foresaw the end of all colonial empires (but who also coveted postwar American bases in parts of the French empire). Despite de Gaulle's expressed aim of liberalizing the structure of the empire in the future, conflict between Roosevelt and de Gaulle over the fate of the empire was built into the situation from the start.

As the events of June 1940 showed, the role de Gaulle envisioned for himself would also bring him into conflict with other Frenchmen who contested his right to speak for all of France, refusing his claim to legitimacy. In June 1940 the most prominent French political personalities in London at the time, Alexis Saint-Léger, Jean Monnet, and Ambassador Charles Corbin, all opposed his ambition. There would be many others later, including some who also opposed the Vichy government. It therefore became his task to take actions that would bring hesitant Frenchmen both within and outside France to support him. If he succeeded, he would become the key spokesman of a reconstituted France that could resume its traditional role as a world power. This ambition would also bring him into conflict with his allies, most notably Winston Churchill and Franklin D. Roosevelt, both of whom, but especially the latter, would look elsewhere for French leaders, while Roosevelt would go so far as to deny the legitimacy of any government created outside France, since only free elections within France itself could confer legitimacy. On New Year's Day 1943 Roosevelt, referring to "our French friends," would write to Churchill: "I don't want any of them to think that we are going to recognize any one or any committee or group as representing the French Government or the French Empire. The people of France will settle their own affairs after we have won this war. Until then we can deal with local Frenchmen on a local basis. . . . And if these local officials won't play ball *we will have to replace them.*"[3]

De Gaulle's support for British action against the French fleet at Mers-el-Kébir in July 1940 made his task much harder, alienating as it did so many potential supporters. So did the failure of the joint Franco-British attempt to bring Dakar and all of West Africa into the Free French fold three months later.

The attempt was an ambitious one. Already de Gaulle, after initially being rebuffed by French leaders throughout most of the empire, had received support in the small southeast Pacific islands of New Caledonia and Tahiti. At the end of August all but one of the territories constituting French Equatorial Africa also rallied to de Gaulle, as the result of daring action by a handful of Gaullist officers, including Hettier de Boislambert, Philippe François Leclerc (who would later lead the Second Armored Division into Paris), and financier René Pléven. Now, if Dakar, the capital of Senegal, would side with de Gaulle, he could envision the whole of French West Africa joining him, and perhaps, despite Mers-el-Kébir, even the entire Maghreb (French North Africa). If this happened, the empire, with its armed forces, would in the main be his, and not under the domination of Vichy. It would be an extraordinary coup that would cement his status as the legitimate leader of a wartime France opposed to Vichy France. Churchill was enthusiastic in his support. He needed a victory, and the rendition of Dakar would eliminate the potential mortal danger of a Nazi seizure of its port facilities—which the Germans certainly envisaged—as well as confirm the path he had followed in supporting de Gaulle.

In the event, everything seems to have gone wrong. Security was lacking, all the planning was improvised, and intelligence was interpreted in the most favorable light. Governor-General Pierre Boisson, who at first had decried the armistice with Germany, nevertheless gave his full support to Pétain and was furious at Gaullist inroads in central Africa. In mid-September, a week before the Anglo-French flotilla approached Dakar, three French cruisers and three destroyers left Toulon in the south of France and slipped through the Strait of Gibraltar unopposed, despite the English commander there having been notified of their passage. Although one was intercepted and turned back, the others outran the British fleet of Admiral John Cunningham, which stood between them and the African coast. They carried troops that were supposed to help reinforce the garrison in Gabon, one of the African states that had so far resisted the Gaullists, but instead they joined the already substantial French naval forces in Dakar. On all the French ships, the memory of Mers-el-Kébir still rankled. Learning of the reinforcements reaching Dakar, Churchill wanted to cancel the operation; de Gaulle, with the Allied flotilla on hand and the agreement of the British commanders on the scene, including General Spears, the British liaison officer, successfully insisted on going forward. His envoys sent to parley with Boisson, or to raise resistance to him, were threatened with arrest, however, and fired upon as they left. Fighting ensued, an unusual heavy fog kept units of the British flotilla from carrying out their contemplated activities, and a botched attempted landing to the southeast was repulsed. In the end, though the British sank three French submarines and one light cruiser, the accurate shore fire heavily damaged three British cruisers, while one battleship was damaged by a torpedo—in what the French ashore called "the revenge of Mers-el-Kébir." De Gaulle, reluctant to have Frenchmen fight other Frenchmen, withdrew. The possibility of French West Africa and North Africa joining the Allies was lost for the foreseeable future.[4]

The results were disastrous for de Gaulle, who was widely and unjustly blamed in the press in both England and the United States. The failure of the British Admiralty to stop the Vichy French flotilla from arriving in Dakar was probably the most crucial factor, along with the fog that kept the French ashore from being awed by the sight of the powerful Allied flotilla and also hindered its actions. In addition, Boislambert blamed British reserve, when a little more effort on the scene might have succeeded. Whatever the case, British newspapers spoke of "miscalculations" and "gross errors of judgment," of "pure folly," of "the lowest depths of imbecility," in the assumption that the appearance of de Gaulle and a British fleet would have been enough to rally Dakar. American newspapers followed suit.[5] American diplomats in Africa, the Middle East, and London reported to the State Department in Washington that support for de Gaulle had been destroyed.[6] De Gaulle sent two missions to Morocco and Algeria to sound out opinion, and members of both were immediately arrested.[7] Roosevelt, informed beforehand by Churchill of the attempt to take Dakar, was sour about it at the time since he was still cultivating Vichy. Its failure, unfortunately, confirmed the president in the view that de Gaulle was an incompetent leader of a dangerously amateurish movement. According to diplomat Robert Murphy (later Roosevelt's special envoy to North Africa), "Roosevelt never lost the distrust of de Gaulle's judgment and discretion which he formed then."[8] General de Gaulle and the Free French could not be trusted with military secrets. Winston Churchill vigorously defended de Gaulle's judgment and actions before the House of Commons, but privately he began to consider other possible French leaders.

French historians and others dispute the legend that Gaullist indiscretions and leaks led to the Dakar defeat. American foreign correspondent Don Cook, in his biography of de Gaulle, concludes, "There was no leak or breach of security that in any way affected the outcome of the Dakar expedition."[9] Admiral Gabriel Auphan in his history of the French navy in World War II confirms that nobody in Vichy, in the Admiralty, or elsewhere had gotten wind of the operation.[10] Boislambert, in his memoirs, provides evidence for his argument that the surprise was actually complete, and quotes one Vichy official who was in Dakar at the time: "If the fleet had penetrated in force . . . while the troops had disembarked at Rufisque [to the north of Dakar], General de Gaulle would have marched through the streets the next day to general enthusiasm."[11] There is no question, however, that Roosevelt believed the stories about leaks, and as a consequence, much later, made sure that de Gaulle was not informed of the date of the Allied North African landings in November 1942 nor, until the last moment, of the Normandy landings in June 1944, both of which obviously involved France's sovereignty. In mid-1942 Churchill did not inform him of a British expedition to the French island of Madagascar, ruled by a pro-Vichy governor. De Gaulle bitterly resented his continued exclusion from these and other major decisions affecting France, which marked him as an unreliable second player in the eyes of his allies. All of this confirmed him in his view that France could not depend on them to recognize and defend French national interests. They were interested only in their own, and these might well impinge drastically on those of the French. French armed forces might have to fight under Allied command, but only a French political authority could see to it that France and its interests were taken into account, and it was up to him to establish that authority.

De Gaulle was deeply disheartened by the Dakar disaster, which he, like Boislambert, blamed on British indecision. Nevertheless, he moved quickly to take Gabon with forces operating out of central Africa, and then took advantage of the precarious position his movement had established there, spending the next six weeks creating the foundations of a new government. The enthusiastic, colorful reception he received from the local populations and French military in the areas revived his spirits. Materially, a land link was now created from British-ruled Nigeria, on the Atlantic coast, to the Middle East: twenty thousand Allied planes were to use it in the next years; shipments from England no longer needed to go around the Cape but could cross the continent to Egypt, while some seventeen thousand primarily African soldiers joined the Free French forces.

Most important, the Free French now had a territory of their own. This meant that de Gaulle could speak to other Allied leaders from French territory, without hindrance from the Allies. His confidence was further restored when the distinguished French five-star general and former governor of Indochina, Georges Catroux, joined him. The British had flown General Catroux from the Far East to England, where Churchill actually offered to have him lead the Free French, thinking that he would have a stronger appeal to the Allies than de Gaulle. But Catroux declined, and when de Gaulle descended from an airplane in the African town of Fort Lamy, in Chad, General Catroux, who had flown to meet him, stood at attention at the base of the ramp and saluted first, recognizing the two-star general de Gaulle as the leader of the Free French. Whatever his military rank, de Gaulle was the chief.[12] Catroux would have his differences with de Gaulle in the future. He was more diplomatic and willing to compromise and was often highly critical of what he considered de Gaulle's harsh and unfeeling tactics, and made his views known. On at least two occasions he threatened to resign, but in the end he continued to support the Free French leader.

On October 24, 1940, Marshal Pétain met Adolf Hitler in the small French town of Montoire, and following their discussions, declared on the radio that he had embarked on the path of "collaboration." Three days later, October 27, in Brazzaville, de Gaulle created a substitute for the aborted National Committee he had proposed five months earlier: the Conseil de défense de l'Empire. What was perhaps most startling was the form of the announcement. "In the name of the people of the French empire, we,

General de Gaulle, chief of the Free French, ordain. . . ." There followed a list of the tasks the council would undertake. It would, in all areas, exercise the general conduct of the war with a view to the liberation of the home-land and deal with foreign powers in all matters relative to the defense of French possessions and French interests. Decisions were to be taken by the leader of the Free French after consultation, if it occurred, with the council.[13]

A month later, on November 16, the announcement was followed by an-other manifesto demonstrating in detail to foreign powers the legal basis on which de Gaulle's movement had come to represent the will of all French people everywhere, regardless of the "pseudo-government" in Vichy. Vichy was now bound by the agreements between Hitler and Pétain. What was more important, the manifesto claimed, was that the Vichy regime repre-sented an unconstitutional delegation of power from the National Assembly to Marshal Pétain, thus nullifying any legitimacy it claimed to have. The new council therefore represented a *legitimate* French authority that would follow the laws of the Third Republic. Until such time as it could account for its acts to the freely designated representatives of the French people, it would operate under a provisional central authority of which de Gaulle assumed the "sacred charge."[14]

In both England and the United States the two moves were controver-sial—in England because they were seen by the Foreign Office as possibly driving Vichy and the rest of the French empire into the arms of Germany when Churchill's ministers were still trying to persuade some of the em-pire's proconsuls to side with Britain. Churchill went ahead and quietly recognized the existence of the Conseil, referring to his approval in June 1940 of de Gaulle's first, failed attempt to form such a council. The Foreign Office asked de Gaulle not to publish the text of his second manifesto in Britain. On January 20, 1942, however, the text was published in the first number of the *Journal Officiel de la France Libre*. Against the protests of the Foreign Office, the French replied simply that the new *Journal Officiel* was an internal periodical of Free France. (The *Journal Officiel* had long been the official journal of the government of France, and creation of a new, Gaullist version outside continental France was another important symbolic step designed to buttress the claim to legitimacy of de Gaulle's movement.) Publication of *the Journal Officiel* and of the text of the mani-festo demonstrated de Gaulle's determination to force the British Foreign Office to cease its quiet negotiations with the Vichy government and accept that it would now work only with de Gaulle as the provisional, and legitimate, representative of France.

For the U.S. State Department, the failure at Dakar appeared to have cruelly exposed de Gaulle's limitations, and as a result the Brazzaville declarations seemed supremely presumptuous. Despite Montoire, the United States recognized only one government as legitimate, that of Vichy, to which most of the French empire still adhered.

Up to this point de Gaulle had had to deal with England, where officials in various ministries distrusted him, but now the United States, whose officials were more strongly opposed to him than were the British, had entered the game. The British knew that the United Kingdom's salvation lay in support from America, and the fact that America was still betting on Vichy and rejected de Gaulle's claim to legitimacy would, in the future, make it difficult for His Majesty's government to give full support to de Gaulle, even when it wanted to.

The French historian Jean-Louis Crémieux-Brilhac notes that while de Gaulle's forces and base were still minuscule at the time of Brazzaville, and his recognition by his allies was grudging, he had done something rather extraordinary in the space of six months. From being a complete nonentity in a world collapsing before the Axis onslaught, he had won his bet that England would hold out, and despite Mers-el-Kébir and Dakar, he had become a highly visible symbol of resistance in England and even the United States—and within France. Starting from nothing, his movement had conquered a territorial base, and he had established an embryonic government that stood for the honor and the future of France.[15] In both Britain and the United States, however, officials who questioned the political meaning of the Brazzaville declarations also took exception to their authoritarian, almost monarchic tone. Another historian of the period, Arthur Layton Funk, asserts that the Brazzaville declarations and the reactions to them set the stage for all future misunderstandings, sowing distrust and mutual suspicion on both sides.[16]

Events in the Middle East were soon to roil the waters further. In May 1941 Germany had obtained from Admiral Jean Darlan, the Vichy prime minister who had replaced Pierre Laval, the right to land men and materiel in Tunis, in North Africa. The British had so far prevented the Axis powers from reaching Cairo and the Suez Canal, but through Tunis the Germans could now more easily reinforce their troops advancing toward Cairo. They were led by the redoubtable "Desert Fox," General Erwin Rommel. Darlan had also granted the Germans landing rights farther to the east, in Syria, from which they could support a pro-Nazi leader who had seized power in neighboring Iraq, and they soon flew troops and materiel into the country. The same month, German troops who had driven the British out of Greece seized the island of Crete, just to the north of Libya and Egypt. A glance at a map shows that a successful pincer movement to secure the Middle East, with its vital transportation routes and its precious oil, seemed in the making, threatening the entire Allied position in the area. (In fact, Hitler was readying his long-planned assault on Russia, and events over which he had no control had brought him into the Middle East in action that, to his mind, constituted a diversion from his major project.) Though the German drive across North Africa through Libya threatened the British position in Cairo and control over the Suez Canal, the British commander in Egypt, while short of men and armaments, nevertheless agreed with the Free French authorities that they had to move into Lebanon and Syria to forestall German domination there. Churchill, earlier, had heard that pro–de Gaulle sentiment was growing in Syria and Lebanon and ordered early action, and he himself sent General Catroux to participate.

The intervention, though ultimately successful, was in many ways another disaster. The Germans, in the face of a counterrevolution in Iraq and with more important needs on the Russian front, had already withdrawn their forces from Syria, but the numerous and better-equipped Vichy French forces loyal to Marshal Pétain fought ferociously against a joint Gaullist-British expedition. Casualties were heavy, the fighting took far longer than planned, and the fratricidal nature of the conflict led to long-term bitterness among Frenchmen, particularly since Free French soldiers sent to parley under a white flag immediately came under fire.[17] As de Gaulle had discovered in his early years, few Frenchmen were willing to abandon their ties to France and home to join an unknown, condemned military man who had been stripped of his rank by the legitimate government of France, and who themselves would therefore be considered legally as traitors. More important, however, were the frictions and suspicions that developed between de Gaulle, who felt his isolation, and the English.

Churchill left the matter of Syria to his subordinates, focusing instead on the crucial battle being fought in Libya against General Rommel's Afrika

Corps. As a result, on the scene in the Levant, the English military who predominated had a relatively free hand, and were impressed with the fact that so many French loyal to Vichy had resisted the Gaullist troops who accompanied them. Consequently they had little use for de Gaulle and paid scant attention to Gaullist interests. On July 14 they signed a truce at St. Jean d'Acre with the Vichy commander, General Henri-Fernand Dentz, that completely overlooked the Gaullists' insistence on a number of conditions—one of which was that they should have been included in the negotiations and certainly in the signing. The truce failed to take into account the Gaullist desire to communicate directly with the Vichy French troops in order to win them over. Instead these troops ended up mostly being shipped back to France, after sabotaging their equipment which the Gaullists desperately needed. The British were more interested in obtaining Arab support through their pan-Arab policy than in the Gaullist desire to reestablish French influence in the area and consequently overlooked or overruled France's insistence on its sovereign rights, a matter on which de Gaulle, in his as yet weak position, proceeded to insist with a fervor that surprised everyone, but that succeeded in getting the British to modify the terms of the St. Jean d'Acre truce.

As a result of these and other matters, an angered de Gaulle, seemingly convinced that the British were using the war to replace French control with British influence, lambasted the British unmercifully. The agreement of St. Jean d'Acre—signed, ironically, on Bastille Day—became a long-lasting symbol of British perfidy. De Gaulle let himself go, launching his accusations in the press, in telegrams back to London, and face-to-face with British envoys in the area. As he traveled back to London, he spoke venomously of British Arabists in the Colonial Office, as well as of the War Office and British intelligence. "Wherever he went," wrote Churchill in a War Cabinet memorandum, "he left behind him a trail of Anglophobia."[18] According to François Coulet, one of de Gaulle's aides, "it was in the spring and summer of that year" that de Gaulle, who had never known the British or their language before May–June 1940, "formed his opinion of his allies. It was a hostile one, and in large part it lasted."[19] What is more, his success in forcing the British to modify the treaty of St. Jean d'Acre confirmed him in his view, contrary to that of the conciliatory General Catroux, that the only way to deal with the British was to "pound the table—and they will give in."[20]

General Edward Spears was in charge of the British delegation in the Levant. He had been the British liaison to de Gaulle and an admiring supporter though wary of de Gaulle's authoritarian tendencies. He now turned bitterly anti–de Gaulle as a result of the Middle East imbroglio, and he and General Catroux, the Free French delegate to the Levant, clashed repeatedly. Spears, wrote British envoy Duff Cooper, became the "most violently Francophobe of all British politicians." As long as he was in the Middle East there was trouble, and many English deplored his attitude as one cause of complications with both the Arabs and de Gaulle. De Gaulle requested his recall, and even the diplomatic General Catroux later wrote that like de Gaulle, he was convinced that Spears was there to carry out a secret policy to displace French influence with British in the area. As long as Spears remained, and as long as Churchill—an old friend of Spears's from the First World War—would not recall him, no one could convince Catroux that this was not the case. In fact, independently of London, Spears did encourage nationalist forces in the area. Duff Cooper wrote, "I therefore considered the presence of Spears as a fatal impediment to improved Anglo-French relations."[21] Moreover, de Gaulle's and Catroux's suspicions coincided with incessant Vichy propaganda about the intention of the British to take over portions of the French empire.[22]

De Gaulle, it should be remembered, was a member of a French military family who shared in all the Anglo-French hostility a long history had bred. For centuries Britain and France had been traditional enemies, fighting on the continent, on the seas, and, until the end of the nineteenth century, over colonies. De Gaulle lived through the 1920s and 1930s, when French and British policy had diverged with respect to Germany, when Britain, as many French thought, had dragged its feet during the "phony war" period, abandoned thousands of Frenchmen at Dunkirk, and refused to send the planes the French had asked for in extremity. De Gaulle had to rely on British support now, but it went against the grain. He would never lose his ability to interpret British policy negatively. (In the face of all this, writes François Coulet, Winston Churchill and de Gaulle nevertheless each took the risk of forgetting the past and betting on each other—even if they occasionally let their differences boil over.)[23]

Back in London, where an exasperated Churchill at first refused to see de Gaulle, the two finally met and appear to have resolved the issues that had so incensed the Free French leader. Nevertheless, intense friction continued in the Middle East itself until the war's end. The sensibilities of the French about their sovereign rights clashed with the fact of British military presence on the scene. It was certainly at this time that de Gaulle hardened in his overall view that the Allies were not about to let France regain its empire, and that it was up to him to block them. This much said, one French historian asserts that de Gaulle, in his obstreperousness, terrified his colleagues in Beirut, Cairo, and London, who considered that a close collaboration with Britain was necessary and that de Gaulle's suspicions were unjustified and his reactions extreme.[24]

British statesman Anthony Eden, reflecting on all this, wrote:

> I had the most sincere admiration for this great Frenchman's qualities. To know him was to understand how exaggerated was the picture, often created in the public mind, of arrogance and even majesty. . . . His selflessness made it possible for him to keep the flame of France alive when in political or more diplomatic hands it must have flickered out. Yet de Gaulle was the victim of his qualities, for the fervour of his faith made him at times too suspicious of the intentions of others. The schemes and the greed not infrequently attributed to Britain and its leading personalities in those years were many of them insubstantial myths. We did not want Madagascar, nor Syria, nor Jibuti. . . . [I]t was to our interest that France should be strong and that the French empire should survive, if possible intact, but I doubt that General de Gaulle ever believed this.[25]

What was also true was that his single-mindedness—"the fervour of his faith"—led him to be terribly difficult. Wrote French bureaucrat Hervé Alphand, when he first came to join de Gaulle in London: "I find in him no desire to please, no care about nuance, no spirit of negotiation. The only maneuver that he seems to know and to employ is that of a tank that forges forward. . . . His rigidity even with respect to the most minor matters is a part of his politics and his personality. He insists that it is the weakened condition in which our country finds itself that forces him to be intransigent."[26] Much later, in the Swiss *Journal de Genève,* the distinguished editorial writer René Payot would conclude that if de Gaulle had bent to his allies' wishes, he would have lost the confidence of his compatriots, and that the foundation of his instinct to be stubborn was sound: he had to convince Frenchmen suffering at home that he was not just an émigré, that he was not just an agent of foreigners.[27]

On December 7, 1941, Japan attacked Pearl Harbor, and four days later, to the relief of Winston Churchill and Franklin D. Roosevelt, Hitler declared war on the United States. De Gaulle saw the consequences clearly, saying to one of his aides: "Well, the war is finished. . . . [O]f course, there will still be operations, battles, fighting, but the war is finished, since the ending is now known. In this industrial war, nothing can withstand the power of American industry." And he added presciently, "From now on in, the English will do nothing without the agreement of the Americans."[28] This meant, in effect, that along with the participation of the Soviet Union, the role of the French would be diminished in the face of the new triumvirate. Biographer David Schoenbrun adds: "De Gaulle did not fear Hitler's victory, which he was certain was impossible. What de Gaulle feared was the victory of Britain and America, with the spoils of victory leaving them the dominant postwar powers in Europe at the expense of a humiliated, powerless France."[29]

It was perhaps in the light of this that two weeks later, determined to rally the French possessions in the Western Hemisphere, de Gaulle sent the head of Free French naval forces, Admiral Émile Muselier, to take two tiny islands held by Vichy, Saint Pierre and Miquelon, off the coast of Canada. There, French army veterans had almost succeeded in rallying the islands to de Gaulle but had been crushed by the local government.

Admiral Muselier was received rapturously by the 1,400 inhabitants. A plebiscite held a short time later gave an overwhelming approval to the action: 783 votes for the Free French, 14 for "collaboration with the Axis," and 215 blank or spoiled ballots.[30] The enthusiasm that erupted in Saint Pierre was widely reported in the United States thanks to the presence of American journalist Ira Wolfert, who had gone along on the expedition. The ensuing ruckus over a tiny affair, however, was almost unbelievable: de Gaulle, with a single highly successful and gratifying minor action, had managed to alienate the United States government even further.

The United States was now at war with Nazi Germany and might have welcomed a small Free French victory over an outpost of collaborationist Vichy. But the American government had signed a secret accord with Admiral Georges Robert, the Vichy high commissioner in the islands of the

French Antilles in the Caribbean, to maintain the status quo of French possessions in the Western Hemisphere so that they would not be transferred to enemy hands, and on December 13, 1941, Franklin D. Roosevelt had sent a personal message to Pétain about the maintenance of all previous agreements in the light of the new developments, that is, war with Germany.[31] Before sending off Admiral Muselier, de Gaulle had consulted the British. The British Admiralty, fearful that a potentially important radio station in the islands could track Allied shipping and might be used to guide German submarines, gave its strong support, and Churchill had happily accepted the takeover, asking only that he be allowed thirty-six hours to make sure the action would be acceptable to the Americans. To his surprise, the American response was a categorical no, and de Gaulle was so informed. But de Gaulle also presumably learned that the Americans were contemplating a Canadian action to take control of the wireless station, and on the grounds that no foreign power could intervene in French possessions, although he had pledged that he would not act without Allied approval, he ordered a reluctant Admiral Muselier to go ahead.

The press in the United States and Britain initially supported the action enthusiastically. But the State Department, and in particular Secretary of State Cordell Hull, exploded. If the American government let the takeover stand, it would alienate Vichy, especially after Roosevelt's personal message to Pétain which had reiterated that the status quo of French possessions in the Western Hemisphere would be maintained, and in the light of the—secret—agreement with Admiral Robert. Somewhat implausibly Hull foresaw terrible repercussions: destruction of the Good Neighbor policy toward the American republics, the withdrawal or forcible removal of Americans such as Leahy in Vichy and Murphy in North Africa who were providing vital information to the Allies. De Gaulle, he told the bemused British ambassador, "had inflicted on Great Britain and the United States unimaginable injury to their military defensive situation in this hemisphere and French Africa."[32] De Gaulle had violated his pledge to the Allies not to act without their approval.

The State Department, on learning of de Gaulle's exploit, had immediately issued a quite extraordinary statement: "Our preliminary reports show that the action taken by three so-called Free French ships was an arbitrary action contrary to the agreement of all parties concerned and certainly without the prior knowledge or consent in any sense of the United States Government. This Government has inquired of the Canadian Government as to the steps that Government is prepared to take to restore the status quo of these islands."[33] Critics, appalled at the notion of returning the islands to the control of collaborationist Vichy France, pounced on the phrase "so-called Free French ships," addressing letters and telegrams to the "so-called Secretary of State" and the "so-called State Department" and likening the department's stance to that of appeasement of Hitler at the time of Munich. The world, after all, was in a parlous state: the Japanese had destroyed much of the American fleet and were advancing through the Pacific and into China, German forces were advancing in North Africa and were deep in the Soviet Union, and German submarines were sinking American and British ships in increasing numbers in the Atlantic—and the State Department had taken the time to propose returning tiny islands seized by the Free French with the almost unanimous approval of their populace to a government that had declared it would "collaborate" with Nazi Germany!

If much of the press in the United States ended up sympathizing with the embarrassment of the American government, the storm that had been aroused over a minor incident seemed to the press, and especially to the British, to be outlandish. Churchill, who was in Washington conferring with Roosevelt at the time, wrote later that far too much had been made of a minor affair. (He also informed de Gaulle that if he had not been on the spot to smooth things over, the American reaction might have been even worse.) Moreover, the Canadians, to the frustration of Cordell Hull, now made clear to the United States government that they would certainly not act to oust an ally from the islands, and Churchill, addressing the Canadian parliament after leaving Washington, condemned the supine men of Vichy while effusively praising those French who resisted under the leadership of General de Gaulle and now gave hope to all of France. Hull characterized the speech as "highly incendiary."[34] The liberal press in the United States excoriated the State Department for its attitude. Nevertheless, in what seems extraordinary in retrospect, given wartime exigencies, Hull continued to advance elaborate plans for the two tiny islands that would result in the withdrawal of Gaullist forces and the introduction of an Allied commission. He threatened to resign if he was not supported, and Roosevelt did support him up to a point. But when the idea of sending an American cruiser to oust the Gaullists was bruited about, Churchill and Eden were forced to protest. In the end de Gaulle won out, simply because an informed public in both the United States and Britain, seeing this war as one of principle, would have been revolted by the idea of ousting the Free French. As one result, Roosevelt came to avoid bringing his secretary of state into policy matters: Hull's overreaction to Saint Pierre and Miquelon had discredited him in the president's eyes.

Nevertheless, there was another consequence. Whatever view one took of the whole incident—and at least one biographer of de Gaulle believed that by his thoughtless action he had missed an opportunity to improve his relations with a United States that was now at war with the Axis[35]—Roosevelt and the top State Department officials had been deliberately flouted, and greatly embarrassed, by the upstart General de Gaulle. Leahy, Hull, Welles, and others, including Roosevelt, would not soon forget. De Gaulle could not be trusted.

In England, too, there was further friction when Admiral Muselier returned. There were many French in England who looked askance at de Gaulle's arbitrary conduct and, with the support of Churchill, sought to have him contained in a broadened committee that would dilute his power. Admiral Muselier had opposed de Gaulle's decision to defy the United States in occupying the islands, and gone on record with his opposition, but felt he had had to obey orders. Now, back in England, he took the lead in trying to weaken de Gaulle's leadership. The War Cabinet supported Muselier's attempt, but de Gaulle acrimoniously rejected any British intervention in French affairs. Nevertheless, quietly, Churchill and Eden secured a compromise. On September 24, 1941, de Gaulle had created a new advisory body, the French National Committee. Muselier was now made a member though his allies were not. De Gaulle, however, relieved the admiral of his command of the Free French naval forces at about the same time, and despite English backing of Muselier, in the face of de Gaulle's insistence that the English could not dictate to the leader of the Free French, the admiral soon disappeared, to emerge later as an anti-Gaullist in North Africa.

Despite these strange and strained circumstances in which the French National Committee was involved so early in its life, its creation was an important step toward the formation of a government-in-exile. Moreover de Gaulle's successful insistence on his independence from the English was another.

With Nazi Germany now at war with the United States, there had been some reconsideration in Washington with regard to relations with Vichy. To the public, Washington's continued Vichy policy and its failure to recognize a de Gaulle who had resisted from the start appeared to condone relations with fascism and totalitarianism. Admiral Leahy himself, as ambassador to Vichy France, had decided that Pétain was spineless in the face of pressures from Laval and other collaborationists. Nevertheless, State Department personnel argued that continued contact with Vichy both provided information as to what was going on in France and was necessary to the ability to keep American diplomatic personnel in Vichy-dominated North Africa—who were there to help prepare Allied landings in the near future. Besides, the affair of Saint Pierre and Miquelon showed that de Gaulle and his organization presented no alternative.

Friction between de Gaulle and the Allies continued throughout 1942 even before the Allies invaded North Africa late in the year. In the Pacific the landing of large numbers of somewhat unruly American troops on the French island of New Caledonia led to irritating conflicts with the Free French military on the island. The conflicts caused the suspicious de Gaulle to believe that the Americans were really trying to take over the island, and to speak for the first time of "American imperialism,"[36] and to incorporate it into his thought. Compounding the situation and increasing his suspicions of the Anglo-Saxons in general, the incident of Madagascar took place at about the same time.

In early 1942 the Indian Ocean island of Madagascar, long a French colony, appeared to Allied strategists to be of increased importance as a result of the fall to the Japanese of the great British port of Singapore, on the other side of the Indian Ocean. The Japanese, having sunk the two British capital ships sent to block them, could now sail into the Indian Ocean with impunity, and if they established a base in Madagascar—after all, Vichy had granted them bases in Indochina—they could control Britain's communication with the Indian subcontinent. De Gaulle himself submitted plans to the Churchill government for a Free French landing with naval and air support by Britain; but the British took the matter into their own hands, landing a small force in the south on May 5, 1942, and when they ran into stiff resistance, ended up treating with the Vichy French governor, allowing him to stay in office. De Gaulle had again been kept out of an operation concerning territory of the French empire. For the British military and for Churchill, another Franco-British operation like that of Dakar and that of the Levant, where French had to fight against French, was out of the question: in the opinion of the British, French participation in the past in this sort of operation had greatly complicated matters. But de Gaulle had not even been informed of the Madagascar operation, code-named "Ironclad," and he was, to put it mildly, hardly happy about it, telling Churchill that had the British landing been coordinated with a Free French one in the north, the whole island would have fallen and his cause, obviously, been greatly enhanced. His movement was becoming widely supported in occupied France, where three months earlier he had sent a secret agent, Jean Moulin, to assemble the various resistance groups that were in the process of forming, and any Free French victory outside France raised morale within. With the Free French controlling Madagascar, the island would have been in the war on the side of the Allies; now it looked as if it would remain largely under Vichy control.

In the light of the New Caledonia altercation and the unannounced British action in Madagascar, an angered de Gaulle, who had broadened his committee in London to contain more civilians, considered various forms of retaliation: moving his headquarters out of London to central Africa, or publicly denouncing the British and American governments. Since late 1941, following the invasion of the Soviet Union, he had seen relations with the Russians (the only term he would use) as a counterweight to the influence of the Western Allies, and following several exchanges, the Soviet Union had sent Alexander Bogomolov as ambassador to the Free French. In the event, de Gaulle even inquired of Ambassador Bogomolov, to whom he delivered an anti-English diatribe, as to whether the Soviet Union would harbor him and the Free French movement.[37] In the end, he took no action. But it should be added once again that de Gaulle did not forgive and forget lightly when it came to the honor and sovereignty of France, which was now, as he and many other Frenchmen saw it, embodied in his movement.

About this time, between May 27 and June 11, a Free French light division commanded by General Marie-Pierre Koenig moved north out of central Africa and repulsed heavy Italian and German attacks on Bir Hakeim, an outpost in Libya, before extricating itself from the surrounding Axis forces. The action gave retreating British troops reeling before General Rommel's Afrika Korps time to regroup. It was strategically a highly important operation, but also a hugely symbolic action for the French (later commemorated in the naming of a Métro station in Paris). It came at a time when not only were the British retreating in North Africa, but also Allied shipping losses in the Atlantic and Mediterranean were at their height, and in Russia the Germans had invested Kharkov, Sebastopol, and Leningrad. Bir Hakeim and American success in repelling the Japanese at Midway Island in the Pacific were the only bright spots of that June.[38] The French success was widely reported and celebrated in both the British and American press, and de Gaulle took the occasion to change the name of the movement from Free French to La France Combattante—Fighting France. Symbolically, the change meant that his organization included not only Free French forces outside France but also the armed resistance within. Churchill personally congratulated de Gaulle. On July 9, 1942, thanks to several developments—Eden's suggestions, the return of Laval to power in France, and the diplomacy of a new French envoy in Washington, Emmanuel d'Astier de la Vigerie (a distant relative of Roosevelt's), who had come out of the resistance in France—Washington appointed a representative to the French National Committee in London, Admiral Harold Stark. The admiral was commander of naval forces in Europe, and he would become a strong de Gaulle supporter. On October 6 President Roosevelt also authorized the extension of the vital American program of Lend-Lease aid to its allies to the Free French.

Sending an American representative to the Free French was an important step. Sending a military man as representative was meant to indicate, however, that the move was not political but merely a means to improve military cooperation. Even so, the State Department, where Undersecretary Sumner Welles had tried fruitlessly to come up with any alternative to de Gaulle, was not pleased by the move. Welles made known his rather strange views to the English ambassador, Lord Halifax. Recognition of Free France, he believed, "would exasperate French public opinion and strengthen the hand of the Germans," and from what he heard from London, "it was very clear" to him that "the Free French movement . . . was rapidly falling to pieces."[39] There is no record of Halifax's reaction.

Despite Welles's curious views, the Free French had gained some advantage that summer—but also lost some. General George C. Marshall, the army chief of staff, was in England in July 1942, along with Admiral Ernest J. King, chief of naval operations, and de Gaulle, anticipating future Allied operations of which he was not being informed, asked to meet with the two American military leaders. The British had requested that details of future action not be revealed to General de Gaulle, and the result was a frustrating meeting from which Marshall took with him a highly negative view of the French leader. De Gaulle, as a result of his argumentative mood, lost the support of someone who could have been an important advocate in official Washington.[40]

Unfortunately, conflict continued in the Levant, where the British wanted assurances that free elections would be held so as to satisfy Arab opinion, while the French insisted that France alone would take care of matters there. The real enmity of British envoy Spears, and the lack of any action on the future of Madagascar, which the British now contemplated occupying in its entirety, both contributed to de Gaulle's continued hostility toward the British. Churchill now heard more and more reports of de Gaulle's views. Then, on September 30, 1942, when the two men met in the presence of Anthony Eden to discuss all that separated them, the discussion rapidly deteriorated. When Churchill exclaimed to de Gaulle that he was not France, de Gaulle answered, "Then why are you negotiating with me?" The exchange ended on such a rancorous note that Churchill was reported to have shouted at de Gaulle that he would "break him like a chair!" while actually breaking a chair.[41] The result was that beginning the next day, for a period of almost a month, until Churchill relented, relations between the Committee and the British government were essentially broken off; the latter, for instance, no longer transmitted Free French coded messages from England to central Africa. Moreover, de Gaulle's intelligence services had reported that the Allies, and in particular the Americans, were contemplating landings in French North Africa, again without informing the Free French. The stage was being set for an Allied victory but also for even more inter-Allied conflict.

On November 8, 1942, American amphibious forces some 100,000 strong landed at seven points on the Algerian and Moroccan coasts, supported by naval and air units. It was a highly complicated and difficult action calling for unusual coordination, since some units sailed from the United Kingdom but others all the way from the United States. For logistical reasons they did not go as far east as Bizerte, in Tunisia, and the omission would have fateful consequences: within days, while pro-Vichy French forces stood by, German troops began to pour into Tunisia. They would slow by months the Allied conquest of North Africa and therefore subsequent moves to land on the European mainland.[42]

The landings were essentially an American enterprise, and Roosevelt had insisted to a reluctant Churchill that de Gaulle be kept out of the operation and not informed until the landings had taken place, telling him, "I am very apprehensive in regard to the adverse effect that any introduction of de Gaulle into the invasion situation would have on our promising efforts to attach a large part of the French African forces to our expedition."[43] In this he certainly reflected Admiral Leahy's view. "Plans for the landing had been kept a complete secret from the so-called 'leader of the French resistance,' who at that time was a highly advertised hero in England and in this country, but who seemed to have few important friends in Africa or in France itself," Leahy later recalled. "[W]e knew that his organization was impregnated with German spies, and if we had given him advance information the Germans might have known it."[44]

To placate de Gaulle the somewhat mercurial Churchill invited him to lunch and told him that since the landings were essentially an American affair, he and Eisenhower, who shared his point of view, had had to accept Roosevelt's insistence, though they personally opposed it. To sweeten the pill, he also announced that Madagascar would now be turned over to the Free French, and reasserted to the man he had wanted to get rid of ten days earlier his full support for de Gaulle's movement as representative of France. The Americans took a different tack. Since the United States still maintained relations with Vichy before the North African landings, the administration had been able to send veteran diplomat Robert Murphy to Vichy-controlled North Africa as a special envoy, supported by twelve vice consuls.[45] They were ostensibly there to observe the carrying out of an agreement Murphy negotiated with General Weygand, the Vichy delegate-general, to supply North Africa with food and other necessities, and to see that none of these were transshipped to occupied France. (They discovered that despite the British blockade, North Africa was supplying Germany with large quantities of vital foodstuffs and raw materials.) In fact, Murphy and his staff were also there to reconnoiter the territories and secure the cooperation of French personnel opposed to Vichy preparatory to the planned Allied landing. Roosevelt and Hull had placed their hopes in Weygand, the French delegate-general in North Africa, despite his key role in insisting on capitulation to the Germans in 1940. They knew he was venerated by the French army; he had kept his distance with regard to collaboration; he would be accepted by French opinion within France and without; and he was apparently convinced that since Germany had lost the battle of Britain and the United States had entered the war, Germany would lose. He would, wrote French journalist Nerin Gun, "become, in a word, a very useful 'anti-de Gaulle.'"[46] He was known to hate the Germans, and if he agreed to turn over North Africa to the Allies, he might also be able to bring over the French fleet units from Toulon.

Weygand happened also to hate de Gaulle, who had stood fast against Weygand's defeatism in the debacle of 1940, and Weygand was also following a policy of suppressing Gaullists in the North African army and administration. In fact under Weygand, North Africa remained a fundamental part of Vichy-controlled France: repressive and antidemocratic Vichy legislation was in full force.

The Germans, however, were suspicious of Weygand and forced Pétain to recall him. He most certainly would never have turned his back on Pétain anyway. Much earlier in the year, before he was sent to North Africa, he had been approached by a member of the American embassy in Vichy with an offer of command of French forces in North Africa if the Americans landed there and supplied his forces. He turned it down and apparently informed Pétain of the offer, thereby making the marshal aware of American plans. When Murphy visited him in Cannes on July 17, Weygand told him, "At my age one doesn't become a rebel."[47]

So much for one American-supported alternative to de Gaulle. There was one other with whom Allen Dulles, the American Office of Strategic Services chief in Bern, had been in contact and helped finance: General Benoit-Léon Fornel de la Laurencie. De la Laurencie, a right-wing nationalist, had distinguished himself in the 1940 campaign, had served the Vichy government, and was a member of the military court that condemned de Gaulle to death. But he had broken with Darlan when the admiral was prime minister, and he had tried to assemble resistance forces within France on the grounds that no one could lead them who, like de Gaulle, had left France. Pro-Gaullist resistants had opposed him, and as a result of public pronouncements he made in favor of the Anglo-Americans, he disappeared, interned by Darlan for the next two years. His being financed by the Americans, however, presumably as a possible alternative to de Gaulle, is still referred to by French historians, who see in it a precursor to further American attempts to supersede the Free French leader.[48]

Failure to enlist Weygand, or de la Laurencie, led to something of a vacuum of leadership in North Africa, where there were certainly Gaullists in the lower ranks—though the Americans thought that there couldn't be many—but there were also many anti-Gaullists, especially in the upper civilian and military ranks, most of whom retained their loyalty to Marshal Pétain. There were also royalists: their leader, the Comte de Paris, pretender to the French throne, was willing to take over North Africa. He had considerable support, but Roosevelt apparently ordered, "As for the Comte de Paris, no monarchic restoration, get him out of Algiers."[49] It was an extraordinarily complex situation. Marshal Pétain, in Vichy, despite the affection and admiration he had developed for the United States when he visited in 1931, had made it clear that an invasion by anyone would be resisted: North Africa was a part of France, and an invasion there would be an invasion of France. Who then could keep the French army from opposing the Americans? Once the Americans landed, hoping, of course, that the French North African army would not resist them, they would have to see to civil government behind the lines. But what or by whom would that government be? American military government was not in the works, so it would have to be government by Frenchmen on the spot. But which ones, among groups that were bitterly divided, but with Vichy officials clearly in command? As far as the Americans were concerned, only one thing was clear: under no circumstances would the government be Gaullist.

Roosevelt's envoy Robert Murphy did his best to find answers to both problems. Murphy and his team of "vice consuls" met with many groups on all levels in what was an enormously complicated set of maneuvers, while also gathering detailed information on what the Allies would meet when they landed. Murphy worked at bringing over wavering French leaders, eventually relying largely on a so-called Group of Five headed by a somewhat shady industrialist named Jacques Lemaigre-Dubreuil. It was in part through Lemaigre-Dubreuil that rather suddenly a candidate appeared who might be counted on to take upon himself both the task of preventing any resistance to the Allied landings and that of securing the cooperation of the North African administrators: an upright, old-school, French five-star general untainted by collaboration, General Henri Honoré Giraud. Although he had given his word to the Germans, Giraud had escaped from German imprisonment and made his way to Vichy, where he met with Pétain—to whom he pledged allegiance and support for his policies, including that of collaboration with Nazi Germany—but who, contacted by Lemaigre-Dubreuil, proceeded secretly to Gibraltar to meet General Eisenhower, newly named commander of the whole North African operation. Their meeting would define the role General Giraud would take in the forthcoming action.

The Americans now pinned their hopes on Giraud. His prestige should make it possible for him to command the French armies in North Africa not to resist. He might be the one to get the French fleet in Toulon to come over to the Allies in North Africa, and he might, in the long run, be the perfect substitute for the contentious de Gaulle. From Vichy, where the United States was now represented by an interim chargé d'affaires, H. Pinkney Tuck, Washington had earlier received a "euphoric" message. Giraud, Tuck declared, was respected by the public, supported by the army, and had an impeccable reputation: "If France decides to fight, Giraud, not Weygand, would be the ideal leader to command a resistance army."[50]

When Giraud turned up in Gibraltar to meet Eisenhower, however, the American commander in chief was startled to learn that Giraud envisioned for himself the role of Supreme Commander of all the Allied forces, which he thought should land in both North Africa and southern France at the same time. He had already done much planning on his own, and insisted that the Allied forces be 500,000 strong. Among other things, he further insisted that landings should take place far to the east, at Bizerte, in Tunis. The general was clearly out of touch with a complicated and evolving reality, and Eisenhower had to persuade him that his role would be the lesser one of commanding the French forces in North Africa, but at the behest of Eisenhower as Supreme Commander of all Allied forces there.

Giraud's arrival in Gibraltar had been delayed by several days; he had then balked at the idea that he, a Frenchman, would not be in command; then he had had to take time to digest his new, proposed role vis-à-vis the Allied forces; and by the time this was worked out, those Allied forces, primarily American, had already landed, to be met with stiff and bloody French resistance, encouraged by repeated broadcast of a call by Marshal Pétain to oppose the landings. Then it turned out that Giraud, who had delayed his departure because of large pro-de Gaulle demonstrations in Algiers,[51] when he finally arrived there, had no influence on the French North African commanders. They remained loyal to Marshal Pétain, who had informed Admiral Leahy earlier that he would order resistance to anyone who landed in North Africa. As a result the French armies paid no attention to Giraud's orders to stop fighting: he was not their commander.[52] It took, instead, the command of Admiral François Darlan, who happened to be in North Africa at the bedside of his son, who had contracted polio. On the grounds that he had the backing of Marshal Pétain, who had sent him a telegram to that effect, the admiral was able to persuade the French army to cease all resistance to the Americans.

It was fantastic: this was the collaborationist Admiral Darlan who had so fatefully refused to let "his" fleet go over to the Allies' side in June 1940, who, during the fourteen months he was Vichy prime minister, had pushed collaboration with the Nazis even further than the hated Laval, had let the Japanese take Indochina unopposed, had authorized the Germans to use airports in Syria and allowed German General Rommel to be supported by shipping supplies through Tunisia. This was the man who had promulgated the anti-Jewish laws in France, the man who, with his knowledge of the British navy, with which he had earlier cooperated, offered to and actually did share his knowledge of British shipping with the Germans, who he was sure would win the war. He was also sure that the Germans would leave France and its empire in a better position than if the British won. He had in fact ordered French troops two days earlier to fire on the Americans.[53]

On the scene General Mark Clark faced French resistance that slowed an Allied advance, brought numerous casualties, and allowed the Germans to begin actively to move fresh troops into Tunisia. To stop the fighting he agreed to let Admiral Darlan assume power as Haut Commissaire en Afrique du Nord "in the name of the Marshal." This took a bit of maneuvering: Pétain had telegraphed his approval of Darlan's earlier stand against the Allies, and Darlan used the telegram of support without reference to its date to justify his later pro-Allied stand to the largely Pétainiste North African officers. In return Darlan, "on behalf of the marshal," ordered a cease-fire that did in fact result in the end of the costly hostilities. Most of the fighting had already stopped, but the rest of the French troops obeyed his orders.

Admiral Darlan had been relieved of his position as prime minister in Vichy some months earlier and had begun to see the change in the whole global situation. He apparently concluded that Germany could not win. Three weeks before the Allied landings in North Africa, the State Department had received confidential information from France to the effect that Darlan might be ready to cooperate with the Allies.[54] In other words, after a little agonizing the admiral was willing to change sides, and the Americans had been informed of it. As a further result he was now disavowed by Pétain. Eisenhower defended the decision to deal with Darlan vigorously in his memoirs. When the Americans met with telling fire as they landed, Eisenhower cabled back to Washington on November 14: "Existing French sentiment here does not remotely agree with prior calculations. . . . The resistance we first met was offered because all ranks believed this to be the Marshal's wish. . . . [O]nly one man has an obvious right to assume the Marshal's mantle in North Africa. He is Darlan."[55] As a result, when a public storm erupted over the decision to retain the former collaborationist Darlan, Chief of Staff General George C. Marshall asked Undersecretary of State Welles not to suggest removing Darlan, "the man to whom General Eisenhower must look for immediate results."[56]

In the next few months the admiral would prove highly valuable to the Allied war effort. Thanks in part to him, ports, railroads, telephone and telegraph communications, and police forces all were secured and made available to the Allies along their lengthened lines leading to Tunisia. This was at a time when many French officers were so anti-British and so loyal to Pétain that they at first cooperated with the Germans in Tunisia and but for Darlan might well have sabotaged Allied communications.[57] Moreover, many in the Arab population supported Vichy because it had put into effect anti-Jewish legislation, and as Eisenhower wrote, without Darlan the Arabs might have interfered with the Allied effort. The agreement left entirely intact the Vichy governmental structures and laws and left Darlan in charge of any changes that might be made.

Ironically, Darlan was able to persuade General Boisson, the commander in Dakar who had earlier repulsed the British and de Gaulle, to bring French West Africa over to his command. Unfortunately, despite his virtually having created the modern French fleet, he was unable to persuade Admiral Jean de Laborde in Toulon to move the French fleet units based there across the Mediterranean to North Africa. Laborde, when first contacted, is said to have replied "merde!" So far as he was concerned, the British and de Gaulle were the enemy. When the Germans, in response to the American invasion of North Africa, occupied the rest of France and prepared to seize the fleet, Admiral Laborde at first declared in an order of the day that the strongpoint of Toulon remained free, its defense was French, and it was subordinate to no foreign command. Five submarines slipped away, but when the Germans prepared to move in, Laborde ordered his men to scuttle their ships, which they did. They sank 220,000 tons: three battleships, seven cruisers, thirty destroyers, and sixteen submarines. Darlan's biographer wrote somewhat bitterly, "The 'unvanquished fleet' was at the bottom of the sea by the will of those who commanded it and without having fought."[58] To many this act—"this grandiose, tragic, nihilistic gesture by French sailors"—was one that could have been avoided. But now the magnificent fleet would never be available to fight against the Nazis, to defend French interests, to carry weight in the future balance of power.[59]

General Clark and Admiral Darlan signed a further agreement on November 22 establishing American and French rights in North Africa and confirming Darlan's position as high commissioner there.

Despite its usefulness in stopping the hostilities, the original agreement with the tainted collaborationist Darlan had provoked an outraged outcry in England and the United States. With the new agreement it now rose in a crescendo—in the press, in Parliament, and among members of other governments-in-exile. Did the record of Nazi collaboration mean nothing in a war to eliminate fascism and militarism? If the Americans, to ease matters, accepted Darlan in North Africa, would they accept Laval in France and other traitors in other occupied countries, like Quisling in Norway or Degrelle in Belgium? Intelligence services reported widespread anger in occupied France. De Gaulle's envoy in Washington, Adrien Tixier, told Sumner Welles that French opinion was overwhelmed by the resurrection in North Africa of a totalitarian regime in the hands of the traitor Darlan. The internal Resistance would lose confidence in the Americans if the Darlan regime was not liquidated.[60] Another Frenchman in Washington, Hervé Alphand, wrote, "All that we could fear for so many months had taken place: no French unity, the most hated traitors maintained in place, the utmost confusion is spread in the minds of Frenchmen who no longer know why we fight."[61]

At the instigation of de Gaulle's envoy to the Resistance, Jean Moulin, Resistance leaders in France published a communiqué addressed to the Allied governments insisting that North Africa's new destiny be put into the hands of General de Gaulle, signed by virtually all the main Resistance organizations. (The Americans managed to get the BBC to refrain from publishing it.)[62] Churchill himself was disgusted: "Darlan," he said, "ought to be shot."[63] Churchill had agreed that America would run matters in North Africa, so he had to accept the Darlan deal. "Being your ardent and active lieutenant," he wrote to Roosevelt, "I should bow to your decision without demur,"[64] but he told de Gaulle what he thought of it and communicated his concerns to the president on November 17 that as a possible consequence there could be "serious political injury," so the arrangement should be only an "immediate expedient," to be superseded as soon as possible.[65] And he was happy enough in the face of fierce parliamentary questioning to let members know that the British government bore no responsibility for the Darlan deal. Stalin, by contrast, sent Roosevelt an approving telegram congratulating him on having brought over people like Darlan into the fight against Hitler.[66] It was somewhat ironic, given the relations the Soviet Union had just established with the Free French. In any event, as a result of the uproar in the press over the deal, Roosevelt, who had vowed he would shake hands with anyone who delivered territory to the Allies, was forced to declare in a press conference on December 16, 1942, that the agreement was only a "temporary expedient," and that it would lead to amnesty for Allied sympathizers, that Allied personnel who had been interned were already being released, while there would soon be restoration of rights to those who had been deprived of them because of race.[67] In fact, the opposite was happening.

The agreement that Darlan had signed gave the Allies control of airports, harbors, and all fortifications, military communications, right of requisition, extraterritoriality for Allied personnel, and wide emergency powers in case of disorder. It also proved, in the long run, grist for the mill of French historians, who saw in it a forerunner of what the Allies were planning for France. Sorbonne Marxist historian Annie Lacroix-Riz still views the agreement as one that was actually intended to apply to all of France.[68] There was, however, never any intention for it to extend beyond North Africa, the one area for which it was intended and to which it applied. In November 1943 an aide-mémoire from the Allies was delivered to René Massigli, the Gaullist foreign affairs commissioner, to the effect that the Clark-Darlan agreement was out of date and they were ready to discuss a new one "as regards our military needs in North Africa" in light of the existence of the newly established French Committee of National Liberation (the CFLN) in Algiers.[69] The discussion continued for months, and de Gaulle declared unilaterally that he was not bound by the agreement. In practice it had already become a dead letter.

Cordell Hull told Gaullist representative André Tixier, with respect to the "Darlan deal," that it had "saved the lives of many American soldiers. . . . [T]he total mounted into very impressive figures. Also, our military plans were advanced at least sixty days . . . and thus we were sixty days nearer the winning of the war. If I were attacked by a thug on the street and someone came to my assistance, I would welcome the assistance of this collaborator in destroying the would-be murderer."[70]

.   .   .

The substantial French North African military forces now commanded by General Giraud, potentially 300,000 strong but needing modern arms, remained intact, supposedly to act in concert with, but not at the direction of, the Allies. Despite President Roosevelt's reference in his December 16 press conference to reforms in North Africa, nothing in the agreement would force the French North African administration to change the Vichy anti-Semitic laws or dismiss fascist personnel and disband their organizations. And in fact the Darlan administration actually proceeded to imprison Gaullist elements and French soldiers who had provided crucial help to the Allied landings, on the grounds that they had disobeyed military commands. Despite objections from some of Donovan's OSS men on the spot, and attempts to keep it from happening, they joined communists, Jews, other anti-Vichy elements and Spanish Republicans who were still in prisons and horrendous concentration camps in the south of Algeria. Eden protested on several occasions to the State Department about what was going on under Eisenhower's watch. Despite censorship, the British and American press managed to report these matters, and as a result the storm at home over continued antidemocratic rule and the maintenance of a Vichyite regime by Darlan in a North Africa controlled by the Allies raged on unabated.

De Gaulle, when first informed of the Allied landings at 6 AM by one of his aides, Colonel Pierre Billotte, is reported by Billotte to have said acidly—and privately—"I hope the men of Vichy throw them back into the sea! One doesn't enter France by breaking in."[71] Nevertheless, de Gaulle publicly took the news calmly, particularly after Churchill at a lunchtime meeting that day had assured him that the lack of Free French participation meant nothing in the long run, that his support for de Gaulle would never waver, and that he himself stood behind de Gaulle. De Gaulle proceeded to speak on the radio in support of the Allied landings, calling on all Frenchmen in North Africa—officers, soldiers, sailors, administrators, and colonists—to help the Allies. Three days later, on November 11, de Gaulle addressed a mass meeting in Albert Hall, in which were assembled not only the notables of the Gaullist movement but also most of the French exiles in England. Here he issued a stirring call for the restoration of true, renewed democracy in France, and for unity of all Frenchmen everywhere.[72] Even some of his opponents were moved to tears. With the agreement of both Winston Churchill and Admiral Stark, the American envoy to de Gaulle, the latter planned to send a delegation to North Africa to work with Giraud, envisioning a rapid understanding. North Africa would soon be flying the French flag with the cross of Lorraine. But when Darlan became the one through whom the Americans would work, de Gaulle called off the visit: he could deal with Giraud but refused to deal with Darlan. And when the terms of the two Clark-Darlan agreements became known, he was, naturally enough, upset; they presaged a long-term Vichyite regime in "liberated" North Africa. Churchill tried to reassure him on at least one matter: since Giraud had agreed to work under Darlan, Giraud's prestige had declined.[73] But de Gaulle was incensed, particularly as he learned of the persecution of Gaullists in North Africa by the Darlan regime, and the British proceeded to censor de Gaulle's pronouncements about the whole operation, forbidding several broadcasts he planned to make and suppressing statements about the necessary elimination of the Darlan regime. Tension between the prime minister at Downing Street and de Gaulle's headquarters at Carlton Gardens reached a new high.

At the same time, however, British opinion in the press, in Parliament, and even in the cabinet grew so strong, condemning the "Darlan Deal" and what it presaged for liberated Europe, and giving such evidence of support for de Gaulle that Churchill addressed a secret session of Parliament in a speech that would not be revealed for decades. He began by decrying the form of government Darlan was running in North Africa, as well as disparaging the admiral himself, and Pétain into the bargain. But he then let himself go in a diatribe against the ungenerous and ungrateful de Gaulle, citing the numerous occasions on which de Gaulle had clashed with the Allies, sown discord among them, and spread Anglophobia. He ended up declaring to the members of Parliament that they should not pin their hopes on de Gaulle, nor should they believe that Britain's duty lay in confiding in him the destiny of France.[74]

From Washington, Gaullist envoy André Tixier telegraphed London that the administration, facing an equal degree of press criticism, was trying to paint the whole Darlan incident in terms of its military value: political differences should not be allowed to hinder the war effort. He also argued that Secretary of State Hull, prior to a possible de Gaulle visit to Washington, had tried deliberately to place a political dilemma before the French leader. De Gaulle, Hull was insisting, should negotiate unity with Darlan. If de Gaulle refused, he would be seen as obstructing the war effort; if he did negotiate, he would lose the support of the Resistance. In either event he would lose. President Roosevelt himself was sensitive to public indignation and to possible political repercussions, since his old Republican political opponent in the presidential elections of 1940, Wendell Willkie, was leading the charge about the immorality of the "Darlan Deal." Washington, it appears, was working hard in whatever way possible to handle and diminish the political uproar it had brought about.[75]

North Africa, following the landings, teemed with plots. Darlan himself faced opposition not only from Gaullists and other antifascists but also from royalists, who supported Giraud, though they also had their own agenda, and Giraudists who wanted Giraud in power. Pétain had disavowed Darlan, so loyal Pétainistes now opposed him; the English despised him; the American president had, after all, declared him merely a "temporary expedient"; and many hoped to get rid of him. On December 24, Christmas Eve, the hapless admiral, who had come to realize his end was near, was assassinated by Fernand Bonnier de la Chapelle, member of a group of young men associated with various pro-Allied North African causes and with clandestine British operations, who had decided that Darlan must be eliminated. Bonnier de la Chapelle had drawn the short straw.

At the White House, Admiral Leahy and others immediately suspected that the Gaullists were behind the assassination, and as a result, the complicated arrangements for a de Gaulle visit to Washington to see Roosevelt were canceled, to Leahy's obvious satisfaction. De Gaulle, who learned of this only two hours before he was to take off, had looked forward to reaching an understanding with the president. He had held several conversations with Admiral Stark, the administration liaison in London, who was impressed by de Gaulle's views on what he hoped to accomplish and by the understanding de Gaulle had shown of Eisenhower's actions in working with Darlan. He had let Navy Secretary Frank Knox know of de Gaulle's views and warmly supported the visit, hoping it might dispel anti-Gaullist sentiment in Washington.[76] Tixier, from Washington, had sent a long telegram to de Gaulle listing the pros and cons of the visit, the latter outweighing the former: "The President would learn first-hand, rather than second-hand, about your character, your orientation, political intentions, your ideas on unity of military action—and it would give the American public an opportunity to manifest its sympathy for you, strengthening your adherents' position."[77] But events had conspired against it. Instead of a visit that might have had momentous results for the Free French leader, the Darlan assassination only increased Washington's distrust.

With Darlan out of the way and his assassin rapidly executed so that no embarrassing revelations might emerge, anti-Gaullist officers in North Africa immediately named the politically inexperienced General Henri Giraud as Darlan's successor. (Giraud had frequently repeated that he had no interest in politics, only in fighting, and allegedly said he had read no book as an adult that was not on military matters. He is also reported to have told the Comte de Paris, "I am profoundly royalist.")[78] Leahy, following a conversation with the president, had had Eisenhower tell the French that Giraud was the only possible candidate the Americans would accept.[79] Churchill, not consulted, was upset: despite his quarrels with de Gaulle, he had seen in Darlan's disappearance an opportunity to create a solid, united French authority that would avoid the presence of two competing French factions. The unseemly haste of the decision, however, meant that any reconsideration of North African policy by the Allies could not take place. De Gaulle was to have no role in North Africa, and the influence of Vichy would, for a while at least, not just remain strong but temporarily increase, as several high Vichy personalities calmly came to serve in Giraud's regime, expecting it to last. Persecution of those who opposed the Vichyite regime increased. Moreover, Giraud had at his command the French army intelligence services that had migrated to North Africa.[80]

For his part, De Gaulle still hoped that he and Giraud could work together. But Giraud, fearing that de Gaulle might have more support in North Africa than anticipated, had no intention of relinquishing his civilian as well as military power. (General Catroux, recently on a visit from Cairo, reported back to London that many Giraud supporters were irritated by his passivity and were moving toward support for de Gaulle.) Giraud allowed his subordinates to mishandle the investigation of the Darlan assassination: he was forced to release most of those arrested—primarily Gaullists and many who had aided the Allied landings—and to apologize for their arrest.[81] At the end of December, when de Gaulle hoped to visit him in North Africa and arrange a repartition of tasks, the Americans, the British, and Giraud himself all kept de Gaulle from doing so, prompting a public blast on de Gaulle's part that increased public opinion in his favor in England and the United States, where the press was in full cry, and that further infuriated Cordell Hull, who protested to the British that they were allowing Gaullists to inflame opinion against him. It appeared now, however, to both Roosevelt and Churchill that something would have to be done to unify the two French authorities, one of which, under Giraud, persisted in blocking any democratic reforms. Among other things, Churchill sent one of his cabinet ministers, Harold Macmillan, to North Africa as minister resident at Allied headquarters, so that he would have a high-ranking Englishman there to advise Eisenhower, equivalent in influence to the American Robert Murphy. It was a significant move, for Macmillan, like Foreign Secretary Anthony Eden, would soon become one of de Gaulle's staunch supporters. "Eden à Londres, Macmillan à Alger, ce fut notre grande chance" (Eden in London, Macmillan in Algiers, it was our great luck), wrote René Massigli, de Gaulle's foreign affairs commissioner.[82]

Changes were in the offing.

CHAPTER 3

Giraud, de Gaulle, and the Committee of French National Liberation

NINETEEN FORTY-THREE BROUGHT VITAL CHANGES TO the world scene. Not the least among them was that General de Gaulle ended the year heading a budding French government-in-exile. By the end of the year, on the other hand, President Roosevelt had become more determined than ever that de Gaulle should be blocked from "seizing" power and that the leader of the cross-channel landings in France should remain in charge of the country and work with whatever local authorities could promise order. The third actor in the French drama—Churchill—spent the year torn between his dependence on Roosevelt and the fact that his cabinet and advisers were more and more convinced that de Gaulle was the one person who could keep a liberated France from chaos. The events that led to this stage of the situation began at a villa in a town in North Africa named Anfa.

On January 14, 1943, Franklin D. Roosevelt and Winston Churchill met in Anfa, outside Casablanca, in order to settle basic issues about future strategy, deciding first on the invasion of Sicily and then Italy, and finally a cross-channel invasion of France, put off until the spring of 1944. They proclaimed the war aim of "unconditional surrender" by the Axis powers.

They also, however, found themselves having to deal with what was for them the vexing problem of France and French leadership. Roosevelt, who treated his outing to Casablanca like a holiday from the cares at home, seemed to think that with his personal charm, he would be able resolve matters.[1]

By the time of his meeting with Roosevelt, Churchill had apparently already decided that there ought to be a central French authority that could deal with the other Allies. It should be headed by an eminent political leader other than de Gaulle or General Giraud, one to whom the two, as military men, would be subordinate. The British had sent a memorandum to Washington to this effect, mentioning the names of several possible political leaders, but received no reply. In fact, as Herbert Matthews wrote to Secretary of State Hull from the American embassy in London on January 1, 1943,

> the British Government accepts the President's and the Department's often enunciated policy that the people of France alone must choose their form of government. But this is accepted with the reservation that some French authority, in effect if not in name a provisional government, must reign in France from the time the Allies first arrive until conditions permit the establishment of that permanent Government and during this period it must be de Gaulle who exercises authority.
>
> British prestige requires that "the one Frenchman who stuck by us in the dark days of 1940" must be installed in France when the day of liberation comes, however fleeting his tenure may be and whatever the consequences for the people of France.[2]

In other words, Churchill's government—if not Churchill himself—was being diplomatic with regard to American sensibilities, while its members kept to themselves their view that de Gaulle was the only real game in town.

Franklin D. Roosevelt had, of course, already reached the opposite conclusion, that there should be no central French political authority, Gaullist or otherwise, and that French armed forces should fight under the Allied High Command. On December 30 Undersecretary of State Sumner Welles sent the president a suggested set of instructions to cable to General Eisenhower and Robert Murphy in North Africa. The sentiments expressed in it would be frequently repeated:

> The government of the United States recognizes the sovereignty of the French people. . . . [I]t will take no step which will in the slightest degree impair the right of the French people to determine with complete freedom their own destinies and to select their own government, once France has been liberated. . . . *[N]o French political authority can exist or be allowed to create itself outside of France.* It is the duty of the United States and Great Britain to preserve for the people of France the right and opportunity to determine for themselves what government they will have.[3]

The doctrine of working with "local authorities" had also previously been made explicit. It would be amended, after the hapless North African experience, to the effect that, if possible, those with whom the Allies worked should be untainted by collaboration. For the moment, at the time of Casablanca, this amendment was most certainly not in force, as the American General George Patton and others mingled amiably with the many Vichy appointees, some of whom had been in North Africa while it was directly controlled from Vichy, some of whom joined Darlan and Giraud there with the assurance that they would occupy key positions, and almost all of whom General Giraud kept in power.[4]

Giraud, strictly a military man, was most concerned with obtaining scarce American arms to bolster his North African forces. While there was little to spare, at the time of the Casablanca conference he obtained considerable satisfaction. He was promised materiel to reequip eleven divisions and the necessary shipping to get it to him—in a memorandum casually initialed by Roosevelt, without consultation with his military leaders or allies, all of whom would be greatly affected by any diversion from their own needs and who would, in the end, slow the process down. There were, after all, priority shipments to Russia, China, and the Pacific front. Roosevelt also initialed a secret memorandum prepared by the Giraudist Jacques Lemaigre-Dubreuil assuring his support for Giraud as the man to realize the union of all French forces and to preserve all French interests.[5] It was a clear expression of support for Giraud as against de Gaulle, although Elliott Roosevelt much later reported that his father, after first meeting Giraud, considered him a "very slender reed to lean on," judging that "a dud as administrator, he'll be a dud as a leader."[6] From Murphy, Eisenhower's political adviser, who went beyond what he was authorized to do, Giraud had also obtained a commitment that the Americans would restore the French colonial empire.[7] In fact, while numerous statements emanating from different American sources made promises to this effect, Roosevelt had little inclination to do so. "Murphy overstepped the bounds in guaranteeing integrity of French colonial possessions," declared Roosevelt. "I don't want to commit myself to their return to France. There is no question of returning Indochina."[8]

In Casablanca the president listened to the sultan and grand vizier of Morocco, who voiced their distrust of Giraud as well as de Gaulle and told him that the Americans should organize a plebiscite for independence. At least one French general reported that Roosevelt seemed to approve,[9] while Macmillan noted the discomfort of both the French and British, including Churchill, who attended Roosevelt's lunch with the sultan and heard FDR discuss the coming end of empire.[10] But since Giraud also failed to impress Roosevelt, the president prevailed upon Churchill to invite de Gaulle to Casablanca to see if it might be possible to hammer out an agreement to unite the two stubborn French factions.

De Gaulle, sensing a trap, balked at an invitation emanating from an Englishman on French soil to meet with Allied leaders on French soil. Such an invitation completely violated his sense of French sovereignty and dignity. In private he told an aide: "They'll try to mix me up in their mud and dirt of North Africa, they want me to swallow Vichy. Nothing doing. I won't walk into it."[11] He replied more politely that he had been seeking a meeting with General Giraud, who had evaded the issue, and that an unprepared one coerced by the British and Americans would not be likely to result in fruitful discussions. Once in December, then twice in January, he had asked Giraud for a meeting, and Giraud had found reasons to put it off, suggesting that liaison officers talk instead.[12] Finally, with a warning from Churchill that he might face reprisals if he did not come, he was persuaded by General Catroux—with a threat of resignation—and by his London committee that he should attend.

He arrived, and was greatly annoyed that on what he considered French soil he was surrounded by hundreds of heavily armed American guards, American barbed wire, and hidden American Secret Service men who were present, behind curtains, when he met with Roosevelt, who insisted on speaking mangled French. De Gaulle, as he had done with Admiral Stark in London, apparently tried to explain to Roosevelt that in the past, when France had come close to defeat, when a governing class or elite failed France, someone from the French masses had emerged—a Joan of Arc in

1429, when the English still occupied much of France, a Georges Clemenceau in 1917, when the French army was swept by mutiny—someone not necessarily in the line of legitimate authority, not elected by the people, but who represented the real, eternal France, and had managed to redeem the situation. He was trying, in other words, to justify his position as the legitimate leader of all the French, even if he had not been invested with this authority by any existing government. His resort to historical analogy was a bad mistake. Roosevelt, who insisted on election as the key to legitimacy, took it that de Gaulle was claiming to reincarnate Joan of Arc and Clemenceau, even though they were very different, and recounted the conversation as a huge joke on de Gaulle. "I almost laughed in his face," Roosevelt remarked to one of his aides when he got back to Washington.[13] Various versions of the story exist, but one is significant. Cordell Hull in his memoirs gives this account: de Gaulle came stiffly into Roosevelt's room and said, "I am Joan of Arc, I am Clemenceau." It shows how deeply many Americans, including Hull, misunderstood de Gaulle.[14] De Gaulle, in his own way, apparently misunderstood Roosevelt. Following his meeting with the president, he told his aide Hettier de Boislambert: "See, today I met with a real statesman [*un grand homme d'état*]. I think we got along well and understood each other."[15]

Previously, in correspondence with Churchill, Roosevelt had flippantly referred to Giraud as "the bridegroom" and de Gaulle as "the bride," whose recalcitrance was making it hard for the two leaders to get the couple into bed with each other. He repeated the terms in a later press conference. De Gaulle, who invariably learned of these matters, was not particularly amused. Nor would he have been amused had he learned that Roosevelt told his admirals and generals that while the Pétain regime was the de facto French government, the only legitimate French leader for North Africa would be Albert Lebrun, the weak president of the Third Republic, then under house arrest in the Italian-occupied zone of France. "I would recognize his government if he returns," Roosevelt said.[16] In the meantime General Giraud was running things, and had received Roosevelt's backing, but would have to be made to change his Vichyite ways.

At the end of the Casablanca conference, before everyone had left, Roosevelt and Churchill managed to maneuver Giraud and de Gaulle into standing up in front of the two Allied leaders to be photographed shaking hands. The widely publicized photograph masked the reality that nothing had actually been accomplished in talks between the two French leaders. De Gaulle refused to come to Africa in a subordinate position, and Giraud refused to purge his Vichyite officers, a condition de Gaulle insisted upon. Nevertheless, Roosevelt had coerced them into signing a brief, noncommittal communiqué to the effect that they agreed on the end to be achieved—the liberation of France and total defeat of the enemy,—and on the unity in war of all Frenchmen.

When Roosevelt arrived home, his critical view of de Gaulle only enhanced, the president repeated to newsmen "everybody is agreed" that neither of the two French leaders could be recognized as the future leader of France: "Let France choose her own government."[17] By "everybody" he presumably meant himself and Churchill. The president's statement to the newsmen was a prelude to his later declaration that until the French could exercise their choice through elections, an Allied military government should be there to prepare the way.

Churchill himself went home furious with de Gaulle for having humiliated him in front of Roosevelt. The president knew that Churchill was financing de Gaulle, yet the general had resisted Churchill's invitation to come to Casablanca, and then bluntly disagreed with Churchill in Roosevelt's presence over the issue of agreement with Giraud and the nature of their joint communiqué. The prime minister may have been somewhat disconcerted when he subsequently had dinner with King George VI, whom he greatly respected; the king advised him to be patient with the difficult de Gaulle, whose views about working with those who had collaborated with the Germans he could well understand.[18]

The Anfa meeting had a near-tragic end: Hettier de Boislambert recounts that as he was flying back to England with de Gaulle, two German fighter planes appeared to their rear, but for some unknown reason—perhaps lack of fuel—turned back. Boislambert was sitting in the rear gunner's seat, preparing to fire. Had he done so, the Germans would most probably have attacked. Gaullism came close to losing its leader, as it had once before, on October 11, 1940, when de Gaulle's plane crash-landed in the swamps of northern Cameroon but left him unhurt, to be rescued several hours later.[19]

Following Anfa, General Giraud should have been riding high. He had secured Roosevelt's backing and the president's personal agreement that his army was now to be reequipped by the Americans. Moreover, he could muster some 300,000 men (two-thirds of them North African Muslims) to de Gaulle's 15,000 or 20,000. Roosevelt's antipathy to de Gaulle had been reinforced, and the president was determined not to let the general assume power in North Africa. Giraud, in February, created the Commandement en chef français civil et militaire, with himself as commander. Later, in July, Giraud accepted an invitation to visit the United States, where he was fêted royally, visiting Fort Benning and West Point, staying in a suite at the Waldorf Astoria in New York, and meeting with every important figure in the administration: Marshall, Leahy, Hull, and others. In a clear indication of the effort to block de Gaulle, everything was done to build up General Giraud's image in contrast to his rival. Roosevelt, in particular, after one of several dinners at the White House, regaled him with accounts of why de Gaulle was not to be trusted with power. François Coulet, the first regional commissioner in liberated France in 1944, writes in a memoir, to indicate something of Roosevelt's position vis-à-vis France, that the president greeted Giraud in Washington as "a French soldier fighting for the Allied cause since, at this moment, France no longer exists."[20] In the meantime, Roosevelt's aide Harry Hopkins had tried to take care of making Giraud more generally acceptable by sending over to Algiers the distinguished French economist Jean Monnet, whom we have seen dealing primarily with supply and production problems, as a political adviser to the general.

Monnet, arriving in Algiers, found the situation complicated: Giraud, by divorcing himself from Pétain, had already alienated many right-wing officers. But Monnet also thought that not many of these would accept de Gaulle. Moreover, he quickly saw that Giraud had no political sense. He determined that whatever political views Giraud had were highly reactionary and that he was not about to alter the Pétainist regime that persisted in North Africa. For two weeks Monnet worked on Giraud when the latter returned from Washington, riding high, so he thought. On March 14, 1943, Giraud finally delivered what he called, ironically, "the first democratic speech of my life," composed almost entirely by Monnet, who deleted most of Giraud's emendations. As Monnet put it, he could not change the general's opinions, but he could make him see the practical necessities: he must outwardly assume a democratic mantle and make democratic reforms if the Americans were to continue to support his army. (Monnet likened the speech to the declaration made in the sixteenth century by the Protestant King Henry of Navarre when he converted to Catholicism in order to be accepted as king of France: "Paris is worth a mass!") Giraud essentially repudiated the 1940 armistice which had been insisted upon by high French officers, spoke of all resistants as heroes, proclaimed the need for French unity under republican institutions, and declared the repressive Vichy laws null and void. It would take time to put the last, important measure into effect, although within a few weeks numerous Vichy officials left office.[21] At the prompting of the American consul in Algiers, Secretary of State Hull issued a statement to the effect that "General Giraud has now confirmed the hopes of this government that his selection as commander in chief of the French forces fighting in North Africa would make possible a greater unification of all groups behind his military leadership. . . . [H]e has been able to remove discrimination in the treatment of those living under his jurisdiction[,] . . . made it possible for all elements to unite[,] . . . has swept aside laws and decrees which were contrary to [France's] traditional republican institutions."[22]

Hull was undoubtedly not aware of what one Frenchman reported to London from Algiers: that Giraud, by his speech, had alienated many of his supporters—those fascist-minded officers who saw in the return of the republic a return of Jews, Freemasons, corruption, and chaos. A number of Giraud's closest right-wing advisers, including the influential Lemaigre-Dubreuil, resigned, to be replaced by more moderate men. The moment was ripe, it seemed, for de Gaulle to come to Algiers, where he would bring a breath of hope and patriotism to an agitated public that might turn one way or the other.[23]

If Giraud's star seemed at least to be on the rise, de Gaulle, in contrast, had been rebuffed by or had further alienated Roosevelt four times in the last few months. Prior to the rather disastrous meeting between the two at Anfa, in October 1942 de Gaulle had sent a long, eloquent, and moving letter to the American president describing his goals, his democratic aims, and the nature of his movement. He explained why, in default of any others, he had assumed the task of representing France; he wrote of the necessity for the French to participate as a nation in the defeat of the Axis powers if a genuine civic renewal were to take place; he assured the president that power would devolve to the people of France once liberation had taken place. In the meantime, with what other person or organization could the Allies deal but the Free French?[24]

Although Gaullist envoy André Philip delivered the letter, de Gaulle never received any reply to what was a major attempt to mend relations—one that, if successful, might have had a great impact both on wartime events and for decades afterwards. There was speculation in the Gaullist camp as to why there was no reply, but the most likely answer is to be found in American archives, only available much later. The anti-Gaullist director of European Affairs in the State Department, Ray Atherton, provided the president with an abbreviated translation, writing in an accompanying note, "It takes some 10 pages of introduction to get down into the very little meat there is in it," and concluding, "I fear General de Gaulle will blindly attempt to force himself and his committee on the French people by foreign arms."[25] It is also possible that the president never read even this devastating—and misleading—summary: he had a habit, when coming upon a paper he did not want to read, to slip it back at the bottom of the pile. (A French commentator in *Espoir,* journal of the De Gaulle Institute, remarks that "the lack of a reply hardly contributes to enhance the personal stature of the person to whom it was addressed.")[26] Whatever the case, it is indicative of how a lower official may have an outsize effect on history.

Shortly after the president told the press that the appointment of Darlan was but a "temporary expedient," de Gaulle decided that there was perhaps another opportunity to improve relations with Roosevelt. He arranged through Admiral Stark that two of his men should meet with the president. One was André Philip, an economist and former socialist deputy who had voted against full powers for Pétain at the time of the defeat of France and who had delivered de Gaulle's letter to Sumner Welles. The other was the gruff Adrien Tixier, who had headed the International Labor Office in Geneva between the wars and had at first been suspicious and critical of de Gaulle but was now a Gaullist representative in the United States. The president agreed, and the first two Gaullist envoys to talk to Roosevelt saw him on November 20.

It was a disaster. Their train was late, so they kept the president waiting. Then, according to Welles, who was also present, Roosevelt began by telling them he was willing to meet with de Gaulle, following which he explained to them why the United States had come to depend on Admiral Darlan. He then went on to say that "so long as the United States was the 'occupying power' in North Africa, the final decisions would be reached solely by the occupying power." He also "expressed it as his policy that until all of France were liberated, the sole decision as to what, if any, Frenchmen would administer the liberated territory was a matter solely for this government to determine." The two Frenchmen, as may be expected, responded angrily, particularly to the term "occupied": French policy was completely different. They envisaged the creation of a provisional government that would administer any "liberated" territory, whether in North Africa or in France. "Liberation" should not result in "occupation." According to Welles, they declared that "they would never 'permit' any French town, village or farmhouse to be administered by foreign powers and that their decision in this regard was final."[27] Welles wrote that there were no thanks for the liberation of North Africa, only recrimination and outright expression of anger. Apparently Philip scolded Roosevelt loudly for naming Darlan high commissioner; he even shook his finger at the president. Roosevelt was appalled at their attitude. He subsequently wired Admiral Stark: "Why did you insist that I receive that man Philip? He had not a word of appreciation."[28] The two French envoys were also appalled. They came away having heard Roosevelt say that America would rule as the occupier in North Africa and, most important, insist that a respect for democracy meant that France had to be governed by the U.S. Army—in other words, occupied—until the French could vote.

The third incident was the subsequent withdrawal of the invitation to de Gaulle to come to Washington after the assassination of Darlan, and the suspicion in Washington that Gaullists were involved. The fourth followed soon after, when Roosevelt seems to have regarded de Gaulle as a figure of fun at Casablanca. There were more incidents. The desertion of sailors from ships under Giraud's control in New York harbor to join the Free French raised another storm in Washington. Reports were made public in the press that de Gaulle's intelligence chief, Colonel Passy, was running an unscrupulous Gestapo-like office on Duke Street in London, where volunteers were interrogated harshly to be sure they were not German spies; one dissident had been tortured and another had hanged himself in his cell.[29] When a Vichy governor was forced out in French Guiana, Admiral Leahy was delighted that a Giraudist replacement arrived there in place of a Gaullist one, whose passage was blocked by the U.S. Navy at the request of Sumner Welles.[30] The action, of course, angered de Gaulle, who saw it as a further attempt to undermine him. The assertion in mid-January by a resistant named Jean Fernand Grenier, who had come to London from France to announce that the Communist Party would adhere to the Fighting French, was a triumph for de Gaulle and his movement, which could no longer be viewed as primarily a right-wing organization. Nevertheless, it did little to endear de Gaulle further to the Washington authorities. The anti-Gaullists could now add communist support and influence to their litany of condemnation.

De Gaulle's representative André Tixier wired back to London that as a result of the arrest of noncommunist Gaullist resistants in France, the Americans were becoming more convinced that de Gaulle was now tied to a communist-dominated resistance within the country. It was indicative of the administration's shortsightedness. The American leaders could not understand de Gaulle's tactics—that fearing a communist takeover after liberation, he deliberately co-opted the communists into supporting his embryo government-in-the-making. But the French writer Henri de Kerillis, who had initially supported de Gaulle, agreed with the administration. Admitting communists, who had sabotaged resistance to the Germans in 1940, was unconscionable.

When Churchill visited Washington in early May, he was bombarded with criticisms of de Gaulle by both Roosevelt and Hull, who supplied the prime minister with highly critical reports emanating from Matthews in London. (In one dispatch Matthews called de Gaulle "this French Adolf.")[31] He also met with Alexis Saint-Léger, the former French Foreign Office official, who explained why he would support the Free French movement only if de Gaulle no longer led it. The result was a remarkable telegram Churchill sent to Foreign Secretary Anthony Eden telling him the cabinet should accept his recommendation to withdraw all support for de Gaulle. Once again, a suggestion for new leadership for the French committee, obviously in line with American thought, emerged. Churchill recommended replacing de Gaulle with a triumvirate of Saint-Léger, Giraud, and Édouard Herriot, the old Third Republic Radical Socialist leader now under house arrest near Paris.

The English cabinet promptly turned down Churchill's request ("and very brave about it in his absence!" Eden wrote rather sarcastically). Eden wired the hapless prime minister in Washington a detailed set of reasons why he was absolutely wrong and an analysis of the American charges. "The latest phase of the Giraud–de Gaulle negotiations indicates that union is nearer than it has been at any time," he wrote, adding:

> We are advised that there is no likelihood of any of the present members of the French National Committee continuing to function if General de Gaulle were removed by us. The same is probably true

of the Free French fighting forces. . . . If we now drove de Gaulle out of public life . . . we would not only make him a national martyr but would find ourselves accused by both Gaullists and Giraudists of interfering improperly in French internal affairs. . . . We suspect that Murphy is becoming impressed by the evidence of rising Gaullism in North Africa. . . . [H]e was as wrong about this as he was about anti-British feeling there. . . . The fact is that Giraud's retention of unpopular men and Murphy's continued reluctance to insist on their removal have helped de Gaulle very considerably in North Africa.[32]

To some observers, paradoxically, the Casablanca meeting where Roosevelt agreed to supply Giraud's army was the beginning of the end for General Giraud, on whom the Americans had earlier pinned such hopes, but whom they now found rather hopelessly rigid. For one thing, the carelessly promised military materiel, though much eventually arrived, materialized only slowly, as other priorities fixed earlier continued to defer deliveries to Giraud's forces, so that he never assumed the military prestige and position eleven well-armed divisions would have given him. Dozens of irritated telegrams passed back and forth between Giraud's headquarters and the State Department in Washington on the issue of the lagging materiel.[33] And both in France and without, de Gaulle's position was strengthening. There was much evidence of his growing support inside the country, and he himself was convinced of it. In April 1942 de Gaulle had issued an important statement of his political purposes, and its circulation had led prominent parliamentarians, including in particular the imprisoned head of the Socialist Party, Léon Blum, to let London know of their full support for his plans for the future. Blum wrote, "The interim government can be created only around one man, one name, that of General de Gaulle . . . the only possible man" (Le gouvernement intérimaire [de la liberation] ne pourra se constituer qu'autour d'un seul homme, autour d'un seul nom, celui du Général de Gaulle . . . le seul homme possible).[34] In November 1942 the State Department received a telegram from chargé d'affaires S. Pinkney Tuck, at the embassy in Vichy, underlining the crystallization of resistance opinion around support for de Gaulle, the fact that former leading parliamentarians opposed to collaboration, like Éduard Herriot and Jules Jeanneney, would accept de Gaulle as head of government, and growing opinion in favor of de Gaulle among officers of the small French army allowed by the armistice with Germany.[35]

As if this weren't enough, a remarkable memorandum from the Office of Strategic Services (OSS), Roosevelt's secret service, run by his own man, General William "Wild Bill" Donovan, should have had at least some effect on the administration, contradicting as it did the views of Hull, Leahy, and the president. Dated April 22, 1943, it read:

> Objective consideration of the report of March 27 1943 entitled "Survey of underground organization in France" by the OSS (Research and Analysis Branch). Organizations reviewed: Libération Française, Libération, Communist Underground, Socialist Underground, Underground Labour Unions. Conclusion: . . . all the resistance movements are converging toward Gaullism . . . in consequence of an evolution *corresponding to the general sentiments of the French people.* . . . [A]ll parliamentarians who have escaped have announced their adhesion to Gaullism. . . . Finally, it is important to note that no organization or even movement exists apart from the Gaullists or those who sympathize with the Gaullist movement.[36]

A month later, on May 15, the "triumphant Philip and Soustelle," members of de Gaulle's entourage in London, brought de Gaulle a telegram from his delegate in France, Jean Moulin, announcing that he had managed to constitute the National Resistance Council, representing all the resistance groups in France, and it had addressed to de Gaulle a message of total support of all movements north and south, all of which agreed that de Gaulle should be installed as president of a provisional government and that Giraud should serve under it as military chief. The French people would never accept de Gaulle's subordination to Giraud.[37] This evidence of full support for de Gaulle from within France would become his trump card with respect to subsequent relations with General Giraud in North Africa.

In spite of all the mounting evidence of support from all quarters for de Gaulle and the major change this indicated, Cordell Hull and Franklin D. Roosevelt "were able" as Hull put it, "to hew consistently to the line we early adopted." And on May 8, a month after the OSS report, and long after Tuck's report, both from within France, Roosevelt wrote Churchill that de Gaulle, who had a "messianic complex," had the idea "that the people of France itself are strongly behind him personally. *This I doubt.*" He went on to explain that they might be in favor of the Free French movement, but if they knew what he and Churchill knew about de Gaulle they would not be for him. As if this personal opinion were not extraordinary enough, he then went on to make an even more extraordinary suggestion: "We might talk over the formation of an entirely new French Committee subject in its membership to the approval of you and me," a body that would be purely advisory. In other words, he was suggesting that he and Churchill dictate the nature of a new French movement and limit its capabilities. It was in this cable that Roosevelt told Churchill he favored a military occupation of France "run by British and American generals," and concluded flippantly: "I do not know what to do with de Gaulle. Possibly you would like to make him Governor of Madagascar!"[38] But however much Churchill agreed with the president on the difficulties de Gaulle presented, he was obliged to respect his cabinet's decision to continue support for the Frenchman. Divergence on what Allied policy should be toward liberated France continued.

As Eden noted, within North Africa, there was growing evidence of Gaullist support, though Murphy attributed it largely to Gaullist propaganda. A new Gaullist newspaper, *Combat,* received an enthusiastic reception. Soldiers in increasing numbers left Giraud's forces to join those of de Gaulle, despite attempts by both Giraud and Allied leaders to stop them from doing so, and cries of "Vive de Gaulle!" were more and more frequently heard in the streets.[39] When North African newspapers and radio stations published the communiqué of support for de Gaulle from the National Resistance Council, de Gaulle's position was further enhanced.

By April 1943, as Eden's memo to Churchill in Washington stated, negotiations for de Gaulle's arrival in Algiers were well under way with Giraud's representatives. Proposals went back and forth. There were delays occasioned by Giraud's wariness of de Gaulle's growing popularity in Algiers and his fear that de Gaulle would be met by massive demonstrations in his favor, and by de Gaulle's conditions for acceptance: that republican liberties would have to be restored, that Vichyite laws be declared null and void, and that free elections be held as soon as possible after the liberation of France.[40] Giraud, as late as mid-April, stuck to his guns: he should lead all French military forces, under the Allied High Command, and he should be the one to ensure public order at the time of liberation, and should name all the top administrators.[41] There was also de Gaulle's haughty insistence that only the city of Algiers would be suitable for his arrival, and his use of an inopportune moment for public ridicule of Giraud's regime. The latter occasioned anger among his own supporters and negotiators, and revealed the depth of division between those who gave their unconditional support to de Gaulle and those who took a more mixed view. General Edgar de Larminat, one of the earliest high officers to rally to de Gaulle, now in North Africa, pleaded with him to come immediately, while General Catroux begged him to come in a spirit of unity, arguing that Giraud was justified in fearing that de Gaulle wanted only to absorb the Giraudists. The purpose of his coming was not to deal with North Africa but to create governmental unity. Privately Catroux threatened to repudiate him if he did not come—and, of course, de Gaulle's ridicule of Giraud reached Washington, once again confirming authorities there in their view of de Gaulle.

On May 13 the Allies, with French participation in the battle, finally received the surrender of the last German forces in Tunisia, thereby liberating all of North Africa. Four days later a French naval squadron that had been tied up in Alexandria, Egypt, ever since the French armistice in 1940, rallied—but to Giraud. Buoyed by this, Murphy and a number of anti-Gaullist Frenchmen, including Admiral Muselier, the man who had led the expedition to Saint Pierre and Miquelon, had urged Giraud to stand fast against Gaullist conditions for unity. Nevertheless, by now Giraud was convinced, against his better instincts—by people such as Harold Macmillan, Jean Monnet, and especially General Catroux—that he had to act to preserve his own position. (His attitude toward inviting de Gaulle is exemplified by an expression he is supposed to have used: "If I let him come in by the door, he won't take long to throw me out the window!") His and de Gaulle's military forces had to be united as quickly as possible if they were to continue to be armed and supplied by the Americans and take part in further action against the Axis.[42]

The result of all the pressures and counterpressures was that on May 17 an invitation, largely crafted by Monnet, Catroux, and Macmillan in a form acceptable to Giraud, was sent to de Gaulle couched in somewhat vague terms but proposing the creation of a new committee headed by the two of them in which each would nominate two others, and to which the fused military would be responsible, through Giraud as commander in-chief. On May 30, 1943, de Gaulle landed near Algiers, to a very different reception than he had had at Anfa: this time, though the arrival was discreet, he was met by the French General Giraud, with French soldiers rendering the honors and a French band playing the "Marseillaise," with American and British delegates *behind* the French. The arrival may have been kept quiet, but in the afternoon enormous demonstrations in the streets of Algiers supported the Free French movement and its chief. The once obscure de Gaulle had come a long way.[43]

De Gaulle arrived with his two nominees: René Massigli, a moderate, longtime member of the French diplomatic corps, one whose support for de Gaulle was cautious and conditional, and André Philip, the labor expert, one of the two Gaullists who had met with President Roosevelt earlier. The next day they met with General Catroux and General Giraud, and with General Alphonse Georges and Jean Monnet, who were Giraud's nominees. General Georges was a conservative if able military man, an old friend of Churchill's from the time of the First World War, whom the prime minister had had spirited out of occupied France with a view to having him participate in any new French authority. Anthony Eden, however, described him as "a reactionary old defeatist," while Macmillan wrote that de Gaulle was infuriated at finding opposite him "an elderly general who had opposed the modernization of the French army and who had then led it to utter disaster."[44] Monnet was generally considered to be a remarkably able "fixer," though back in Washington, Cordell Hull distrusted him as not anti-Gaullist enough.

On June 4, 1943, the seven men announced the creation of the Comité français de la libération nationale (the CFLN) after two days of often acrimonious discussion and shouted arguments about responsibilities and threats of walkouts but finally an agreement, still opposed by Giraud, to sack the last of the Vichy North African commanders. General Catroux was added to the committee, and Giraud and de Gaulle were named rotating co-chairs. The committee formally declared that it would be the central French power in the conduct of the war effort, that it would exercise sovereignty in all areas not controlled by the enemy, represent French interests everywhere in the world, and hand over its functions to a provisional government created according to the laws of the republic at the time of total liberation of French territory at the very latest. The committee solemnly undertook to reestablish French liberties, the laws of the republic, and the republican government by destroying the arbitrary regime and the personal power now imposed on the country.[45]

The creation of the CFLN and the statement of its purposes was a giant step both in creating a wartime central French authority—virtually a de

facto government-in-exile, widely seen as such—and in declaring the role
it would have with the liberation of France. The *Echo d'Alger* headline of
June 4 read "Une Journée décisive pour l'histoire de la France." Historian
Don Cook remarks: "De Gaulle . . . was clearly in a mood of exhilaration,
wielding power on his own from French territory, free of London, free to
move about within his own domains without seeking Anglo-Saxon permission, free to communicate with Moscow and the entire French Empire,
free to mold French affairs to his own will at last."[46] The committee sent a
memo to all of the Allied states asking that it be recognized "as the body
qualified to ensure the conduct of the French effort in the war as well
as the administration and defense of all French interests."[47] The committee members, and the press in the United States and England, expected a
rapid reply. To the two most interested parties, however, the meaning of
the committee's formation was not clear nor was the committee, in the case
of Roosevelt, even desirable. Churchill reassured a wary Roosevelt that the
makeup of the committee was such that it would dilute de Gaulle's power
and very likely override him if he tried to act beyond his authority.

Incredibly, all through the month of August 1943 and during a meeting
between Roosevelt and Churchill in Quebec, the two allies negotiated
arduously over an acceptable recognition formula. Foreign Secretary
Anthony Eden, his envoy Macmillan in North Africa, and members of the
British Parliament had worked hard to convince an obstinate and reluctant
Churchill that some form of recognition was necessary; all the other governments in exile had already recognized the CFLN, and public opinion
required one. Eden, convinced that a strong France would be necessary to
Britain after the war, did all he could to get Churchill to agree to work on
Roosevelt. In Algiers, Macmillan wrote that both Eisenhower and Murphy
"continue to plug in telegrams about this," that is, advising immediate recognition. Eisenhower, along with members of his staff, had come to the
decision that de Gaulle, not Giraud, would best contribute to the military
effort, and recognition would help de Gaulle, while Murphy had cabled
Washington that the composition of the committee showed that it was quite
conservative. Finally, with respect to recognizing the committee, Churchill
had sent Roosevelt what Macmillan called "a really wonderful telegram,
urging him to do so."[48]

At the same time, Roosevelt and Hull plied Churchill with all the reasons they could muster to oppose recognizing the committee. Recognition
would mean the abandonment of the local authorities doctrine and policy;

it would mean that the CFLN would have to be consulted on matters pertaining to France and the empire, and that the Allies would have to consult with French political leaders, not just the military authorities. The CFLN could claim membership on inter-Allied committees, could insist on participation in planning the invasion of France, could lay claim to large sums of French money frozen in the United States. Recognition would probably mean abrogation of the Clark-Darlan agreement on North Africa.[49] In North Africa, Macmillan noted in his diary, "If the President knew how much this policy [of continued support for Giraud] is disliked and even despised by the American Army here, I think he would get a rude shock."[50]

An anti–de Gaulle press campaign by the U.S. government backfired badly.[51] Roosevelt wired Eisenhower that if necessary American armed forces would intervene in Dakar should de Gaulle try to replace Governor-General Boisson, the man who had earlier repelled the Anglo-French effort to land there and had later rallied to Darlan as governor-general of North Africa. Within a few days he, Roosevelt, might break with de Gaulle! The reason for FDR's surprising support for Boisson appears to be that Roosevelt had sent an American envoy, Admiral William Glassford, as his personal representative with the rank of minister to see about building up Dakar as a wartime antisubmarine base but also as a postwar UN base under American control, and Glassford and Boisson had established cordial relations.[52] For Undersecretary of State Welles, it was also a matter of keeping out the British, who might otherwise supplant the Americans. "We might lose the position which should belong to us at Dakar," he wrote. Under a de Gaulle regime, he pointed out, the French would "brook no outside interference in the administration of their colonies."[53] De Gaulle, of course, was aware of Roosevelt's intention to keep control of this particular French colony—and of others.

Anthony Eden's response to Roosevelt's message that it might be time to break with de Gaulle was to note in his diary: "FDR's mood is now that of a man who persists in error. It has all that special brand of obstinacy, like Hitler at Stalingrad." The Americans, he thought, had mishandled the French problem from the beginning; their treatment of de Gaulle would soon make him a national hero.[54]

Whatever the American president might feel, it was now impossible to get rid of de Gaulle, and when Roosevelt and Churchill met in Quebec, an unwilling Roosevelt was forced to agree to make some statement about the new French committee. What the two men came up with—and the

English version was more generous than the American one—was a grudging welcome to the establishment of the committee, references to the need for it to work within Allied war plans, and a recognition that it represented the administration of those overseas French territories that accepted its authority, but with a proviso that this declaration did not constitute recognition of a French government. The American version ended with a repetition of the commitment to let the French choose their own government and officials when the time came. Churchill had worried that the Russians would be more generous, and that if the Western Allies did not come up with something acceptable to the French, the latter would turn for support to the Soviet Union. In fact, the Soviet Union did pronounce itself more positively disposed, to the effect that it recognized the committee as the guarantor of the interests of the French republic and as the unique representative of French patriots fighting Hitlerism. In Algiers, de Gaulle privately, and favorably, took note of the Russian position, while the other Allied declarations received a muted public approval. In the United States, pro-Gaullist newspapers like the *New York Herald Tribune* were highly critical: "In comparison with the broad and simple formula which the Soviet Union has adopted . . . the elaborate qualifications deemed necessary by the Western Allies would benefit by a tone of cordiality. This tone, unfortunately, the State Department did not see fit to adopt."[55] Nevertheless, Macmillan wrote, "de Gaulle now found himself Prime Minister of what was in effect, the Provisional Government of France."[56]

Following another one of several crises and disputes among its members that almost destroyed the committee, an enlarged committee emerged on June 13, with the arrival of several more Frenchmen from London and France, ready to take over ministerial affairs as *commissaires*. What this meant was that the committee had begun to organize itself as a shadow government, with specific ministries—Interior, Foreign Affairs, Finance, Labor, and so on—and people named to head them. According to Monnet, the new members were ready to assume administrative tasks without being necessarily committed to one or the other of the two generals.[57] Nevertheless, de Gaulle's tide seemed to be rising. Gaullist officials were moving into administrative offices at various levels, and despite efforts by Giraud, and a word from de Gaulle warning against the practice as one that would create more trouble, soldiers were increasingly leaving Giraud's forces to join de Gaulle's. Many of the officers might be Giraudist, but, Macmillan wrote, "according to our information the French troops were . . . overwhelmingly Gaullist."[58]

A second Gaullist newspaper, the *Marseillaise,* was receiving wide distribution, and de Gaulle's publicity people were active. (Roosevelt cabled to Churchill: "De Gaulle is, without question, taking his vicious propaganda staff down to Algiers to stir up strife between the various elements," while Hull told Churchill, "I wished to point out with emphasis the poisonous propaganda activities of the de Gaulle organization.")[59] To Roosevelt's annoyance the Boisson affair in Dakar was settled when Boisson resigned under pressure from de Gaulle. In the meantime Giraud alienated supporters in the American military with his insistent demand that equipment be delivered for his troops, while he demonstrated a lack of ability to organize the complex handling and disposition of the equipment as it was landed in North Africa.[60] Macmillan notes that by June 1943, both Eisenhower and his deputy Walter Bedell Smith, and even Robert Murphy, "were beginning to feel that Giraud was really no good. He was stupid and vacillating, always preferring the discomforts of a fence to the horrors of a decision."[61] In fact the American military's preference for dealing with de Gaulle was becoming quite apparent. On July 6 Eden noted that he had heard from Algiers that both Eisenhower and Murphy were advocating immediate recognition of the new CFLN. But Eisenhower also apparently found it necessary to wire back to commander in chief George C. Marshall in Washington that the rumor that he wanted to go ahead and recognize the CFLN on his own was false; he knew that recognition was a matter for the president to decide.[62]

In the United States, French refugees such as Geneviève Tabouis and others had hoped that unity of the two factions would result without one trying to dominate the other. One of the most prominent noncommunist Resistance leaders in France, Henri Frenay, arrived in England and reported his view that in de Gaulle's absence, Carlton Gardens, the Gaullist headquarters, was in considerable disarray, with new, younger Gaullists in the Resistance bitter at the hold on power of older ones. They were asking, he wrote in one memo, "Are the Gaullists of London intent on remaking France by themselves or for themselves?" It was indicative of the breach between some members of the internal Resistance, who were on the firing line, facing possible arrest and torture, and who resented directives from the external Resistance, safe in London. It was indicative also of the breach between Frenay and de Gaulle's man Jean Moulin, whom Frenay regarded as too procommunist, and too authoritarian in imposing London's orders on the Resistance. More important, perhaps, was what Frenay wrote in a second memo: it was time for de Gaulle to be generous, to be ready to make sacrifices, to seek genuine fusion with, not absorption of, the Giraud faction. He could understand the factors that irritated de Gaulle and made him intransigent, including the obstructionism of the Americans and the general climate in North Africa. But the quarrel of the generals diminished the French in the eyes of the world and should come to an end; the triumph of Gaullism should be one of the spirit and not of political maneuvering. The Giraudists, who shouldn't look to Allied support, which made Giraud appear to be America's man, were like many French who had supported Pétain at first but had since come around, and should now be accepted as genuine resistants.[63]

In absolving Giraud of his past allegiance to Pétain, Frenay joined the administration in Washington which had fêted Giraud while he was there, as well as the French journalists in the United States who had wanted de Gaulle to accept Giraud as an equal, and Robert Murphy, who also stood by Giraud. Murphy had written President Roosevelt that in conversations with Giraud he had determined that the general was against the Vichy laws, the dreadful concentration camps, and the laws against the Jews, but had to proceed slowly: "I am more convinced than ever of . . . his desire to make a clean break with undesirable ideas and policies and his sound judgement on certain phases of the North African situation, especially the Moslem question."[64]

If all this were true, it would certainly be a "clean break." While a prisoner of war in Germany, Giraud, convinced of the correctness of Marshal Pétain's National Revolution, had written a report to Pétain about the 1940 defeat in which he blamed the British, the Popular Front with its uniting of Freemasons, unions, and bolshevists, and its concomitant sapping of French virility.[65] To General Catroux, at the Anfa meeting, he said acidly, "You, do you believe in democratic principles?"[66] Later, in North Africa, Giraud wrote a memo to the CFLN in which he repeated his earlier arguments that at the time of liberation, the military commander should be in control of the government, the prefects and the police, a position rejected by the committee.[67] In the Archives nationales there is a document dated June 21, 1943, purporting to represent the real views of General Giraud as made known in a speech to a corps of officers by Giraud's *chef de cabinet militaire*, General René Chambe. Presumably Giraud would, when France was free again, restore Marshal Pétain as well as the Révolution nationale, which would, to the extent possible, bring back the laws against Jews, Masons, communists, and Gaullists. In the meantime, he meant to penalize soldiers who deserted to de Gaulle's forces. Whether the document is genuine apparently cannot be determined.[68]

In light of all this, Roosevelt's support of the conservative Giraud against de Gaulle appears to have been flawed from the outset. It was based, however, on the president's continued view that the French should simply provide troops to the Allied commanders and forbear from politics. For this purpose Giraud, whatever his political views, would do.

De Gaulle gave a rather remarkable explanation to one of his entourage about Roosevelt's support for Giraud. It was based, he said, on three considerations: that Giraud was a first-rate man, when he had actually just the characteristics of a sergeant major; that success in ridding North Africa of the Germans would give Giraud enormous prestige in metropolitan France; and that there were no Gaullists in North Africa. By now, however, Roosevelt was beginning to see his mistake, and de Gaulle would welcome a meeting with him.[69]

Despite what others might think, the single-minded de Gaulle, now sure of his support in France *and* in North Africa as well as the rest of the empire, where several further areas had rallied to his movement, was impatient with the idea of shared political authority with Giraud, a good military commander who had no political sense and undoubtedly held the reactionary views attributed to him. De Gaulle was angered that Roosevelt had tried to maintain Boisson in office in Dakar, which de Gaulle now knew Roosevelt coveted as a postwar American base. Roosevelt, unable to avoid meddling in French affairs, had also—in what Harold Macmillan called "a most extraordinary telegram"—actually ordered Eisenhower to see that Boisson and other Vichy officials who had come to North Africa to serve in Giraud's government were not pursued in justice, despite their previous activities. Boisson, after all, had opened fire against the joint British-French force at Dakar, thereby prolonging the whole African war, and under his direction Allied prisoners had been badly mistreated. A second official, Marcel Peyrouton, was the Vichy minister of the interior who had signed de Gaulle's death warrant. A third, Pierre-Étienne Flandin, had briefly served as prime minister in the Vichy government when Pierre Laval had been removed by Pétain.

The tone of Roosevelt's telegram greatly upset the Allied leaders in North Africa. "Please *inform* the French Committee as follows," it read. "In view of the assistance given the Allied armies during the campaign in Africa by Boisson, Peyrouton and Flandin, you are *directed* to take no action against these three individuals at the present time." Eisenhower knew that the attempt to dictate to the committee on such a matter would be angrily rejected as an unwarranted interference in internal affairs and provoke a potentially catastrophic crisis. Through General Marshall, and with the support of Winston Churchill, he was able to get Roosevelt to tone down his message, merely requesting that the committee defer action until after liberation, and authorizing Eisenhower to negotiate the matter. Eisenhower was able to do so, and the men were comfortably lodged until their postwar trials.[70]

Despite what many thought at the time, the issue between the two French leaders was not just a conflict of personalities, nor of ideologies, nor a simple maneuvering for power, but rather one of fundamental concepts. For de Gaulle, as we have seen, what was needed was a strong, recognized political authority that would, among other matters, determine the use of French troops and would be able to define, insist on, and defend French interests in the face of the Allies as well as forestall Roosevelt's desire for AMGOT in France. Giraud simply wanted to rearm French soldiers in order to fight within the Allied ranks. This, of course, was what Roosevelt wanted, and he and Hull saw the clash between Gaullists and Giraudists as impeding the war effort, with de Gaulle to blame. American military in the area, however, were having more and more difficulty with Giraud, especially when, after the fall of Sicily, they wanted to use French troops in Italy and Giraud created difficulties. (In the event, in November some four French divisions under General Alphonse Juin would join the other Allies in the Italian campaign and fight brilliantly.)

In the meantime developments in North Africa had served to secure de Gaulle's authority within the CFLN. If some of his followers in both London and the United States were alienated by what they thought were his maneuvers in arrogating power to himself, a series of events had much to do with precipitating the change. With the Allies in Italy, de Gaulle was told that he would be invited to send a delegate when and if the Italians decided to surrender. Italy, after all, had attacked France back in May 1940 and continued to occupy part of the country, and French troops were now fighting in Italy. On September 4, 1943, however, after the overthrow of Mussolini, a new government under General Pietro Badoglio signed an armistice agreement with the British and Americans, and de Gaulle was not informed until four days later. The Allied High Command told him that Giraud had been constantly in touch with the negotiations, but when Giraud was asked why he hadn't kept the committee abreast of the affair, he denied having been kept informed.[71]

Another affair also further weakened Giraud. Earlier, without notifying the committee, Giraud had quietly sent arms to the communist underground in Corsica, the island to the south of France which had been occupied by the Italians, and where a noncommunist Resistance group had been broken by the Italians; its leader had committed suicide. On September 8 Corsican communist-led patriots with whom Italian troops had been negotiating since the Italian mainland surrender announced the liberation of the town of Ajaccio and asked for help. When the Allied High Command told Giraud they could spare no equipment, Giraud finally told an angered de Gaulle what he had been up to. The committee feared a bloodbath, since several thousand German troops had landed in Corsica, but it authorized Giraud to send the poorly armed contingents for which he could scrape together transport, first on a submarine and then on two French destroyers. With Italy having surrendered a month earlier, the partisans had the help of 85,000 Italian troops, and the island was liberated within three weeks. German troops also evacuated the nearby island of Sardinia. Although most accounts credit Giraud with demonstrating his military abilities in the campaign, OSS operative Carleton Coon, who accompanied the French troops, would later argue that Corsica was not really liberated by the Allies, but that the operation was "largely an act of occupying territory that the Germans did not want." All the French and Italians did "was annoy them on their way out."[72] The Germans, however, had provided a strong covering defense of Bastia as they reembarked from there, requiring considerable fighting.

Whatever may be the case, it was Giraud who had seen to clearing the first Axis-occupied French territory by French military action. He had spent three days in Corsica himself overseeing the operation, and it should have redounded to his benefit. But he had moved without authorization of the CFLN in an action that had real political consequences: he had done so in conjunction with the communist-led partisans, who took the opportunity to try to install communist mayors in most towns. It was precisely this end that de Gaulle and the committee wanted to avoid when France was being liberated. In Corsica, through adroit maneuvers by Gaullist supporters, the communists were subsequently shunted aside, but Giraud's judgment was, to put it mildly, brought into question. What Eisenhower noticed was that when Giraud visited the island in early October, the central square, place du Diamant, had been renamed place de Gaulle, and when Giraud toured in an open car, the wild crowds cheered "Vive de Gaulle!" De Gaulle's subsequent tour of the island a few weeks later was in the form of a triumphant procession: to his evident pleasure he was greeted with unbridled enthusiasm everywhere he went. It was an important development that would have results later, when Eisenhower, by the time of the invasion of France, differed strongly with Roosevelt over what de Gaulle's role should be.

De Gaulle was never one to make a joke. But when he arrived at the airport after his tour, he told his aide that back in the 1930s a war minister had said contemptuously that the irritating upstart Colonel de Gaulle ought to be sent away to Corsica. Well, he continued, "here I am!"[73]

Back in Algiers, events, as one general put it, followed the "recipe for an artichoke that is eaten leaf by leaf."[74] General Giraud came back from Washington with an exalted view of his status in the eyes of the Americans, not realizing perhaps that in his absence de Gaulle had cemented his position in terms of a smoother running of the nascent government, as well as getting the committee to dismiss some four hundred pro-Vichy military and naval officers.[75] On his return Giraud came up with ideas unacceptable to de Gaulle as to the future of the committee. He balked at first but, after complicated maneuvers, agreed to a committee decree of October 2 that maintained the co-presidency but created the position of head of government, which would be occupied by de Gaulle, and established a commissariat of defense, which would give orders to the commander in chief, the position retained by Giraud. It made sense to most members of the committee. Five weeks later, at the request of the newly created Provisional Assembly, whose members expressed the view that there were too many generals on the committee, de Gaulle asked for the resignation of all members of the committee so that he could reform what had virtually become his government. When he had done so, Generals Giraud and Georges found themselves excluded, though Giraud retained his position as commander in chief, but with reduced powers. Giraud's refusal to resupply a British-equipped French division with American equipment so that it could join the fighting in Italy hardly endeared him to the Allied High Command, which had made it an urgent matter. Eventually, in April 1944, having refused to merge his own intelligence services with those of the London office—a key issue—he was relieved of his command. The committee named him inspector general of the armies, a position he would not accept, and he simply faded out of the picture.

Jean Monnet, the man who had been sent from Washington to work as political adviser to Giraud, concluded that the politically naïve Giraud could have remained commander in chief of the French army but for his unwillingness as a five-star general to serve under a two-star general. He had also tried to retain the political power accorded him almost by accident at the time of Darlan's assassination. It led him, wrote Monnet, "to lose everything because he wanted to cede nothing."[76] De Gaulle was now the single head of the Committee of French National Liberation, and the head of the French armed forces. His victory was complete. On September 17, 1943, the CFLN created by decree a Provisional Consultative Assembly, whose members began to emerge from clandestinity in France in October and November, or who had been Gaullists in North Africa, or who came from other parts of the empire. It marked the beginning of the creation of a real representative provisional government with a highly argumentative and divided assembly.[77] Some commentators argued that de Gaulle created it only to enhance his democratic credentials, some that he had little regard for the heated partisan disputes that characterized it. There is little question, however, that he cooperated with it.

That same month, September 1943, the CFLN sent a crucial document to the American administration and to the British, outlining in detail its plans for how it would operate as the liberation of France took place and how it would cooperate with the Allied armies in furthering the military effort.[78] It represented an important and detailed attempt to resolve the knotty problem of civil administration behind the Allied front lines, but it assumed that the French committee would take on the responsibilities involved, and as a result the committee, like de Gaulle a year earlier, never received an acknowledgment or an answer from either government. The document, however, apparently received the approval of the Allied High Command and, discreetly, that of Churchill. The latter, in deference to Roosevelt, never argued with him about it, and Roosevelt apparently let the document lie on his desk unanswered. Roosevelt, in fact, pursuing his own line of reasoning, on September 7 had proposed that no further arms be sent to the French Army of Africa if "our prima donna is to seize control of it from the old gentleman." Marshall dissented strongly from the president's suggestion in view of the usefulness of the French divisions in Italy and on the grounds that Eisenhower needed more French divisions for forthcoming operations in France itself. As a result the arms continued to flow.[79]

The lack of an answer to the September memorandum from the CFLN rankled. As Roosevelt's telegram to Churchill of May 8, 1943, and his follow-up letter to Secretary of State Hull demonstrated, he still entertained the idea of establishing a military government in France. Some of those around him did not share this view—people like Secretary of the Army Henry Stimson and his deputy John J. McCloy, who was much more favorably inclined than his boss, along with Secretary of the Treasury Henry Morgenthau and others. But as long as the president persisted, tentative planning might go on, but no one could accept the CFLN's views. The result was that the French committee received no answer, the document approved by so many others lay on the president's desk, and French certainty that the United States still planned an AMGOT for France was only reinforced.

Roosevelt had had to accept that Giraud was not the man he had hoped for. The administration would have to deal with the committee. But the moves taken to eliminate Giraud, which cost de Gaulle the support of French émigrés such as Geneviève Tabouis and Henri de Kerillis in the United States, meant that Roosevelt and the State Department now viewed the CFLN with increased distrust, even though by the end of 1943 thirty-seven countries had recognized it, and it had taken on the form of a genuine government, with ministries, working committees, and, under the direction of René Cassin, a juridical committee that examined all laws and decrees.

In September 1943 the Allies created a Mediterranean Commission on which France would be represented, and the CFLN responded enthusiastically. Vital French interests in Italian affairs, among others, would not be ignored. But a decision at the Moscow Conference of October 1943 on postwar planning, attended by Secretary of State Hull, replaced the Mediterranean Commission with a new European Advisory Commission made up of the United States, England, and the Soviet Union. It would work on postwar European affairs, but France was not invited to be a member.

(Back in the United States, journalist Walter Lippmann commented on the absurdity of not having a French representative at the Moscow Conference and then on the European Advisory Commission.[80] For decisions on European affairs to be accepted, France had to be in on the decisions.)

Once again the British acted to relieve the French by securing the creation of an advisory council for Italy, with French participation. Although it operated at a lower level, for the moment it relieved French feelings. "The extreme sensitiveness of the French," wrote Harold Macmillan, "was of course natural—if rather tiresome. It explained many exaggerations and emotional outbursts."[81] To Washington it merely meant that the French, and especially de Gaulle, were troublemakers who interfered with agreements that could be reached by others. Roosevelt wrote in an irritated and somewhat arrogant vein to Churchill: "For the life of me I cannot see why France is entitled to anybody on the Allied Control Commission for Italy. His [de Gaulle's] presence there will, we know from experience, cause controversy and more trouble with the French Committee. . . . I wish you and I could run this Italian business. We would not need any help or advice."[82]

If the Italian affair was another one of the string of events that helped determine Roosevelt's attitude toward de Gaulle and de Gaulle's distrust of the United States, events in Lebanon further muddied the waters in late 1943. De Gaulle had suspended the Lebanese constitution and dissolved the Lebanese parliament but was forced by the British and Americans to restore the government. It was on this occasion that Roosevelt wrote a memo to Hull that ended with a passage cited earlier: "The Lebanese affair illustrates the general attitude of the committee and especially de Gaulle. The latter now claims the right to speak for all of France and talks openly of plans to set up his Government in France as soon as the Allies get in. . . . [T]he thought that the occupation when it occurs should be wholly military is one to which I am increasingly inclined."[83] In February 1944 Roosevelt—perhaps unwittingly, though the French did not think so—demonstrated his attitude toward de Gaulle when he officiated at a ceremony turning over a new destroyer to Admiral Raymond Fénard, chief of the French naval mission to the United States; in his remarks he simply omitted any mention of the Committee of French National Liberation and of its president, Charles de Gaulle.[84]

Over the wartime years Anthony Eden, Harold Macmillan, and Duff Cooper all ensured that de Gaulle would continue to be supported by the

British government, despite Churchill's growing deference to Roosevelt, with his increasing distrust of the Frenchman and determination to intervene in French affairs. Eden, the foreign secretary, Harold Macmillan, the resident minister in North Africa, and Duff Cooper, who succeeded him and later became ambassador to the French Provisional Government, all had their difficulties with the irascible, temperamental, and stubborn French leader, and all acknowledged their problems in their memoirs. But as a result of their constant contact and work with the French, they remained certain of one thing: de Gaulle was the man whose authority would be recognized by the French, who could establish a working French administration that would prevent chaos and a possible communist takeover during the liberation of France, and would as a consequence provide them with a partner on the continent with whom they could work in the postwar period—however difficult a partner he might be.

Events in 1943 had ensured that de Gaulle would be the sole head of the French Committee of National Liberation. The committee was now recognized as a provisional government-in-exile by numerous governments. But to Roosevelt, it had become an organization that ought to be kept from seizing power in France.

Against this background of mistrust, misunderstanding, and hostility in England and in the United States, preparations had long been under way at a lower level to deal with the problem of Allied civil administration in France at the time of liberation. They were colored by the experiences in North Africa and subsequently in Sicily and Italy. The French watched these preparations with considerable apprehension.

CHAPTER 4

Allied Preparations for Civil Affairs in France

AT THE SECOND PEACE CONFERENCE IN THE HAGUE, IN 1907, the participating powers, including the United States, signed a convention that included, in the annex to the convention, a section on the powers of a country that occupied territory of another in case of war: "The authority of the legitimate power having in fact passed into the hands of the occupant, the latter shall take all measures in his power to restore and ensure, as far as possible, public order and safety, while respecting, unless absolutely prevented, the laws in force in the country."[1] Clearly, the terms of the convention posed numerous problems that would be subsequently discussed at length: Was it applicable to a territory "liberated" from another country as well as to one "occupied" by another country? Did the latter part mean the occupant was legally required to observe, for example, the Nuremberg laws enacted by Nazi Germany if it occupied the country at the end of World War II, or, for that matter, when it occupied French North Africa, where Vichy-imposed anti-Semitic laws were the law of the land?

Americans had had some experience in occupying other countries. In 1918, following World War I, American soldiers temporarily occupied a part of the German Rhineland. In a report prepared after the end of the occupation, Colonel Irwin L. Hunt, officer in charge of civil affairs, Third Army, wrote a memo that might have been written yesterday:

The American army of occupation lacked both training and organization to guide the destinies of the nearly one million civilians whom
the fortunes of war had placed under its temporary sovereignty. . . . It
is extremely unfortunate that the qualifications necessary for a civil
administration are not developed among officers in times of peace.
The history of the United States offers an uninterrupted series of
wars, which demanded as their aftermath, the exercise by its officers
of civil governmental functions. Despite the precedents of military
governments in Mexico, California, the Southern States, Cuba, Porto
Rico, Panama, China, the Philippines and elsewhere, the lesson has
seemingly not been learned. In none of the service-schools devoted
to the higher training of officers, has a single course on the nature
and scope of military government been established. The majority of
the regular officers were, as a consequence, ill-equipped to perform
tasks differing so widely from their accustomed duties.[2]

The administration of occupied territory, he concluded, was not only something that might be a normal part of wartime activity but also something
that required extensive preparation. The army should therefore develop
competence in civil administration among its officers during peacetime.

In the 1920s and 1930s the peacetime U.S. Army dwindled to only the
nineteenth largest in the world, while the United States, as a result of disillusion with the aftermath of the Great War, retreated into legislated isolation: never again would it be drawn into "foreign wars." Instead it would be
prepared to defend the Western Hemisphere—the Americas—on the sea,
with a powerful two-ocean navy. Nevertheless, as the 1930s wore on, with
war clouds gathering, students at the Army War College who were interested in the Hunt report suggested that it was time to produce manuals on
military government. As a result, in 1939 the Office of the Judge Advocate
General published two field manuals, *The Rules of Land Warfare,* with a
substantial section on civil administration, and in June 1940 another new
one, FM 7-25, *Military Government,* a statement of purposes, policies, and
procedures.[3] In the next two years, when the American armed forces began
their enormous and frenzied expansion and the Japanese attack on Pearl
Harbor finally brought the United States into the war, military government seemed the least of the army's preoccupations. A few men, however,
foresaw a time when Allied armies would force the Germans and Japanese

to retreat, and the problems of administration would arise in liberated territories. Field manual FM 7-25 might have to be applied.

In the meantime, in London, following the Allied decision made at the January 1943 Casablanca conference to invade western Europe in 1944, the English Lieutenant General Frederick Morgan was appointed chief of staff to the Supreme Allied Commander, who would be named later. Morgan set up his staff under the acronym of his title, COSSAC. (Once Eisenhower was named to command Operation Overlord—the invasion of France—in early 1944, COSSAC became SHAEF, Supreme Headquarters, Allied Expeditionary Force.) Morgan's major task was to begin the planning of Overlord.

It was an enormous enterprise: the fitting together of thousands of pieces of the puzzle as to what equipment and what men would be where at what time, who the men would be, what the equipment would be, how they would be moved at that proper time, what supplies would be necessary and where should they be at what time, what casualties could be expected and how to handle them. The issues were endless, and were complicated by the fact that COSSAC was an integrated Anglo-American staff. The views of different men of different nationalities with different interests had to be melded. Morgan also tells us: "Of all the many and varied facets of COSSAC's great task the most vexatious and the least satisfactory was undoubtedly all that complex activity known collectively as Civil Affairs. . . . The collection, organization, and training . . . presented continual difficulty, but the evolution of policies and procedures on which the staff was to function was a perpetual nightmare."[4] He quotes a Major Sullivan: "There were plenty of affairs, but the difficulty was to keep them civil." And, he adds, echoing the comments of the American, Colonel Hunt, in 1920: That so late as 1943 we at COSSAC should have been forced to break new ground . . . argues unmistakably that our normal preparation and training in peacetime both in the United States of America and in the British Commonwealth is gravely deficient. The culmination of almost any campaign must surely consist of the reinstitution or institution of some form of public administration. . . . It seems thus unavoidable that military officers must be trained to this end."[5]

The varied missions of civil affairs were bound to be complicated and sometimes contradictory. Order and security had to be maintained behind the lines in such a way that there would be no hindrance to the military effort, and at the same time the liberated areas would have to contribute to the military effort in the form of secure transportation—which often had to be reconstructed or needed heavy maintenance—and secure lines of communication. Liberation and occupation both entailed emergency feeding of the civilian population, provision of medical care and control of disease, the provision of housing, the resumption of civilian production and employment—often necessitating the supplying of specialized equipment—acquisition of raw materials for military needs, and then the restoration of civilian control and delegation of powers to the civilian agencies of the occupying power and ultimately, in the case of liberated countries, to their own civilian authorities.[6] One great source of continuous conflict was clear and could only be settled on the spot: there was bound to be disagreement between the fighting men of the armed forces and civil affairs officers over allocation of shipping and transport generally, for any ships devoted to food and relief and reconstruction supplies required by the civil affairs detachments meant one less ship carrying munitions and other equipment that might be desperately needed by the army. One barrel of oil for civilian use meant one barrel less for army tanks and trucks. If conflict over supplies was inevitable, so was the issue of who would decide.

The British had already had some experience in late 1940 in the Italian colonies they had conquered in Africa—Eritrea, Cyrenaica, and Italian Somaliland—and in early 1941 the British War Office inaugurated courses at St. John's College, Cambridge, "to train officers in postwar reconstruction and other matters incident to military operations in foreign countries."[7] Judged too academic and too far removed from the expertise available in London, the Cambridge courses were replaced in January 1943 by the Civil Affairs Staff Center at Wimbledon, which became the main training ground for civil affairs officers for northwest Europe. Subsequently schools were opened at Shrivenham in Wiltshire, primarily for training Americans, and at Eastbourne, by the sea in Sussex, for training British officers. (Canadian civil affairs officers received training at the Royal Military College of Canada in Kingston, Ontario.)[8] In the meantime, back in the United States, Brigadier General Allen Gullion, Judge Advocate General, a Democrat and formerly administrator of the New Deal National Recovery Act for Honolulu, suggested to his seniors in the General Staff that the time had come for procurement and training of military government personnel in the American armed forces.

Soon after, two American officers who had attended a course in Cambridge in October 1941—the first American officers to receive military government training—reported on their experience. In consequence, despite the resistance of personnel who, after Pearl Harbor, felt that officers should not be diverted from far more pressing military needs, in early 1942 a School of Military Government was set up at facilities contributed by the University of Virginia in Charlottesville. They cost the U.S. government $75 a month. The school was headed by General Cornelius W. Wickersham. Officers and civilians were rapidly commissioned as faculty, with competence in the fields of engineering, accounting, law, economics, sociology, and the like. Courses were to be given in the international law of military government and in the history, culture, language, and government of countries that might soon be occupied, to which were added courses on handling the practical problems of civil government. A distinction was also made between "military government," which would operate in enemy countries, and "civil affairs," which would operate in friendly territories. On May 11, 1942, fifty officer-students began their first training.[9] There developed, however, widespread dissension at top levels in the American government over who should run the whole enterprise.

The army's viewpoint was made clear in a memo from Jesse Miller, director of the Military Government Division and aide to General Gullion, addressed to the undersecretary of war: "The prime direction and administration of military government belong wholly to the military command. If there is one outstanding lesson to be learned from prior experience in military government, it is the unwisdom of permitting any interference by civilian agencies with the Army's basic task of civilian administration in occupied areas. . . . In those important American experiences . . . where civilian influence was permitted to be exercised, the results were . . . demoralizing, costly, and ludicrous."[10] The War Department and the army thought they had matters in hand, and would be able to avoid the bitter disputes that had characterized every major war in the past over whether civilians or the military should govern occupied or liberated territory. They were mistaken. Several New Dealers were by no means in agreement with the idea that the governing of civilians, friendly or enemy, was a job for the military. According to one historian, "newspaper reports on the School of Military Government had described it disdainfully as the Army's 'school for *Gauleiters*,'"[11] and several of the president's advisers bitterly attacked the army's planning. President Roosevelt, in particular, felt that the administration of civil affairs in liberated or occupied territories needed first-class civilians, and through numerous meetings stuck to his guns: in this war, in particular, occupation of Italy, France, and Germany would require the elimination of fascism in all its forms, and thus the democratic reconstruction of administrative and political systems, a task for which he did not think the army was suited.

The director of the School of Military Government admitted that the most vulnerable point of the program was that there were not enough "high-class students." (In England, where the corresponding training was now taking place at Wimbledon, one report lamented that the students "tended to be elderly, often eccentric, often weeded out of other military outfits."[12] It was also in England, somewhat later, that AMGOT was said to stand for "Ancient Military Gentlemen on Tour.")

In spite of Roosevelt's views and those of several angry New Dealers, three developments ensured that the army would retain the military government or civil affairs function in the initial stages of any occupation. The first was simply that civilian departments had not organized for the job, thus leaving the field to the military. Although in mid-June 1943 the president reiterated his desire for a rapid introduction of civilian control, by November, in a letter to Secretary of War Stimson, he acknowledged that the failure of civilian agencies to prepare made this impossible.[13] By this time Charlottesville was turning out 175 graduates every three months, while the ten universities in which three-month courses had been set up were taking in 450 students a month.[14] The second was that following the North African invasion in November 1942, General Eisenhower had found that the presence of several different civilian agencies—the Board of Economic Warfare, the Agriculture and Treasury departments, the Lend-Lease Administration, and the State Department—had badly confused the situation there. The military command in place, he concluded, should control all civilian agencies. The third was that the English, who had decided to rely on the military for occupation duties, were a year and a half ahead of the Americans in preparing for military government and civil affairs, and the two countries had to coordinate their activities. The Americans would almost be forced to follow the British lead.

Finally, a compromise was reached: in the zone of military operations, the army's military government or civil affairs officers would retain control. Subsequently, in a second zone, where military operations had ceased but logistical needs and proximity to the zone of military operations would leave army officers in control of certain functions, civilian agencies would move in but still be coordinated by delegates from a new War Department Civil Affairs Division. The new division was created in March 1943, headed by Major General John Hilldring, who reported directly to the secretary of war. The personnel of all stripes would serve under the local military commander and work with local personnel and officials.

The North African experience showed that in addition to the need for coordination of civilian agencies by having them report to the military commander, and the need for an enormous quantity of civilian supplies, wide use of local personnel was also essential. The question was, which local personnel? In North Africa, Eisenhower, who had not wanted to be involved in local politics, found himself in the midst of it. Basically, there had been no planning for civil affairs prior to the North African invasion, since it was assumed that the Allied armies would be entering territory where there were no hostile troops and where a friendly administration would be in place, and therefore the Allies could rely on the existing administrative apparatus. After the aborted attempt to put General Giraud in charge, Eisenhower and General Mark Clark had initially relied on Admiral Darlan and numerous Vichy appointees. The uproar in the Allied camp made it clear that in the future, the Allies might have to rely on local authorities, but not on those who had been obvious collaborators. Nevertheless, the question of which French or locals to work with could not be avoided. Eisenhower, to his exasperation, found he could not escape political decisions, given the imbroglio already described in chapter 3.

Meanwhile in Sicily and Italy, twenty-one years' worth of Fascist administrators simply disappeared and had to be replaced, and at least temporarily, this meant by AMGOT personnel, who assumed detailed administrative functions and, again, were immersed in political issues. According to Harry Coles and Albert Weinberg: "In many cases all of the machinery of modern life had ceased to exist; there was no government, no police, no food supply, no water, no electric light, no transportation and no organized medical service. . . . [T]he dead had to be buried, the streets cleaned of debris, water and food brought in etc."[15] Allied planners "had underestimated the prospective destruction. . . . Chaos reigned[,] . . . rubble, ruin and filth were on every hand and looting was rampant. In a word, everything had to be done and generally there was little with which to do it. Directives, manuals and wise saws were less relevant in such a situation than had been expected, and improvisation was the order of the day."[16] The civil affairs officers in Italy "were by and large an extraordinary group of people—politicians, financiers, lawyers, inventors, professors, philosophers, artists, and poets. . . . [They] learned much of politics from their colleagues, the British. They learned even more about politics in Italy because every major problem which confronted them in that land of excitable people, including the economic problems, had its political element. They learned politics in large measure from the people they governed, past masters at politics."[17] What had been a more or less theoretical issue became clear and concrete: "Military necessity demands relief of civilian distress," yet since both demanded resources, the struggle to allocate those resources between the two needs was a constant one. Shortages of shipping and port facilities and the presence of masses of refugees all served to complicate civil affairs. Although preparation for civilian relief had begun in England, no one had really anticipated that food for civilians would be "the keynote for the success of military government after occupation." Planners had essentially thought that relief and very simple rehabilitation was all that would be required.[18]

A lesson had been learned in Sicily, however, and the English were well ahead of the Americans in their planning for northwest Europe. The Combined Civil Affairs Committee meeting in England assumed that the theater commander would supply civilian stocks from army stores for a minimum period of perhaps up to six months until civilian agencies could pitch in. But whereas the Americans began with the assumption that 6 million tons of relief supplies would have to be made available for the first year after liberation, the British, in discussion with governments-in-exile, had come up with a much higher figure.[19] No one, of course, could be certain how it would all play out, but in Washington at least one major decision was reached, requiring considerable maneuvering: as in the case of civil affairs, the president laid the responsibility for the "initial burden of shipping and distribution of relief supplies" directly on the War Department, which would require the cooperation of the civilian agencies involved—the Department of State and the Foreign Economic Administration, among others.[20]

In the meantime the English, their preparations for northwest Europe well under way, never considered civilian control of civil affairs: everything would be under the War Office. In June 1942 the War Office created the Administration of Territories (Europe) or AT(E) Committee, which "was to play by far the most important part in shaping policy and principles for civil affairs and military government."[21] It would be transmuted into General Staff 5 (G-5) when SHAEF was later established under General Eisenhower. Its membership included representatives of the War Office, the Foreign Office, and the Board of Trade and of inter-Allied relief organizations, and delegates from the American embassy, the U. S. Army, and military headquarters preparing for the invasion of Europe. In the summer of 1943 a Directorate of Civil Affairs with multiple branches emerged as the British counterpart to the American Division of Civil Affairs, with which it began to cooperate closely, and to which American officers were assigned from the American headquarters in England, ETOUSA (European Theater of Operations, USA).

As planning for northwest Europe began, one issue was settled. Although some officials would continue to argue about the matter (and despite French writers' continued use of the term AMGOT), there would be no AMGOT, as such, in the liberated countries as there came to be in Sicily and Italy. There, a line of command outside the normal military channel had been established, and AMGOT officers who actually took over local administration acted on their own, with their own line of communication to their superiors (though, naturally, they had to communicate and cooperate with nearby armed units). Given the fading away of Fascist administrators with virtually no one to replace them, a genuine military government was established. In the course of 1943 this pattern was decisively rejected as far as northwest Europe other than Germany and Austria was concerned. France, Norway, Holland, Belgium, and Luxemburg were not enemy countries; they were to be liberated, not conquered.

The Foreign Office was highly conscious of foreign sensibilities, and civil affairs staffers also pressed home the point: in negotiations with the countries to be liberated, AMGOT as practiced in Sicily and Italy simply would not do. As a result, in mid-1943 the United States and Britain, with some measure of foresight, and after complex negotiations, signed joint civil affairs agreements with representatives of the governments-in-exile for Norway, Holland, Belgium, and Luxemburg. They defined the new pattern to be followed. In the zone of military action, civil affairs officers would operate alongside the armies, attached directly to army units, carrying out "civil affairs" functions but working through local personnel. Behind this area, the governments-in-exile would take over. There, the agreements read, the respective governments would "resume their full constitutional responsibilities for civil administration . . . on the understanding that such special facilities as the Allied forces may continue to require . . . will be made available for the prosecution of the war to its final conclusion." The returning governments would be relied on to weed out collaborators and other undesirables, and would restore democratic rule. The agreements "reconciled the necessities of military operations with the turning over of civil affairs to governments in such a way as to not hamper military operations."[22] Civil affairs units would move forward with the armies, leaving behind only a nucleus to deal with logistical and transportation issues and help out local authorities to the extent possible.

The political issues appear to have been resolved for at least some countries. When COSSAC became SHAEF with the naming of General Eisenhower as Supreme Allied Commander in early 1944, some of the officers he brought over with him from the United States, including General Julius Holmes, who had experience with military government in the Mediterranean theater and became deputy chief of G-5 (the public affairs staff), tried to resurrect the AMGOT pattern. Their views were soon rejected by Eisenhower's chief of staff, Lieutenant General Walter Bedell Smith.[23]

From the point of view of French officials, the most significant and explosive point was that the Allies negotiated no such civil affairs agreement with them, since the American government maintained that such an agreement would imply de facto recognition of the CFLN as the legitimate French government. De Gaulle and his entourage were incensed, and their suspicions about what was being planned for France only increased. The fact that negotiations had even been opened with the other countries but not with France fed their distrust. Surely the AMGOT that Roosevelt was known to favor was in the works.

It was for fear of French reaction that there had been hesitation in opening civil affairs negotiations with the other countries. Now, however, despite the tension with the French, planning for the others went ahead at full speed. Lengthy discussions at several levels and the resolution of numerous disagreements led to the creation of elaborate inter-Allied committees and divisions to supervise civil affairs and the provision and shipment of relief supplies to liberated countries.[24] In August 1943 the British created four separate organization known as "country houses" to study the specific problems of civil administration and relief for France, Belgium, Holland, and Norway. They expanded considerably over time—the French house totaled 240 men, including 90 officers—and many of those assigned to the country houses eventually became civil affairs officers themselves, attached to military units. As a result of in-house research they also produced considerable documentation, in the form of both books and papers, to guide civil affairs officers once liberation of the Nazi-occupied countries began. (At least one historian reports that there was so much in them they often went unread.)[25]

The first publication, *ATE Plan for French Participation in Civil Administration of Liberated Territory in Metropolitan France,* was soon discarded: it upset the Gaullists, who obtained a copy and found themselves relegated in it to an advisory role, and it was rejected by American officials for several reasons, chief among them that it was intended to be signed by the CFLN, with whom no written accord was acceptable. It was also about this time that Brigadier General S. Swinton Lee, the British officer who headed the French house, gave a lecture to civil affairs staff members in which he drew a clear distinction between "liberated" areas and "occupied" areas, pointing out that in liberated areas, as soon as the situation permitted, the civil affairs officers should hand over services to indigenous authorities. They should also be aware of and sensitive to what the people had gone through under German occupation and would go through in the fighting that would accompany liberation. But he also repeated what had been said in the first, discarded *Plan for Metropolitan France:* in the war zone, as outlined in the Hague Conventions of 1907 that dealt with—among other things—the responsibilities of belligerents in territories they occupied, the commander in chief would have virtually dictatorial powers. Although French advisers would accompany the civil affairs officers, the latter would have full executive power.[26] This was not what the French wanted.

Subsequently, in providing the country documentation that the civil affairs officers needed, the "country houses" also unwittingly provided further ammunition for Gaullist suspicions and fears in the form of the "Zonal Handbooks." Often attributed to the Americans, the handbooks were in fact a British production: an American version simply added a preface by General Walter Bedell Smith. These were twenty-two sometimes voluminous handbooks, basically reproducing information taken from French local directories, providing detailed documentation on all French communities. They identified, among other things, local functionaries and their political affiliations, local schoolteachers and priests (with the location of their schools and churches), newspapers and their affiliations, the location of government offices, fire and police stations, movie houses, garages, industries, and stores of all types, ending—to the amusement of French commentators, who failed to note that they reproduced French guidebooks—with the location of brothels. The only added material was, in the American edition, the Walter Bedell Smith preface, and in all of them an English introduction that provided stereotypical characterizations of the local populace, affording much amusement for the French: "Inhabitants of the south are happy, scatterbrained, and lazy," "Basques are inveterate smugglers," "Normans are naturally taciturn and reserved," and so on.[27]

The "Zonal Handbooks" seemed to provide even more evidence to the French of Allied intentions actually to administer the French localities and to repeat the Italian AMGOT experience. Why else were the communities described in such detail? Long after the war, numerous French authors would use the existence of the handbooks to support their view that an AMGOT had really been in the works for France.[28] At this point, when General Hilldring, commanding the Charlottesville school, invited the French to send several officers to classes at the school, the first reaction in Algiers was that they would most certainly not participate in American plans to install AMGOT in France. Several eventually attended, however, and reported, rather surprisingly, that they found nothing to complain about. In England, de Gaulle's associate General Paul Legentilhomme and others visited Wimbledon to assure themselves that no AMGOT was being prepared.[29] Algiers, however, was not reassured.

In the meantime, the subject of civil affairs for France was being debated at a higher level. Despite increased Anglo-American cooperation and planning, at this point the clear divergence between British and American views became apparent. In early September 1943 the English sent the American commanding general who preceded Eisenhower a proposed agreement with the CFLN in the form of a directive to the commander in chief. Citing the changes under way among the French in Algiers, where a quasi-governmental administration was emerging, the agreement suggested that the British and Americans should now negotiate directly with the CFLN and recognize that it would take over administration in France. In Parliament that month Anthony Eden replied to questioners, "It was our intention from the earliest possible moment after the landings, when the military position allowed, that the administration should be turned over to the friendly government." When asked, "Does that apply to France?" Eden replied, "Certainly."

"Will you use the National Committee?"

"Of course we shall. We are in relation with the Committee."[30]

Citing Roosevelt's view, however, the Civil Affairs Division in Washington rejected the British draft, arguing: "It is too much in the form of an agreement. . . . [O]ur troops will possess the power and authority of an occupying force." The British proposal attached too much importance to the CFLN.[31] In short order, in reaction to the British suggestion, the division drew up a very different directive, which was approved by the president and Secretary of State Cordell Hull. Hull took it with him to the October 1943 three-power Foreign Ministers Conference meeting in Moscow, where, despite Eden's earlier statements in Parliament, the three foreign ministers initialed what became known as the "Dunn-Wright" agreement and passed it on for consideration by the newly created three-power European Advisory Commission, which did not include any French representation.

Although this top-level agreement declared that France would be treated as a friendly liberated territory, it also stated that the commander in chief would have all the rights of military occupation: "He shall proceed upon the basis that there is no sovereign government of France." While his civil administration would be "as far as possible French in character and personnel . . . he and his authorized deputies shall appoint or affirm French official and judicial personnel in temporary office. Selection will be based solely on efficiency and loyalty to the allied cause. . . . Obnoxious political organizations will be suppressed and leaders detained by the Commander in Chief when in the interests of the allied cause or the maintenance of order." While the CFLN would be invited to attach qualified French liaison officers to the commander in chief's staff, they would be consulted only "as far as possible about appointments of French citizens to administrative and judicial posts." And once more, the memorandum reiterated the aim of creating conditions "permitting re-establishment of representative French Government in concordance with the freely expressed wishes of the French people."[32]

The Free French London office managed to obtain a copy of what was supposed to be a confidential agreement. To the French, coming on top of everything else, it was and remained an obvious, clear expression of Anglo-American intent to install AMGOT in France, and some French would frequently refer to it to buttress their view. It certainly represented President Roosevelt's view.

Anthony Eden (who does not mention the agreement in his memoirs) must have initialed Dunn-Wright without carefully considering it, for on March 4, 1944, he observed: "The President's absurd and petty dislike of de Gaulle blinds him. It would be folly to follow him on this."[33] To him and to most Americans already in England, including the American envoy to the CFLN, Admiral Stark, and to General Eisenhower himself, the Dunn-Wright agreement seemed like nonsense.

Eisenhower, despite subsequent references to it, was clearly opposed to putting it into effect. En route from North Africa to England by way of Washington to take over his new position as Supreme Commander for the invasion of France, Eisenhower found that Secretary of War Stimson and his influential undersecretary John J. McCloy shared his point of view: in preparation for the landings he should be able to remain in direct touch with the Resistance through the CFLN, and he should deal only with the CFLN, which ought to have primary responsibility for administration in liberated territories. McCloy was willing to go further, advocating recognition of the CFLN as the de facto government of all of France as soon as some part of the country was liberated.[34] Eisenhower, who was impressed by the enthusiastic reception de Gaulle received when he visited liberated Corsica in October 1943, among other things, tried to make clear to President Roosevelt, when he finally met with him, that the Dunn-Wright agreement was a nonstarter. The president, however, had already told Secretary of State Hull that in light of the lack of agreement with the British, he would make no final decisions at that time. With Eisenhower he used one of his usual methods in dealing with someone who raised a contentious issue. He remained noncommittal.[35]

The confusion was complete. Just before leaving North Africa, British envoy Harold Macmillan ruminated about the "unrealistic" and "dangerous" planning that was taking place in England and the United States. "The right thing" he wrote in his diary, "was for the CFLN[,] which was in effect the provisional government of France, to take over at the earliest possible moment. They, and not the British and American officers, were the natural people to administer metropolitan France and to assume full responsibility for its government"; he told this to Secretary of State Hull, who stopped in Cairo on his way to the Moscow conference. Hull's reply is not recorded.[36]

Both in the United States and in London, many officers actively involved in preparations for the landings shared Eisenhower's view of the whole matter and tried to allay French apprehensions and secure Gaullist cooperation. In July 1943 Eisenhower, from North Africa, had written to General Marshall in Washington to deny rumors that he wanted or planned to recognize the CFLN: such a decision was up to the president. Nevertheless, he concurred with a Murphy recommendation sent to Washington that General Giraud's visit might be the occasion for the United States to announce recognition of the CFLN "as the body which is collectively responsible for the representation of French interests until such time as a national government is established."[37] Naturally, in light of Roosevelt's opposition, this was another recommendation that got nowhere, but it was an early indication of General Eisenhower's emerging views.

Perhaps the most important event to occur in the whole evolving situation was one only briefly mentioned in most accounts of the period: an impromptu personal courtesy call General Eisenhower paid to General de Gaulle on December 30, 1943, shortly before Eisenhower left North Africa to assume command of SHAEF. De Gaulle recounts the incident in his memoirs, and French historian Jean-Louis Crémieux-Brilhac calls the result of the cordial meeting a "gentleman's agreement" that was, in essence, an accord of mutual cooperation, including a promise by Eisenhower that French troops would be among the first to enter Paris and that he would in effect recognize de Gaulle's authority as the only one to treat with in France. Eisenhower even apologized for his early suspicions about and attitude toward the Free French leader, and de Gaulle by his own account told Eisenhower: "A la bonne heure! Vous êtes un homme! Car vous savez dire 'j'ai eu tort'" (Good! You are a man! For you know how to say, "I was wrong"). De Gaulle, it appears, now knew that he had some formidable foes, among them the president of the United States and the American secretary of state. But Eisenhower, the commander in chief for the invasion, supported him, and he had the backing of the military establishment in Washington and the United Kingdom. Lieutenant Commander Harry Butcher, Eisenhower's naval aide, described the meeting as a "love fest."[38]

On January 19, 1944, Eisenhower tried again to persuade Washington to accept his argument. Assessing the situation that he found in England, he reiterated the view he had expressed to Stimson, McCloy, and the president in Washington, this time in a cable to the Combined Chiefs of Staff. It was essential, he wrote, for planning and preparation of operations that he should be allowed to enter into discussions with the French regarding arrangements for civil affairs. To avoid becoming embroiled in French politics, he wanted to use French authorities, and the *only* authority available to work with was the CFLN. His aide Walter Bedell Smith had recently written to a correspondent, "I am far from being pro-Committee or pro–de Gaulle, as you know, but I believe we will have to use some vehicle, and I don't see a better one at the moment."[39] Eisenhower wanted to have the CFLN designate a spokesman with whom he could deal. The War Department and the British War Office and Foreign Office were unanimously in favor of opening such negotiations.

Unfortunately, following the latest Lebanon and Syrian affair, when Gaullist forces suppressed a nationalist uprising (see chapter 3), a wavering Roosevelt withdrew an earlier directive that might have allowed this and drafted one that reflected once more the idea of local authorities and his position that the French must express their own views when the situation was ripe following liberation. Planning would go on under the terms of the Dunn-Wright agreement, and there was to be no civil affairs discussion with the CFLN pending further authorization from the president. Optimistic rumors had circulated in Washington to the effect that a change in policy was in the offing, but the president specifically denied them in a February 10, 1944, press conference.[40]

Hervé Alphand, one of the French envoys in Washington, had shared in the optimism, telling the London office and cabling Algiers that the inter-Allied proposal in line with the views Eisenhower had expressed earlier in Washington and repeated in his cable of January 19, 1944, was now on the president's desk. The press was on the right side, and all the departments concerned were in favor, though the president still hesitated. Roosevelt's hesitation, Alphand was sure, was in part a result of Alexis Saint-Léger's campaign against recognition. When the president's February press conference came, of course, it was a cold shower. In Algiers, in the wake of Alphand's earlier optimistic cables and others from Jean Monnet, the disappointment was profound.[41]

There were, nevertheless, further attempts to change the president's mind. Three months later, on May 10, 1944, eighteen Socialist Party members of the Consultative Assembly, only recently escaped from France and certainly cognizant of opinion there, addressed a letter to the president, to be passed through State Department channels. They thanked him ardently for his support for France and his expression of sympathy for the imprisoned president of the Socialist Party, Léon Blum, but urged him to acknowledge that the only organization the French would accept at the time of liberation was the French National Committee of Liberation.

> Hesitation on the part of the British and American Chiefs of State to place confidence in the Government and Consultative Assembly in Algiers may give hope and strength to the Vichy usurpers and their associates. . . . [S]ince the Algiers Government has made arrangements for the installation of local authorities and for taking on measures to aid the liberation armies, any collaboration with other groups or individuals could only end in trouble and disorder prejudicial to the United Nations. . . . While the French people will receive the Allied armies with enthusiasm, if liberation should take the form of occupation, faith would suffer and friendship be wounded.[42]

There appears to have been no reply to the letter, but in the *Washington Post* on March 20, 1944, the authoritative voices of correspondent Harold Callendar and columnist Ernest K. Lindley supported the presidential view. Lindley wrote: "There may emerge in some districts or areas patriotic French leaders who do not pay allegiance to the Algiers committee. . . . [T]he supreme Allied commander should be left free to act as circumstances and overriding military necessities dictate."

By this time, in contrast to the views of some of the French officials in Algiers, and whatever the views of Roosevelt or Hull in Washington, most French officials in England understood that although they might have objections to other aspects of civil affairs planning, in fact AMGOT as such was not in the cards. In July 1943 the French had established the Service militaire d'études administrative (SMEA) in London, headed by Pierre Laroque, a former minister of labor and a founder of the Resistance network Combat, to coordinate activities relative to civil affairs, and to deal with Brigadier General Lee, now in charge of the "French House," where civil affairs planning for France took place.[43] After a first conversation with Lee in August 1943, Laroque wrote to Algiers that he found a "very great understanding and a sincere concern to reply to French preoccupations."

The civil affairs preparations, he wrote, were strictly for within the confines of the military zone. In the rest of liberated areas, and as soon as possible, the whole of administration would be turned over to French civil authorities. What needed to be pinned down was the extent of Allied and French authority within the military zone, where Lee, representing the Allies, still seemed to foresee that the Hague Conventions would operate, giving authority to the Allies.[44]

The French, in contrast, insisted that they would apply French martial law within the military zone, since the area would be not "occupied" but "liberated." In a September report to the authorities in Algiers on what the first four French trainees at Wimbledon learned, Laroque insisted that the issue must be resolved, since the classes there, taught by Americans, still referred to the Hague Conventions as applying within the military zone. The English appeared more flexible. He noted, however, that they all assumed—too optimistically, as we have seen—that inter-Allied agreements would soon be reached that would settle the issue in favor of French views.[45]

Laroque subsequently talked to Major General S. Woodward Kirby, the British civil affairs director, who told him he hoped the French would send him more personnel for civil affairs training at Wimbledon, since the British and Americans wanted to keep their own personnel to a minimum. The French should be able to take over as soon as possible, Kirby assured him. While seeing to the beginning of the training of French officers in the Service des affaires civiles, Laroque complained to de Gaulle in Algiers that he lacked sufficient numbers to ensure that they could assume administrative duties inside the military zone.[46] By the end of January 1944 he wrote again to Algiers to sum up his discussions with the British. He had come to realize that *no* AMGOT was intended for France, so there was no need to try to block it. The original French assumption that there would be an extended military zone in which French civil affairs couldn't operate was also outmoded, though it was time to get an agreement on the limits of the combat zone, as well as an assurance of French sovereignty within the zone in the choice of public officials and in making sure that French nationals would be subject to French judicial powers under French martial law. (André Philip, the Commissaire de l'intérieur, had already established that the Allies intended the zone to be only about twenty miles wide, and that behind it "the administration would be left entirely to French civil authorities.")[47]

Laroque continued that the Allied Combined Chiefs of Staff were ready for a wide collaboration with the French authorities, Eisenhower was prepared for French representation at all levels on the same basis as the other Allies, and the problems of the civilian population would be put entirely in the hands of the French in the shortest time possible. Admiral Stark, the American representative to the CFLN, had again asked Washington to let him negotiate civil affairs matters directly with the CFLN. The CFLN, Laroque wrote, perhaps discounting opinion in the White House, had really become the organization that Eisenhower and the Allies counted on.[48]

Not all French officers shared Laroque's or Philip's optimistic point of view. Back in Algiers, late in 1943, Colonel Claude Hettier de Boislambert, one of de Gaulle's earliest and most trusted aides, recently escaped from imprisonment in Vichy France, had been put in charge of creating the MMLA—the Mission militaire de liaison administrative—the corps of French officers who would accompany Allied troops at the time of liberation to ensure cooperation with the local administration and themselves supervise the multiple tasks associated with civil affairs. In addition to other matters, the MMLA was intended, as Boislambert saw it, to *devancer* the Americans, that is, to be ahead of them: "We must be able to substitute ourselves completely for what the Allies envisage."[49] Laroque made sure that Boislambert, who came to London on de Gaulle's orders in early September 1943, received copies of his reports. It is not clear, however, that Boislambert was actually convinced at the time by Laroque's attitude and explanations about Allied intentions. Like many others, he must have been cognizant of President Roosevelt's stubborn refusal to let any civil affairs agreement be negotiated. Later, however, the sympathetic Brigadier General Lee, head of the French Country Section at SHAEF, surreptitiously handed Boislambert the top-secret "Civil Affairs Handbook" on May 15, 1944, only weeks before the invasion, and Boislambert had a mixed reaction to it. While he wrote that "the general lines of conduct . . . were much in line with what the CFLN and the French people wanted," he took strong and specific exception to several sections giving to the Allies legislative, judicial, and executive powers within the military zone of operations which he felt impinged on French sovereignty and of course conflicted with the CFLN view that French martial law would be applied there by French officials. He communicated these objections to Lee, and—most important—within a few days these sections were revised to his satisfaction, reasserting MMLA authority over such matters within the military zone.[50]

In light of later charges about American intentions, this was a highly significant development. In addition, at an earlier dinner with a friendly Eisenhower on May 8, he was assured that no infringement on French sovereignty was intended, that the Allies really wanted to work through the French, and that as far as Eisenhower's headquarters was concerned, this meant—informally—working with de Gaulle's organization in England not only on military plans but also on civil affairs. "I think I can trust you," he reports Eisenhower telling him.[51] In the months previous to D-Day his MMLA officers not only received their own training but also attended courses at the British civil affairs school. Given General Lee's changes to the "Civil Affairs Handbook," all French apprehensions should now have been laid to rest. Nevertheless, several years later Boislambert wrote in his memoirs in a very different vein, recalling that having examined the book handed to him by Lee, he realized that the English and American governments—apart from specific individuals—"wanted . . . a total take-over with no control by us of the administration of France in its most minor details."[52] It is this startling change that has entered French consciousness. (For the most plausible explanation, see chapter 7.)

While the situation was evolving in England, on April 9, 1944, Secretary of State Hull had given a speech, remarkable for him, that appeared to have signaled, finally, a change of heart in Washington and certainly encouraged both the British and Eisenhower at his headquarters.[53] It was, Hull said in his speech, "of the utmost importance that civil authority in France be exercised by Frenchmen, should be swiftly established, and should operate in accordance with advance planning as fully as military operations will permit." The United States could not recognize the CFLN as the government of France, but the president was disposed "to see the CFLN exercise leadership to establish law and order under the supervision of the Allied Commander-in-Chief. . . . [T]he Committee will have every opportunity to undertake the civil administration, and our cooperation and help in every practicable way in making it successful." He even went on to say that the CFLN had been "a symbol of the spirit of France and of French resistance."[54] When de Gaulle was asked at a press conference in Algeria on April 21 whether Hull's speech meant that the situation was now such that the French authorities could organize the administration of France, de Gaulle replied dryly that French administration depended only on the

French, so the question was settled in advance, and the sole issue was that of cooperation of the French administration with the Allied command on the matter of military operations.[55] On March 14 the CFLN had communicated to the Allied governments its statement on the civil and military powers it would assume both within the military zone and behind it, and its observation that the CFLN, in cooperation with the Allies, would determine the extent of the military zone.[56]

On April 26, 1944, six weeks before D-Day, British and American SHAEF officers concerned with civil affairs hosted a meeting with French authorities, including General Marie-Pierre Koenig, who commanded the French Forces of the Interior, Colonel Passy, commander of de Gaulle's intelligence services, Hettier de Boislambert, organizer of the MMLA, and others, all of whom were welcomed on Eisenhower's behalf. They were informed that the Supreme Commander "was most anxious that as far as military operations permitted[,] nothing should be done in France which was not in keeping with the wishes of the French." As a result, and after a lengthy discussion, a number of joint committees were created to work out procedures in a number of areas. A week later, on May 3, 1944, Foreign Secretary Anthony Eden told the House of Commons that His Majesty's government being in full agreement with Hull's April 9 statement, the Supreme Allied Commander was now pursuing conversations with the French military mission to work out detailed arrangements with respect to the administration of liberated territory. When asked by one M.P. whether this meant "that the authority with which we deal in liberated France will be the French Committee of National Liberation?" Eden responded: "Yes, sir. I do not know of any other authority except Vichy, and we have no intention of dealing with Vichy in any circumstance whatever." He then went on point out that the CFLN had repeatedly declared that in due course the French nation would make its own choice of government."[57]

On the scene, in England, from where the invasion would be launched, it appeared that the American Supreme Commander, Dwight D. Eisenhower, and the British government, with Secretary of State Cordell Hull on board back in Washington, were all agreed that the Allies would work with de Gaulle's French Committee of National Liberation on the issue of civil affairs. Only details remained to be ironed out. If these included the precise authority given to Allied civil affairs officers within the military zone, even this appeared to pose no problem, since General Lee had agreed to changes in the "Civil Affairs Handbook" requested by Boislambert with respect to this. In spite of President Roosevelt's views, agreement with the CFLN, so necessary from Eisenhower's point of view, was now possible.

Events often confound expectations. Indeed, as Robert Burns put it, the best-laid schemes o' mice an' men gang aft agley. The liberation of France was no exception. Hull would later write in his memoirs, "The President, having approved my speech of April 9, had backed away from my statement that we were disposed to see the French committee exercise leadership to establish law and order."[58]

CHAPTER 5

French Preparations for Liberation

WHILE THE ENGLISH AND THE AMERICANS STRUGGLED to define their policies toward liberated France, General Charles de Gaulle and his organization moved to define their own.

In the space of over three and a half years de Gaulle had risen from a position of near anonymity and almost solitary defiance of constituted authority to become the leader of the French Committee of National Liberation, now considered by almost all but Franklin D. Roosevelt and some of his advisers to be a legitimate French government-in-exile. De Gaulle had done much of what he set out to do: gain a French territorial base from which he could speak freely, gain control of a standing army, and win formal recognition by numerous countries. Now, in the face of continued opposition from the head of the most powerful of the Allies, he had a further task: prepare to be ready, on the scene, in liberated France, to take over the administration of the country as a whole, so that no one else could attempt to do so.

Within France itself a great change had taken place over the years of the occupation. The sense of hopelessness, the anticipation of having to live in a Europe under German domination for the foreseeable future, had largely evaporated. By 1943 the Pétain regime in Vichy had lost practically all popular support and resorted to a harsh repression of the growing number of resistance groups that began to emerge once the sense of hopelessness was gone. There was at the outset no single "Resistance": over time groups with different political orientations and goals formed. The communists, before the war, had always been the most tightly organized of political parties. At the outset of hostilities, when the Nazi-Soviet pact of August 1939 was signed, the party had had to cease all opposition to Germany. Once Hitler launched his attack against the Soviet Union, however, it could revert to its original opposition to fascism in all its forms. Energized by the Soviet Union's unforeseen success in resisting Nazi Germany after its early massive losses, the communists soon became the core of perhaps the most prominent Resistance groupings.

Until the end of 1941 there was virtually no contact between de Gaulle and the various diverse, still nascent resistance organizations. None of these had contacted de Gaulle, who remained a shadowy figure to them. But in London it became clear that the French National Committee could not be the voice of France without ties to the emerging resistance. Considerable discussion took place about what the relationship should be between the London office and resistance groups, and what the role and strategy of the resistance should be within France. Early in the discussion, the committee decided that one element of any action to bridge the existing gap must be to try to bring the London Free French into a position of leadership of the entire resistance. (Among other reasons, the Gaullists wanted to ensure that the communists could not successfully put themselves in charge.) Unity became a watchword to be found in one document or pronouncement after another. Unity in France had been broken by the German invasion and by treachery, and could be restored only through a national revolution, one encompassing the resistance and led by de Gaulle. As a matter of strategy de Gaulle therefore determined that the attempt had to be made to bring to the resistance organizations some form of unity; then, if possible, they should be persuaded to accept guidance from London; and finally, they should be prepared to coordinate their action with that of the Allies once the Allies landed in France. Unity of the resistants behind de Gaulle would put the Allies face-to-face with the only possible representative of France: a Gaullist-led Resistance. It was in all a daunting but imperative task.

At the end of November 1941 Anthony Eden sent de Gaulle a message indicating British agreement to a plan to unify the groups, and on January 1, 1942, de Gaulle dispatched his envoy Jean Moulin to parachute into the south of France, to get the resistants to close ranks. "It is essential that the internal resistance form a single entity, coherent, organized, concentrated," de Gaulle wrote, while Moulin declared, "It's a question of using power against the Germans, against Vichy, against Giraud, and perhaps against the Allies."[1] Given the recalcitrance of some of the groups, the task took over a year. In the southern unoccupied zone Pierre Frenay, who would become highly critical of Moulin, nevertheless was instrumental in helping him bring the three main groups together: Combat, Libération, and the Franc-Tireurs. In October came a fusion of resistance groups in the north. De Gaulle named General Charles Delestreint commander of what would become the Armée secrète. Later, when former members of the dissolved French Armistice Army joined in, it became the Forces françaises de l'intérieur—the FFI. In January 1943 the clandestine Communist Party sent a delegate to London to announce that the party adhered to La France Combattante; on March 30, 1943, Jean Moulin returned to France with instructions from de Gaulle to create the Conseil national de la Résistance (CNR) and to bind it to the London committee. Ultimately, overcoming mutual suspicion and antagonism, he succeeded. It had not been easy.

There were always tensions and disputes, both political and personal, within de Gaulle's headquarters in London.[2] There were also always conflicts between resistance groups in France, which often had a very different view of the future. For good reason the socialist-led ones were particularly wary of the communist ones, and when the communists announced their adherence to Gaullism, there were leftist revolutionaries who felt that the communists had betrayed the necessary forthcoming revolution that should accompany liberation. Resistance leader Emmanuel d'Astier joined Henri Frenay, the founder of Combat, in accusing Jean Moulin of being authoritarian, a dictator, too pro-communist, while Moulin distrusted Frenay as too linked to Vichy, to Allen Dulles, who headed the American Office of Strategic Services mission in Switzerland, and to General Giraud, whom some Resistance leaders still supported. D'Astier, Moulin thought, was too much of an ambitious opportunist. There was always the issue of whether to accept those who had previously worked for Vichy, or to remain *pur et dur* (pure and tough). It is certainly true that as liberation approached, different groups, especially the communist Franc-Tireurs et partisans, maneuvered to get into power when the time came.[3]

Equally significant were the tensions between the Resistance members in France, on the one hand, many of whom were arrested, tortured, deported, or executed, and the leadership in London, which, largely isolated from the hardships within France, now presumed to give the Resistance its orders. Many on the scene in France were convinced that only they could legitimately represent the future and a true ideal of a renewed France. The new prefects, mayors, and other authorities should come from *their* ranks; *they* should form the core of the new structure of the state. Renewal was more important than technical competence. "Resistants complain about choices that, in their eyes, overestimate the prestige of the central [London] authorities, and underestimate that of the Resistance," wrote Charles-Louis Foulon.[4] Claude Bourdet, a journalist, former member of the Popular Front of 1936, and a co-founder of the Resistance group Combat, would write "The insurrection [at the time of liberation] will go well if persons from outside don't come to upset the natural course of events, give directives that disagree with our own[,] . . . in a word, reduce the Resistance, which has been until now the center of clandestine political life, to the ranks of a simple pawn on the chessboard of regional power."[5] A 1943 Resistance memorandum stated clearly:

> It is up to the people of France itself, guided by the Resistance movements, to impose its will, first on the Allies, then on the National Committee of Liberation, because it is, alas, too certain that a number of the committee's members, consciously or not, will play the Americans' game, or that of reaction. . . . [In the short time after the end of combat] before the Allies take in hand . . . the local administration[,] . . . the people will have to impose its will. . . . In the brief lapse of time, power will have to change hands. It is thus absolutely impossible . . . to foresee a coordinated and centralized action.[6]

Much later, in a 1974 book on the liberation of Normandy, a former FFI Resistance leader complained that in fact the choice of officers made by de Gaulle's Provisional Government of the French Republic (GPRF) at the time, in 1944, in both Brittany and Normandy, included too many who were "indifferent, even hostile" to the Resistance, and that one major official chosen by London "did not hide his disdain for the clandestine army and his systematic animosity directed at the Resistance."[7]

Despite the widespread view that the local Resistance groups should be prepared to seize power before anyone else arrived, Moulin was able to persuade the groups to cooperate and at least nominally accept the leadership of de Gaulle's organization in London. On May 15, 1943, when de Gaulle had still not arrived to talk with General Giraud in North Africa, the newly formed National Council of the Resistance (CNR), at whose first meeting Moulin presided, demanded that a provisional government be formed in Algeria with de Gaulle as its leader and Giraud as his military commander.[8] The support of the entire internal Resistance, throughout France, was probably the strongest card in de Gaulle's deck with respect to his approaching contest for leadership with General Giraud, and ultimately with respect to the Allies. Some observers, particularly in the United States though also in England, argued that the united Resistance supported de Gaulle as a symbol but might well not support him as a political leader. There was at least some basis to this view, given the diversity of opinion and ambitions of the Resistance groupings.[9] Nevertheless, they had clearly endorsed de Gaulle.

It should be noted that the British Broadcasting Corporation, by giving air time for foreign broadcasts to de Gaulle's headquarters in London, played an enormous role in stimulating support in France for the previously unknown de Gaulle, in helping de Gaulle propagate the vision of a free France that would emerge with the defeat of the Germans, and in providing vital communications between the London headquarters of the CFLN and the Resistance in France.

June 1943 witnessed the creation of the Comité français de libération nationale, under the joint leadership of de Gaulle and Giraud, with the resulting transfer of the emerging government with its "ministries" from London to Algiers. This left London with what was essentially an embassy along with the offices concerned with the Resistance. Despite the slow, grudging, and limited recognition given to the new CFLN by the United States, most other governments now saw in it what de Gaulle had wanted: a genuine government-in-exile, with its own ministries, its territorial base, its own army, and of course its own policy in relation to French interests. When de Gaulle emerged as its sole leader, he became, in essence, the head of both internal and external French opposition to Germany and Italy. On September 17, 1943, as we have already seen, the CFLN brought into being the Provisional Consultative Assembly with some one hundred members, of whom almost half came from Resistance organizations (many having been brought out of France on a daring flight by two British bombers). Others were representatives of the older political parties, members who had re-fused to vote full powers to Pétain. Still others represented trade unions and units of the empire. It was the first French deliberative council since Pétain had dissolved the parliament in 1940, and it first met on November 3, 1943. It would have primarily deliberative and advisory powers and was to be discharged once matters were regularized in France, but while frac-tious and occasionally disorderly, it exercised considerable influence.[10]

André Philip, who acted as go-between for the Assembly and de Gaulle, noted the feeling of many in the Assembly that it served de Gaulle primar-ily as means of impressing others with his democratic credentials, and that he needed to treat it with more respect. "Your intelligence is republican," Philip wrote to de Gaulle, "but your instincts and your guts are not." Never-theless, the British Foreign Office judged the Assembly's independence as "very encouraging from the democratic point of view,"[11] while on return-ing from Algiers, Harold Nicolson, a member of Parliament, wrote in the *Spectator* of December 5, 1944, that de Gaulle had surprised even his fervent admirers by his adaptation to a parliamentary system which, unlike that of the Third Republic, had a question hour, to which de Gaulle had to respond. Nevertheless, there remained one major difference between de Gaulle and a large number of the deputies: de Gaulle had little use for the old Third Republic, with its parliamentary supremacy, quarreling par-ties, and weak executive, and desired a strong presidential system, a view shared by neither the old republicans nor the communists and socialists.

As far as President Roosevelt was concerned, all these moves toward democracy meant little. In Washington, Alexis Saint-Léger argued in a long memorandum he sent to Roosevelt on January 31, 1944, that all the ac-tions taken by the CFLN were illegitimate, given that a law of 1872, the so-called Loi Tréveneuc, established the proper constitutional method for restoring government through a convocation of local councils—the Con-seils généraux—if the legitimate government could no longer operate. The Provisional Assembly meeting in Algiers, after all, was only appointed, not elected, and therefore had no legal standing.[12] Convocation of the Conseils généraux could not take place until the country was completely liberated. The president may or may not have read the memorandum. In any event, it fit right in with his preconceptions.

In May 1944 Vincent Auriol, former minister of the Popular Front and future president of the republic, read out to the Assembly "with tears in his eyes" a declaration from the National Council of the Resistance to the effect that in its view, "the French Committee of National Liberation, faithful image of the nation at war, now constituted the legitimate government of France."[13] Reflecting this judgment, the committee recommended to the Assembly that it be renamed. On June 3, a day before French troops entered Rome alongside the Americans and British, and three days before D-Day, by unanimous vote the Consultative Assembly accepted the recommendation and renamed the Comité français de libération nationale. It became finally—and triumphantly—the Gouvernement provisoire de la République française.

The American government did not approve. Prior to this action, when the committee was considering the name change, its members wanted to reassure the Allies that such a change in no way indicated an effort to perpetuate itself at the time of liberation. In Washington, Jean Monnet approached Assistant Secretary James Dunn at the State Department to find out what the American reaction would be to the change, given the assurance that the committee insisted it would give way to the popular will when the time came. Dunn (author of the abortive 1943 Dunn-Wright agreement in Moscow) was unequivocal: "There is no possibility of this government dealing with any 'provisional government' since no such government exists. . . . The use of this title for any purpose would create many difficult questions." It was unfortunate, he continued, that there had not been any discussion of the name of the committee at the time. In other words, the French should have sought American permission. The Office of War Information, the U.S. government's wartime propaganda arm, was instructed by President Roosevelt that it should not use the term "Provisional Government" in any way with reference to the French National Committee, even in quoting official documents.[14] Three days after D-Day, when Commissioner of the Interior d'Astier broadcast to the Resistance on Radio France and then asked that his speech be rebroadcast over the more powerful United Nations Radio, the request was refused because he had, in fact, used the forbidden term—"Provisional Government."[15]

Long before the American government proved so huffy, extensive French preparations had been taking place to create a whole administrative apparatus that would take over within France at the time of liberation, thereby preventing chaos or a communist takeover—or an American military government.

On March 15, 1943, André Philip, as CFLN commissioner for the interior, had received a memo titled "Considerations on the Problems of French Government at the Moment of Liberation of the Territory," signed only with the code name "Unir," but providing something of a blueprint for what the CFLN would do, and rejecting a series of possible alternatives.

It began by noting that as the North African imbroglio demonstrated, improvisation would be disastrous. What would need to be done must be carefully prepared in advance. Within France a variety of groups were pondering the future and getting ready for action. As a result, the risk of confusion, competition, rivalry, and disorder was very real. Outside France there was a lack of unanimity and a risk of seeking false solutions that bore little relation to French reality.

One solution, still envisaged by some, was to maintain the Laval government now in power in Vichy. It would be perilous to change governments at such a difficult moment, the argument went, and some in the government had surreptitiously helped dissidents and escapees, and had cooperated with the Germans primarily to prevent even harsher conditions from being imposed on France. Laval himself had let the word spread that he had been in contact with the Americans and had said, or allowed it to be said, that he was playing a double game. Whatever the truth of this, such a solution did not hold water. The years of shame, of servitude and suffering, prohibited it. (The memo did not explicitly note that the Resistance would surely have opposed this option by force.)

A second solution would be to maintain old Marshal Pétain in power, with a government purged of collaborators and staffed by resistants. There were some working for this. Pétain himself had thought of it, and let Admiral Leahy and other Americans believe that he had supported the Resistance and would be acceptable to the French at the time of liberation. Admiral Leahy certainly continued to believe until the bitter end that Pétain would be the *only* acceptable leader. Pétain, however, had a staunchly reactionary peacetime background and had launched "collaboration" at Montoire, with all else that followed: support for the Anti-Bolshevik Legion, repression in the unoccupied zone, and his call for resistance to the Allied landings in North Africa, Madagascar, and Syria. His weakness, imposture, and treason, the memo continued, had made him a useful instrument in the hands of the Germans, with whom he would surely disappear.

A third possibility, return to the Third Republic, might seem logical, but the France of 1943 was not the France of 1939. As a result of years of humiliation, suffering, and reflection, almost all Frenchmen wanted a return to a regime of liberty, but 80 percent did not want a return to the Third Republic, associated as it was with corruption, disorder, treason, and defeat. Many in the Resistance held the view that a genuine social revolution must take place at the time of liberation, and this meant the sweeping aside of the old elites.

Only a fourth possibility now stood any real chance: the creation of a government with de Gaulle at its head. Following the debacle in North Africa, people turned instinctively to the man who had nourished hope and incarnated the idea of France. Any attempt at a government without him at its head, whatever its makeup, risked civil war.

In conclusion, read the memorandum, the Gaullist movement must carry out four major tasks. First, de Gaulle himself must do more to clarify his vision of the future—to describe the form of a Fourth Republic that would become more than a symbol, a synthesis of the republican ideal with new men and new structures. Second, a government must be created that could take power at once, to forestall its adversaries within and without and prevent anarchy or adventurism. Third, a powerful, qualified person must make ready a team in Paris itself to provide de Gaulle with trusted colleagues and heads of the great public services. Finally, preparations should be made for an immediate referendum to give authority to the Provisional Government that would allow it the several months necessary for the election of a new Assembly and the preparation of a new constitution.

De Gaulle's organization wasted little time in addressing the issues raised in the memo. The first, the creation of a vision of the future, was embodied in numerous documents and declarations to the effect that it would restore republican liberties, and in the creation of the Provisional Government, with the Consultative Assembly, and the insistence that it would last only as long as it took for the French people as a whole to create a new government. De Gaulle himself had declared that a "national insurrection" would take place upon liberation, following which a new government would take charge. Many in the Resistance had their own views of what this government should be but agreed for now that it should be led by de Gaulle.

The second issue, that of creating a shadow administrative apparatus for the whole of France, was tackled almost at once. It was complicated, first, by the necessity of obtaining the support of the different Resistance groups, which, as we have seen, insisted on their (competing) prerogatives in the choice of new personnel, and second, by the difficulties of communicating between London headquarters, the CFLN in Algiers, and the various groups in France. One memorandum read:

> If London complains about lack of communication from Algiers, envoys in France never stop complaining. Passy [the head of de Gaulle's intelligence services, usually based in London but on a mission in France with Pierre Brossolette to seek out cadres for the new administration] experiences the problem: he sends almost 80 telegrams and one mailing and receives only 3 insignificant responses. . . . Jacques Bingen [another Gaullist operator sent to France in April 1944] is bitter about receiving not a single reply to his 100 messages. . . . [T]he CFLN cannot find out whether the death of Jean Moulin on the 28th of August 1943 can be confirmed.[16]

Moreover, the arrests and deaths of officials either engaged in the process or due to be named to positions of authority were a blow to the whole organization. Jean Moulin, Pierre Brossolette, and Jacques Bingen were only three prominent Gaullists who committed suicide rather than reveal information to the Gestapo when arrested,[17] while General Delestreint, head of the Forces françaises de l'intérieur, was arrested and executed. In the last year before liberation the German authorities and new Vichy French militias cooperated in decimating the Resistance and killing many of its supporters throughout France. Repression and assassination became more savage as liberation approached. In combination with vastly increased Allied bombing, this made the year one of real terror. Matters were made even more difficult by the fact that although Algiers was the seat of government—de Gaulle and most of his cabinet and the Provisional Assembly were all there—London was the main center of communications with groups inside France and the base from which arms and delegates and sabotage teams were sent into France. British officials imposed severe limits on the weight of packages that could be sent by air between London and Algiers, and as of April 17, six weeks before the planned D-Day landings, in the interest of security, the British government forbade any coded communications between England and the outside world, including diplomatic communications abroad. While all the governments-in-exile protested this measure, applied to the French, it meant that Algiers and London were virtually cut off from each other. De Gaulle, of course, was outraged, given that French forces would be fighting alongside the other Allies, and on French soil, and he reacted strongly, ordering that negotiations in London between his headquarters and the other Allies cease, since he could not be informed about them.

An additional complication was that given the probable chaotic situation at liberation, extraordinary powers would have to be exercised at first by any Gaullist administration but must not be publicized, lest de Gaulle's opponents seize upon the decision as proof of his authoritarian tendencies.

Nevertheless, in time, and despite all these difficulties, the various groupings and offices in Algiers, London, and France managed to cooperate in creating an administrative apparatus that the new French Provisional Government could install throughout all of France when the opportunity arrived. There is, it should be noted, little in American documents and accounts that shows any awareness of the extent to which in such difficult circumstances the French at so many levels had worked out detailed plans for their post-liberation assumption of authority in place of the Vichy administrators. In fact, on the scene in the first liberated areas, Allied civil affairs officers were sufficiently ignorant of all the French planning that sometimes they didn't know what to make of Gaullist appointees who arrived to establish their authority.[18] The lack of French liaison officers, whose numbers were limited by de Gaulle at the last minute, seems to have contributed to the confusion.

What is astonishing, writes the historian Jean-Louis Crémieux-Brilhac, is that the various French parties were able to create this administration while in exile. The various *ordonnances* creating the offices and defining their roles and powers were prepared under the aegis of a Commission du débarquement, directed by Henri Queille in conjunction with a Conseil juridique under Commissioner René Cassin, and were published in Algiers. Little was left to chance. De Gaulle had strong views about what the new administration should look like. One historian writes, "A long period of work ended up with a synthesis acceptable to the clandestine Resistance, but always close to the Gaullist conception of the state."[19] In the process an insistence that new personnel be named with the *consent* of the Resistance evolved into acceptance that they be named *after consultation* with the Resistance. It was a key development in Gaullist planning for a state where authority would once again be centralized in Paris.

In 1941 the Vichy regime had instituted regions comprising several departments, with regional super-prefects.[20] The Gaullist committee charged with working out the details of the new structures and with the appointment of new people realized that the regions, though created by Vichy, would now, with Gaullist-appointed *commissaires régionaux,* provide a useful way of quickly creating an authority linked to the central government that could prevent chaos in newly liberated areas. They would, in other words, be the instruments for reasserting control from the center as against any attempt to assert authority emanating from within the different regions. After numerous aborted attempts at working out details of the matter, the institution of regional commissioners was created by an *ordonnance* of January 10, 1944, that defined the extraordinary powers they could temporarily exercise on their own if no communication was possible with the central government. In order to be able to respond to the necessities of the moment, they would have broad authority to suspend laws and regulations and to take any measures necessary to maintain public order and restore a functioning administration—which meant naming or dismissing administrators and seeing to their proper functioning, as well as acting on behalf of the *commissaire à la guerre* in dealing with military matters in their region. They would be "the essential actors in the restoration of the state in 1944," and naming them was an essential first step. Since there was considerable back-and-forth as to who would be acceptable and capable, it took until well beyond D-Day before the list was complete, though a first, secret list was prepared and signed by both de Gaulle and Giraud in October 1943. The remarkable story of how each new commissioner reached his own territory to replace the Vichy super-prefects in the chaotic conditions of 1944 is retold by Charles-Louis Foulon, who concludes: "The success of putting into place these clandestine *responsables,* the speed and facility of the changeover, testifies to the quality of the preparations. With the German retreat, one of the dreams of the Resistance is realized: Vichy simply crumbles."[21] All but five were already in their territories by the time of liberation. Consequently they were almost all already familiar with the local situation and ready for their takeover of power.

In the meantime Gaullist officers from London—Émile Laffon, long a member of the Resistance, and Michel Debré, who would become a regional commissioner—were sent to France to conduct a massive search to find enough untainted candidates who could be named departmental prefects, as well as to see to the screening of local mayors and other officials. Alexandre Parodi, another resistant, created the Comité général d'études (CGE) within France to work out judicial reform at the time of liberation (it sent its proposed *ordonnances* to Algiers for ratification by the CFLN), and in March 1944 de Gaulle put him in charge of the clandestine administration. By the time of D-Day, Debré, with five hundred nominations, was able to name a full slate of prefects for all the departments. One third were former prefects, one third came from the private sector, and the rest came from universities, ministries, and so on. As a result of the difficulties of communication (Laffon had a hard time getting out of occupied France to report to London), only thirty had been approved by the CFLN in Algiers by the time of liberation. But the list of acceptable officials was there.

On instructions from the London offices at Carlton Gardens, the Conseil national de la Résistance had also seen to the creation in each of the ninety-five departments in France of a Comité départemental de la libération (CDL), made up of members of Resistance groups. These were essentially to serve as a liaison between the Resistance groups and the authorities the Gaullist government was creating and intended to put in place. The CDLs were supposed to control the "national insurrection" that would break out as the Germans were leaving, but then become provisional consultative assemblies to the new prefects, regional commissioners, and municipal councils appointed from the center. While the CFLN gave strict instructions that all the departmental and local levels of government and the CDLs were to act at the behest of the regional commissioners, who were the representatives of the state, certain Resistance leaders tried to insist that regional and local authorities take into account the views of the CDLs, "which represent," wrote a Resistance spokesman, Emmanuel d'Astier de la Vigerie, "popular sentiment, and without whose assent, local assemblies could not be created that would have any authority."[22] The CDLs, however, never achieved the stature such Resistance leaders as d'Astier claimed for them: popular support for the revolutionary aims of many resistants proved not to be so great. The regional commissioners ultimately acted on the basis of instructions from the central government and passed those instructions on down the line. The principle represented by de Gaulle's insistence on unity under a new central government had won out by the time he reached Paris in September 1944, though he subsequently had to take decisive action and tour the country to make sure the central government's authority would be put into effect (see chapter 7).

One thing was sure: by the time Allied armies reached any part of France, they would find acceptable mayors, city councils, prefects, and the representatives of the Provisional Government already in place or ready to take office, not those other, popular non-Gaullist leaders on whom Roosevelt counted and whom he had assured Secretary Stimson would emerge. A May 1944 memo from the French London offices to Algiers concluded, "The CFLN has worked for putting into place at the instant of liberation a civil administration enjoying the confidence of the population, worthy of that of the Allied military authorities, and ready to take all measures necessitated by the exceptional circumstances of the moment."[23] As for the point made in the earlier memorandum that a strong government should be ready to take over in Paris the moment the city was liberated, the Algiers apparatus was organized into ministries called, in the absence of a true government, *commissariats*, which replicated all the regular French government ministries, along with their subordinate offices. They would be ready. (The decision to call the ministries *commissariats* was made in order to reassure everyone, but especially the Allies, that their existence was still only provisional.)

One final organizational move was the creation, under Claude Hettier de Boislambert, of the Mission militaire de liaison administrative—the MMLA—(described in chapter 3) and his move to London in September 1943. Indicative of the infighting among the French is that one of Giraud's officers in North Africa tried to undercut Boislambert by sending a first contingent of MMLA officers who were all Jews, an attempt to reinforce anti-Gaullist propaganda to the effect that de Gaulle was surrounded by Masons and Jews.[24] The planned number of MMLA officers was reduced when it became clear that they would operate only in the military zone since the CFLN civilian personnel under the *commissaires de la République* would be ready to take over in the civil zone. Boislambert's officers received their own training as well as training at the British civil affairs school at Wimbledon. On April 19, 1944, Boislambert moved all the MMLA trainees and personnel to a camp at Camberley, outside London that needed enormous refurbishing but that would allow all of them to get to know one another and share procedures. By bringing them together rather than leaving them dispersed in the other training centers, Boislambert could give them a single order that would get them on the move. They would be attached to the Allied armies at all levels to organize the support that the French authorities and the civilian population would furnish to the Allied troops in their operations.[25] It is significant that Boislambert wrote back to de Gaulle at the end of October, after a month in London: "In all quarters, there is no longer any question of AMGOT. A different organization would play its role." Civil affairs officers would operate in the military zone and turn power over to French authorities as soon as possible.[26]

In March 1944 he prepared a report in which he wrote: "Allied intervention in what concerns French administration and civilian population will be limited as soon as Allied command is convinced that military operation will not be hampered by installation of civilian authority." He had had contacts with all levels of the SHAEF command. All the Allied commanders envisioned MMLA personnel working alongside them and had come to appreciate what these would do for them. All the Allied civil affairs officers, Boislambert continued, would have taken a course from an MMLA officer. In addition, special attention was being paid to the protection of historic monuments, a task whose importance could not be overestimated: the loss of a Mont Saint-Michel or a Chartres cathedral would be "irreparable." A special corps of Allied officers, equipped with lists of historical monuments, museums, libraries, and so on, were charged with such protection, with instructions that such buildings not be used for military purposes, such as command posts or for billeting troops.[27]

Boislambert was helped by his friendship, knit during the 1940 military campaign, with General Morgan, who, as Eisenhower's adjunct, organized the material side of the forthcoming invasion. MMLA personnel and civil affairs officers were in constant contact, and numbers of MMLA officers took training courses with both the American and British commands. Wherever there was a detachment of civil affairs officers, there would be an MMLA member. Since French administrators would take over behind the military zone, the civil affairs officers and MMLA would essentially operate only in the military zone.[28]

As the day of liberation approached, despite internal conflicts between the communists and others, disputes over control of competing intelligence bodies, and unrest over the declining role of General Giraud, the CFLN appeared to be ready. A series of official *ordonnances*, such as one of March 14, published in the *Journal Officiel* on April 1, 1944, defined in detail the duties and powers of officials from the highest—the regional commissioners—to the lowest, at community level, within both the military and civilian zones.[29]

The question of command relationships was not completely resolved: French forces would be under the command of SHAEF but also responsible to de Gaulle, as of April 4, chief of the French armies. Allied generals could raise issues about the use of their troops through their governments, but since the Allies still did not recognize the CFLN as a government, its commanders could not do so. What was lacking was American recognition of what the CFLN's role should be as France was gradually liberated, as well as any formal civil affairs agreement such as had been signed with other governments-in-exile.

To Eisenhower, the lack of a civil affairs agreement with the French was both ridiculous and alarming: it could cause real problems in the wake of the Allied advance. De Gaulle shared Eisenhower's point of view; the lack of such an agreement would cause trouble, though the issue of recognition was no longer essential. On May 25, ten days before the Allied landings, he told the English envoy, Duff Cooper:

> We are not in a position of entreating anything. The London and Washington formulas for recognition of the French government have little interest for us at this point. . . . The essential matter for us is recognition by the French people, and this is now a fait accompli. . . . As far as the attribution and exercise of French administration in liberated territories, there is no longer any issue either. We are the French administration. . . . In this, too, we are not demanding anything. There is either us or chaos. . . . We will accept no supervision of or encroachment upon the exercise of our powers.[30]

This was something he would repeat in times to come.

CHAPTER 6

D-Day

W INSTON CHURCHILL WAS VERY MUCH ON EDGE AS D-Day approached. The whole gigantic organization for the invasion was receiving its final touches. But the prime minister was well aware of what the Allies faced. As of March 1, intelligence showed that in the West, behind the enormous German coastal fortifications and beach obstructions, the Wehrmacht had 1.6 million men: ten armored divisions, one panzer-grenadier division, and forty-eight infantry divisions, along with several Waffen-SS divisions.[1] Churchill could remember the 1915 failure of the Allied landings he had launched at Gallipoli in World War I; that failure had cost him his role as First Lord of the Admiralty. Closer to home was the disaster of the Dieppe raid on the French coast in mid-August 1942, when the Allies suffered unforeseen heavy casualties—60 percent of personnel on the ground—and the Royal Air Force lost more than twice as many aircraft as the Luftwaffe. He could hardly forget the difficulties of the January 1944 landings at Anzio in Italy, when the forces on the beachhead were pinned down by the Germans and failed to achieve their objectives. "It is told," wrote General Frederick Morgan, "that even the great British lionheart lost many an hour's sleep from his small allowance, tortured by thoughts of the Channel clogged with British and American corpses." Morgan went on to observe: "Sicily was one thing. Normandy quite another."[2] Even the weather was bad. The one thing that could cheer the prime minister was that the Allies had command of the skies.

Deception had also worked: Hitler still expected a landing to the north, at Calais, and had kept nineteen divisions there. German propaganda, however, adroitly exaggerated the defenses available.

Eisenhower was perhaps more optimistic, although, as we have seen, he drafted the note he never had to use, announcing the failure of the Normandy landings. Whatever his state of mind, though, he was primarily and deeply involved in making final decisions. Previous months had brought struggles over the extent of his authority within the complex Allied command structure. There had been conflict over bombing strategy and over the diversion of necessary landing ships from other areas such as the Mediterranean and even the Pacific. The British preference for intensifying the fight in Italy clashed with the needs involved in the so-called ANVIL landings on the Mediterranean coast of France. These were at first planned to coincide with the Normandy landings, so as to divert the Germans from a concentration of their forces there. ANVIL would make use of Allied forces in North Africa, including the French First Army. In the event, an uneasy compromise had been reached by postponing ANVIL.

By early June, for General Eisenhower and most of the other people involved, the majority of problems had been resolved, and only one vital issue remained: the specific date of Operation Overlord, which was dependent on the phases of the moon, the tides, and the weather. Nevertheless, behind the scenes there was in fact that other troubling problem: the issue of civil affairs to the rear of the battle lines in France. As far as de Gaulle was concerned in far-off Algiers, his governmental administration would be ready to take over as the troops moved forward, but he would insist, further, that within the military zone French sovereignty must be observed—that is, Gaullist administrators would administer French martial law in Gaullist-appointed courts. (Martial law for France had been declared by the CFLN in Algiers on February 29, 1944.) He needed no Allied recognition, since the CFLN was now the Provisional Government of the France in which the landings would take place.

There was, however, one obstacle that greatly irritated Eisenhower: he was still not allowed to negotiate an agreement that would ratify the French role. He was not formally empowered to allow de Gaulle's officers to exercise their authority within the military zone, nor was he allowed to turn over control behind this zone directly to the CFLN. And there was one other extremely important matter: coordinating action of the French Forces of the Interior (the FFI) with the Allies' landings. General Marie-

Pierre Koenig, who had led French forces at Bir Hakeim and then at El Alamein, was now in London, where he commanded both the FFI inside France and also French naval and military forces outside the country destined to be used in liberating France. He was, however, in an impossible situation vis-à-vis SHAEF, the Allied Supreme Headquarters: although his forces were to act at the behest of SHAEF, and Eisenhower wanted him to give directions to the French Forces of the Interior, Koenig did not have the same status as other Allied commanders. As a result he was not allowed to know Allied plans in detail. Moreover, for the last few weeks before the landings, for security reasons, he was not able to communicate in code with his government in Algiers. As a consequence of this last measure, an angry de Gaulle had ordered Koenig and his able ambassador Pierre Viénot to make no additional agreements with the Allies until subsequent notice, a measure that obviously further complicated planning for the invasion.[3]

In light of all else with which Eisenhower had to deal, this was hardly a situation that made him happy. He had come to respect de Gaulle, and as far as he was concerned, he wanted an agreement with the only authority that existed—de Gaulle's CFLN. Such an agreement could and would resolve so many issues. His aide Walter Bedell Smith had told Eisenhower what he already knew when he first arrived to take over SHAEF in January: there was no other authority with which he could deal. They tried again to convince Washington. On January 7 General Smith repeated his view in a telegram to the War Department. Then Eisenhower took his turn on January 19: "It is essential that immediate crystallization of plans relating to Civil Affairs in metropolitan France be accomplished. This requires conferences with properly accredited French authorities. I assume that such authorities would be representatives of the Committee of National Liberation."[4] On the twenty-third, General Smith chimed in again:

> If we are to avoid political and social confusion and excessive commitments in personnel and supply after entry on the continent, we must be able to deal with some form of government of Metropolitan France. The French National Committee, whatever its faults may be, represents the beginning of civil government in France, and has received the allegiance of practically all of the French resistance groups and its present seat, Algiers, is actually by law a part of Metropolitan France. Consequently, the Committee seems to be the logical

vehicle. General Eisenhower discussed this matter on an informal
basis with the President, the War Department and the State Department while in Washington recently, and found them in general agreement with his own ideas.[5]

President Roosevelt, however, still unwilling to agree, continued to avoid
the issue. Secretary Stimson's War Department, well informed through Admiral Stark in London, who had met with Resistance leaders, nevertheless
told Eisenhower that he should do what he wanted to make the Resistance
helpful to him. As a result, Eisenhower's headquarters issued a directive
to the effect that planning should be based on the assumption that the
"National Committee will in fact be recognized as the National Authority
for France, and that it will command the allegiance of the local government
authorities who will act in its name."[6] On May 23 Eisenhower addressed a
telegram to Algiers asking for some five hundred French liaison personnel.
Two days later he asked General Koenig, in London, for an initial eighty.[7]
Given Roosevelt's mood, the moves were somewhat premature.

In England almost all members of the British cabinet—like
Eisenhower—were eager to have SHAEF deal directly with the CFLN,
and Eden's responses to parliamentary questioning (see chapter 4) were a
clear indication of this. Duff Cooper wrote in his diary "It seems intolerable
that one obstinate old man should hold up everything this way."[8] Churchill,
however, remained unwilling to counter Roosevelt's views. On March 15,
a day after the CFLN in Algeria had issued its detailed *ordonnance* on the
activities it would undertake upon liberation, President Roosevelt finally
responded to the requests for a decision with a lengthy memorandum directed to Eisenhower.[9] It could not have made the general, his entourage,
or the British very happy, not to speak of the French. Among the goals of
the invasion, wrote Roosevelt, would be "the fostering of democratic methods and conditions under which a French government may ultimately be
established according to the free choice of the French people." In order to
do this, he informed Eisenhower:

> As . . . Allied Commander, you will have the ultimate determination
> as to where, when, and how the Civil Administration in France shall
> be exercised by French citizens. . . .
>   You *may* consult with the French Committee of National Libera-
> tion and *may* authorize them in your discretion to select and install

the personnel necessary for such administration. . . . You are, how-ever, *not limited* to dealing with said Committee. . . .

Nothing that you do . . . shall constitute a recognition of said com-mittee or groups as the Government of France *even on a provisional basis.*

Moreover, incredibly, Eisenhower was actually instructed to obtain from the committee agreement to a series of restrictions on its purpose, to the effect that

it has no intention of exercising indefinitely in France any powers of government, provisional or otherwise, except to assist in the estab-lishment . . . by democratic methods . . . of a government of France according to the free choice of the French people. . . .

It favors the reestablishment of all historic French liberties. . . .

It will take no action designed to entrench itself or any particular group in power pending the selection of a constitutional government by the free choice of the French people.

Eisenhower, in other words, was to tell de Gaulle's French Provisional Gov-ernment how it was to behave. In addition, the president's memo made it clear that Eisenhower should enmesh himself in French politics in de-termining with which groups other than the CFLN he should deal. The British were upset, convinced that this could only cause confusion and perhaps make the CFLN refuse to negotiate further. The Supreme Com-mander should not be saddled with the "heavy political responsibility" of deciding with whom to deal.[10]

There were two important points in Roosevelt's memorandum, how-ever, that contradict what some Gaullist writers were later to assert. First, he wrote: "When and where you determine that there shall be set up a Civil Administration in any part of France, so far as possible there shall not be retained or employed in any office any person who has willfully col-laborated with the enemy or who has acted in any manner inimical to the cause of the Allies." And second: "You will have no talks or relations with the Vichy Regime except for the purpose of terminating its administration in toto." Both items contradict claims by French observers ranging from Annie Lacroix-Riz and Charles-Louis Foulon to Charles de Gaulle himself that the Americans might use collaborators or work with the Vichy regime.

They also meant, however, that Eisenhower was essentially being directed to make decisions as to who was to be allowed to govern France.

Curiously enough, to confuse matters more, three weeks later, on April 9, Secretary of State Cordell Hull delivered the speech that seemed to go much further than the president had ever been willing to go: "We have no purpose or wish to govern France or to administer any affairs save those which are necessary for military operations. . . . [C]ivil authority in France should be exercised by Frenchmen, [and] should be swiftly established. . . . We are disposed to see the French Committee of National Liberation exercise leadership to establish law and order under the supervision of the Allied Commander in Chief."[11] Apparently Hull had reluctantly been won over by the argument that opposition to de Gaulle would only serve to strengthen the general's position in the eyes of the French people, and that the resulting widening rift this would bring between the Allies would be disastrous. For everyone concerned the question immediately arose: Had Hull's speech been cleared with the president? Did it foreshadow a change in policy?

The answer was not clear, and as a result of the speech there ensued an exasperated exchange between London officialdom and Washington, in which London wanted to change the word "may" to "should" in Roosevelt's directive telling Eisenhower, "You *may* consult with the French Committee of National Liberation and *may* authorize them in your discretion to select and install the personnel necessary for such administration." The change to "should consult" would have drastically altered the meaning of the directive. Roosevelt stuck to his guns: he flatly rejected the proposed change. The word "may" was to remain.

In the United States the press was in full cry.[12] On February 9 Walter Lippmann had pointed out in the *Washington Post* the logic of the matter. If the administration insisted on free elections in France, someone would have to organize them. The Americans could certainly not do it, and the only and obvious candidate was the CFLN. Who else could there be? Moreover, France—meaning the CFLN—must be in on all decisions on the future of Europe. Otherwise there would be continued conflict and chaos.

A month later Lippmann weighed in again, writing of the president's misjudgment and its consequences: "We should never have permitted ourselves to quarrel with de Gaulle. We should always have dealt with him, quietly until we had overcome the resistance of Vichy in North Africa, and then openly and warmly as the champion of the French nation. We should have recognized the French Committee . . . and sought its advice and assistance in our dealings with all European questions." A few journalists, such as *Washington Post* columnist Ernest K. Lindley, took the opposite tack and supported the president and his policy. Harold Callendar in the *New York Times* also remained skeptical about de Gaulle. Callendar had written earlier of the "French farce" with respect to the infighting between Gaullists and Giraud supporters, while *Times* columnist Drew Middleton had, according to one French observer, insulted de Gaulle, writing of his dining on the black market to give himself the strength he needed.[13] Prominent *Times* editorial writer Arthur Krock had also long been bitterly critical of de Gaulle. But on February 4, 1944, an editorial in the *Times* called for recognition of the CFLN as the provisional government of France. (Callendar, in North Africa, reported the positive reaction there.) In the *Washington Post,* foreign correspondent William F. Shirer was among the critics of Roosevelt's policy: one of his columns was headlined "US Attitude toward French Committee Is Stubborn and Unwise." He went on to note the complex problems of restoring a functioning society behind the lines. Who was better suited to do this: hastily trained American military personnel, or Frenchmen who had fought alongside the Allies? He noted, among other things, that forty-five of the one hundred members of the Provisional Assembly had left France only in the fall. They knew the situation there, and the CFLN had constructed a provisional administration.

A *Washington Post* editorial referred to the spread of wild rumors about, for example, cooperation with Vichy, or about making Eisenhower seek out Frenchmen other than Gaullists who could be trusted. It stated: "A considerable measure of responsibility [for these rumors] rests upon the President. He has had before him for many weeks a plan of collaboration with the CFLN which, in the opinion of the War and State Departments and of the British government, would effectively safeguard our own interests and interests of the French people as well. But he has done nothing about the plan." On March 28 Samuel Grafton wrote in the *Chicago Sun:* "There was a time when recognizing de Gaulle would have demonstrated our spirit of enterprise. Later it would have proved our spirit of practicality. But today we have waited so long it has become comical. And yet we still wait."

The French press, of course, was vehement. In *Combat* on June 3, 1944, one columnist wrote that letting the Allied High Command choose the local authorities they would work with, like Darlan or Badoglio, or others whose subordinates had worked with French fascists, such as Marcel Déat or Jacques Doriot, "revolted the French people, and appeared to them absurd, dangerous, and intolerable." Beyond its immorality, it provoked the danger of disorder and civil war. "The Allies should open their eyes and see that in France, in any case, the people's choice has already been made."

Against all the hopes raised in Britain by Hull's April 9 speech, and despite the public and diplomatic pressures, President Roosevelt obstinately refused to revise his position. At a cabinet meeting in May he declared that if anyone could give him a certificate proving that de Gaulle was representative of the French people, he would deal with him, but that otherwise he had no intention of changing his position.[14]

The British, before the upsetting exchange over the word "may," had welcomed Hull's speech as a preliminary move to making a change in Roosevelt's policy. On May 8 Eden wrote to Prime Minister Churchill that a decision now had to be made. The Allies had to deal with the French committee. There was no other authority with whom they could work, and clearly the Combined Chiefs of Staff had been ready to go ahead until the president had drawn back. The consequences of a breach would benefit no one but the Russians.[15]

Three days later, in a telegram of May 11, an exasperated Eisenhower made a final attempt. The situation produced by the president's policy was "potentially dangerous." The only body that could "effectively assist us in the fight against Germany," he told Roosevelt, was the CFLN. SHAEF had been having extensive discussions with its military and naval representatives with respect to such matters as security of lines of communication, billeting, supplementary currency, the furnishing of local resources, labor requirements, distribution of civil supplies, and "most important of all, the initial approach to the French population." Eisenhower counted on the CFLN "to explain to the French people and reconcile them to the necessity of our bombing program."[16] The horrific effects of high-altitude American bombing, which frequently missed its target and caused enormous civilian damage and thousands of deaths, provided grist for the mill of Vichy's most able anti-Allied propagandist, Philippe Henriot. Bombings in Normandy caused 52,000 civilian deaths and left 40,000 badly wounded. For Frenchmen whose towns had been destroyed and people about them killed, the knowledge that this was done by those out to liberate them hardly endeared the ones doing the bombing to those who were being bombed.[17] Eisenhower needed the Gaullists to try to mitigate the political damage.

The suspension of coded communications, Eisenhower went on, had produced a condition under which none of various questions could properly be dealt with. General Koenig, he pointed out, "feels very keenly the fact that he is denied even the most general knowledge of forthcoming operations, although French naval air and airborne units are to be employed, and much is expected from French resistance."[18] Among other units, De Lattre de Tassigny's First French Army was the largest Allied force among those designated to land on the south coast of France shortly after the Normandy landings, and General Philippe Leclerc's Second Armored Division was scheduled to join General George S. Patton's Third Army in Normandy at about the same time. (De Gaulle would write regretfully, "How short it is, the sword of France at the moment the Allies launch the assault upon Europe!")[19] In light of Roosevelt's position and the communications cut-off, the French had balked at further negotiations. Eisenhower noted in his telegram that there were two possible solutions to the impasse created by the president's position. The better choice would be to invite General de Gaulle to London so that Eisenhower could deal directly with him on all these pressing matters; the alternative was to allow the resumption of coded communications between high French officials. It was British envoy Duff Cooper in Algiers who, desperate at the sight of an almost complete breakdown in relations, had suggested the visit to Churchill and Hull, and Eisenhower jumped at the suggestion.

Strangely enough, the president, unwilling as he was to recognize the French committee or to allow a civil affairs agreement with it, nevertheless had no objection to inviting de Gaulle to London, as long as he would be made to stay until after Overlord was under way—an almost insulting reflection of Roosevelt's long-standing lack of faith in French security. But once again he reiterated to Eisenhower his view that in the interest of democracy, the Allies must not impose de Gaulle upon the French. Appalled, British Foreign Office officials had learned that in February, Admiral Leahy had again told the president that only Marshal Pétain could rally the French people at the time of liberation.[20]

Winston Churchill, facing public pressure to deal directly with de Gaulle, was nevertheless incensed by de Gaulle's decision to keep General Koenig and Ambassador Viénot from dealing with the Allies as a result of the cut in coded communications, and by an angry speech de Gaulle had delivered in Tunis on May 7, in which he had excoriated the Allies' attitude on the matter of civil affairs and referred to the need to maintain a permanent alliance with that traditional ally, "dear and powerful" Russia. As a result, following Roosevelt's lead, the prime minister tried to explain to Parliament why, although his government supported the right of the CFLN to establish civil government in liberated areas, it could not recognize the CFLN as the legitimate government of France. Despite all his eloquence, he was not successful: he faced a wave of criticism from both sides of the House. Harold Nicolson, a member of Parliament and editor of the *New Statesman,* found it impossible to understand why the British and American governments acted to thwart the French committee. He called the policy "an error . . . unjust . . . inopportune . . . grotesque . . . absurd." It would be discourteous if adopted toward a neutral country, but when adopted against an ally that had managed to right itself and regain its rank among nations, it was inexplicable. "The USA and the UK commit a grave political error in not recognizing the CFLN, particularly at a moment that French soldiers are our allies and our equals on the battlefield," declared Nicolson. His Majesty's government followed the lead of the United States, which was administering "every snub which ingenuity can devise and ill-manners perpetrate."[21] Why, asked another member, couldn't the government be more firm in *demanding* of the Americans that the government of de Gaulle be recognized as soon as possible, while another member expressed his regret that the prime minister had said he could do no more in this matter.

Over the course of the next three days the London *Times,* which had argued ten months earlier that delay in recognition was an error, as well as the *Manchester Guardian,* the *Daily Mail,* and the *Economist,* all repeated their themes: it was not only time that the British government recognized the CFLN but also imperative that it do so. The *Spectator* declared, "The CFLN is already the provisional government of France." For the *Sunday Express,* "the return [of France] to greatness and power is essential to the stability of Europe," while the *Chronicle* argued that recognition would enable the French people to install democracy. Not to recognize the CFLN meant allowing Goebbels and Vichy propaganda full play.[22] Churchill, upset, wired the president that public opinion was more and more aroused and insistent that the French be a part of the liberation, particularly after the courage and success of French troops in combat in Italy. Could Roosevelt send someone of high rank, such as Undersecretary of State Edward Stettinius, to help explain to members of his cabinet, to members of Parliament, and to the press the basis of his policy, in order to help him, Churchill, to stand up to them, and at the same time be present for negotiations with de Gaulle if and when he came to London? In this case Roosevelt was of no help, replying: "The simple fact [is] that I cannot send anyone to represent me at the de Gaulle conversations with you. . . . I hope your conversations with General de Gaulle will persuade him to contribute to the liberation of France without our imposing his authority over the French people."[23]

Churchill, despite his reservations and resentment, ultimately acquiesced in the decision initiated by Eisenhower and endorsed by Roosevelt to invite de Gaulle to England a few days before Overlord was slated to begin. Eden prevailed in getting him to send a cordially worded invitation, and to dispatch his own personal four-engine York transport plane to Algiers to fetch him, and another one for his staff. "I give you my personal assurance," wrote Churchill in extending the invitation, "that it will be in the interest of France." (One reason for inviting de Gaulle was the thought that any statement he made at the time of the landings would be in some way more under the influence of the Allies if he were to make it in London rather than in far-off Algiers.)

Churchill knew that the invitation, under the circumstances, and with its conditions, would be taken as insulting. And in fact De Gaulle told British envoy Duff Cooper, who delivered the invitation, that there was no reason for him to go to London if there were not to be tripartite negotiations leading to a civil affairs agreement. The invitation, he declared, was just a machination to get him to deliver a message to the French that would make it appear he was in agreement with the British and Americans when he clearly was not. Cooper assured him that with the American ambassador, John G. Winant, in London as well as envoy William Phillips, a political adviser to Eisenhower, there could be tripartite talks. There was, however, another long-standing impediment, the matter of what de Gaulle called the "fausse monnaie." The Americans were insisting on issuing French francs for use by occupying troops, but refused to include on them any mention of the Provisional French Government, which would imply recognition. In fact Roosevelt had refused Secretary of the Treasury Henry Morgenthau and Undersecretary of Defense John J. McCloy's insistence that at least the words "République française" and the slogan "Liberté, Égalité, Fraternité" be printed on the notes, though he finally relented on the latter. "Émis en

France" would be printed on them, with the slogan in tiny letters. As far as the French were concerned, the issuance of a currency was a sovereign matter of great symbolic importance: only the French government could issue currency to be used in France. If the United States issued it, it had to be under the imprimatur of the Provisional Government, with a clear indication on it to that effect. In the past, as the CFLN pointed out, it had provided French francs to Allied troops for use in parts of the empire, and if an agreement could be reached, it would do so again. The issue had been a bone of contention for some time, with some State Department people, such as Assistant Secretary Breckinridge Long, ridiculing the French for their stance: "He [de Gaulle] is fussing because we are expending invasion francs in France instead of some currency he would agree to spend and authorize!"[24] But Eisenhower himself had been reluctant to issue the francs in their approved form in what he considered to be a flagrant violation of French sovereignty, and de Gaulle had become more and more adamant, declaring—and ordering—that the money not be accepted by French officials in France.[25]

De Gaulle continued to equivocate about the invitation to London. Shortly before the date for the possible trip, he held a cabinet meeting in which he expressed his opposition. He was, however, outvoted four to eleven, and René Massigli, his conciliatory commissioner for foreign affairs, threatened to resign if he didn't go. And so, at the last moment, he agreed—but as military leader he would not take any ministers with him. Duff Cooper believed that he, too, had been persuasive: "The argument which seemed to have most effect on the General was that simply as a soldier it was his duty to help the battle which was about to take place."[26] Cooper breathed a sigh of relief at the airport when he saw de Gaulle, the last to arrive, take his place in the prime minister's York transport plane, along with his aides Gaston Pawleski, Hervé Alphand, and Geoffroy de Courcelles.[27]

As the French historian François Kersaudy writes, the battlefield in London in the next seventy-two hours would be as ferocious as—if less bloody than—the battlefields in Normandy.[28]

De Gaulle was greeted at the airport by a military band playing the "Marseillaise." Churchill had established his headquarters for D-Day in a railroad train near the coast, much to the discomfort of his staff: there was only one telephone, usually being used by General Hastings Ismay, the prime minister's chief military assistant, and one bathtub, usually occupied by the prime minister. On de Gaulle's arrival the prime minister, much moved, descended onto the rails to welcome the French leader with open arms. De Gaulle responded rather stiffly, perhaps because Marshal Jan Smuts of South Africa was in Churchill's party. Smuts had recently made an anti-French speech in which he had declared that France would no longer be an important international player. Nevertheless, a pleasant lunch ensued, during which de Gaulle expressed his admiration for the fact that after all the United Kingdom had gone through during the war, it could still launch such a gigantic undertaking.

Once discussions got under way, however, they heated up when Churchill suggested they now talk policy.[29] De Gaulle stiffened: What was the point if there was no American representative there to sign an agreement? When it was suggested to him that he could ask to visit Washington to clear up matters with the president, he grew even angrier. He had sent proposals for an arrangement months ago and there had been no answer. Now he was told he should ask if he could visit the president when all along, clearly, the president hadn't wanted to see him and offered the excuse that as a head of state he could not invite de Gaulle—but that he would entertain a request from de Gaulle to visit him! De Gaulle had no need to pose his candidacy for taking power in France. The French government already existed, and he was its leader. With the landings about to take place, he could understand the need for haste in seeking cooperation between the French government and the Allied military, as he had suggested nine months ago. But without American representation, nothing could be done. The Allies had made their preparations, and he had learned they were ready to issue a currency that had no value and would not be recognized in France. "Go ahead, make war, and use your fake currency!" de Gaulle exclaimed. Churchill, exasperated, took the occasion to tell de Gaulle that whenever he had to choose between him and Roosevelt, he would always side with Roosevelt, and he was certain the House of Commons would support him. But Laborite minister Ernest Bevin, long a de Gaulle supporter, intervened to tell de Gaulle that Churchill had spoken only for himself, and not even for the British cabinet.

Dinner over, the uncomfortable party prepared to break up. Before leaving, however, a melancholy Churchill toasted his guest, "To de Gaulle, who never accepted defeat." De Gaulle replied, "To England, to victory, to Europe."

Churchill and Eden now took de Gaulle to Eisenhower's headquarters in a nearby forest, where Eisenhower and Walter Bedell Smith greeted him cordially and laid out for an admiring de Gaulle the amazing details of their vast plan. Eisenhower pointed out that given the tides and the phases of the moon, if the landings did not take place between the third and seventh of June, they would have to be put off for a month. But the weather forecasts were bad for the four-day period. A diplomatic Eisenhower asked de Gaulle for his advice. Flattered by the request for his suggestion, de Gaulle replied that if he were in Eisenhower's position, he would go ahead. Bad weather posed less of a threat than a delay of several weeks that would heighten tension and would compromise secrecy.

They were about to part when Eisenhower told de Gaulle that after other Allied leaders spoke to the people of their occupied countries, he would then speak to the peoples of Europe, and address the French. He hoped that de Gaulle would follow him with his own speech. He handed de Gaulle a mimeographed copy of the speech he planned to deliver. De Gaulle exclaimed: "You, a proclamation to the French people? By what right? And to say what to them?" When he glanced at the speech, he was even more acerbic: "You speak to the other peoples as commander in chief, as a soldier with a military task, in a way that has nothing to do with their politics. But you address the French in an altogether different tone." Eisenhower, wrote de Gaulle later, "gave the appearance of taking charge of our country, for which he was, however, only an Allied general in charge of troops, but who had no title to intervene in its government."[30] Moreover, there was no mention in the speech of either General de Gaulle or his movement, now officially the Provisional Government of France. This was wholly unacceptable. To de Gaulle, it represented nothing short of the imposition of an AMGOT in France.

Here accounts differ. French General Antoine Béthouart, who was present at the meeting, declared that Eisenhower had said the text "had been approved by his government and that he couldn't change any of it." Historian Milton Viorst confirms this account.[31] Anthony Eden writes of a "misunderstanding: "De Gaulle thought he was being asked to comment." Duff Cooper, however, who was also present, writes: "Eisenhower gave de Gaulle the text of the radio speech he was going to make and asked for suggestions and corrections. De Gaulle took it away with him."[32] As de Gaulle himself recalled, Eisenhower told him the speech was only a draft and that he was ready to modify it to take into account de Gaulle's suggestions. When de Gaulle sent Eisenhower a corrected version the next morning, on the fifth, he was told it was too late: 40 million copies had been printed, ready to be dropped on France.

Writing much later, French historian Jean-Louis Crémieux-Brilhac throws considerable light on the story. Eisenhower apparently did not know that an earlier draft had been prepared by his staff explicitly mentioning the MMLA, the Provisional Government of the French Republic and its Provisional Assembly, and its president, de Gaulle, but that the draft had been rejected by the State Department, which had concocted the new one. When the British had asked for some modification of the new speech, they had been refused.[33] In any event, the incident could only lead to further ill-feeling. As Duff Cooper put it, "it was one of the many causes which contributed to what was almost a disaster."[34] Churchill invited de Gaulle to ride back with him to London on his train since de Gaulle was staying at the Connaught Hotel, where he had resided before moving to Algiers. De Gaulle refused: he would ride back in his own car. Churchill felt chilled.[35]

It was June 5, the weather was bad, and Overlord had been put off until the following morning. For the men around Churchill, and for the men around Eisenhower, the waiting period before they would take action could not have been a more nerve-wracking time. Field Marshal Sir Alan Brooke wrote in his diary: "At the very best it will fall so very far short of . . . expectations. . . . At the worst it may well be the most ghastly disaster of the whole war. I wish to God it were safely over."[36] Late in the afternoon Churchill received word from Charles Peake, who represented the Foreign Office at SHAEF, that when de Gaulle had been told the moment had come for the speeches to be made to the peoples of the occupied countries, the general had refused. Moreover, on the grounds that there was no civil affairs agreement, he also refused to send his MMLA liaison officers along with the first waves of Allied troops. Later in the day, at Duff Cooper's urging, he relented insofar as the MMLA was concerned and allowed twenty men to go. In fact Boislambert had already dispatched thirty, and by the end of the week, despite de Gaulle's original refusal, there were eighty in place.[37] With respect to the speech, it seems that Peake had misunderstood the general, who had actually told Peake he would not speak after Eisenhower's speech had been delivered, since he would seem to be endorsing Eisenhower's order to the French people to obey him, Eisenhower. He, de Gaulle, head of the French Provisional Government, would speak later at a time of his own choosing.

Churchill, however, was told only that de Gaulle had refused to speak. Enraged, on edge, well through his day's ration of whisky, the prime minister began to dictate a memo ordering that de Gaulle be sent back to Algiers immediately, "in chains if necessary." It appears that his minister of information, Brendan Bracken, managed to calm the angry prime minister and persuade him to destroy the memo. Bracken later told Eden, who had received a lengthy call from Churchill berating him for opposing and bullying him at a time like this, that Churchill had called him a "lackey of the Foreign Office."[38] And so, as a French journalist wrote later, "for him [Eden], as for Pierre Viénot [the French ambassador], began, before the longest day, the longest night."[39] It was "the worst night of their lives," they were quoted as saying by Crémieux-Brilhac, who continued, "Who could believe that the prime minister of Great Britain and the head of Free France passed the night of the landings vituperating the one against the other?"[40]

At ten thirty that night, as airmen were preparing to drop parachutists on Normandy and land gliders in the dark, and landing ships drew near to the coast, Ambassador Viénot drove through a darkened London to the Foreign Office at Anthony Eden's request. There Eden told him that at this crucial moment, as a result of de Gaulle's refusal to broadcast to France, as well as his refusal to send the MMLA, relations were at a breaking point. Astounded, Viénot replied that de Gaulle had never refused to speak. The issue was only one of timing. On the question of the MMLA, however, he defended de Gaulle's position: it was that of his government, but he had relented and allowed a limited number to go. After some further discussion, during which Eden asked the ambassador to press de Gaulle to revoke his decision about the MMLA, Viénot left the Foreign Office and went directly to the Connaught Hotel, where an astonished de Gaulle repeated that he had always intended to speak to the French people, either from there or from Algiers. In the case of the MMLA he had acted correctly. But as they talked and reviewed Anglo-French relations, de Gaulle became more and more violent: the invitation to leave Algiers and come to London had only been a trap, Churchill was a gangster who now revealed his methods—and on and on—while Viénot tried to contradict or mitigate some of what the general spewed forth. A livid de Gaulle insulted his ambassador. "Jamais de ma vie je ne me suis fait engueuler de la sorte" (Never in my lifetime have I been chewed out in this manner), said the ambassador later.[41] When de Gaulle told him that he couldn't trust him to report correctly to Eden what he had said, Viénot replied: "I do not accept that you speak to me this way. . . . You can relieve me of my position." De Gaulle calmed down, but Viénot also told the general he had made a mistake in failing to inform the British several months earlier that the MMLA could operate only under the terms of a civil affairs agreement. When de Gaulle asked Viénot what he would tell Eden, the ambassador replied that he would say there had been a misunderstanding, that de Gaulle would certainly speak, but that the MMLA issue was the result of a CFLN decision taken earlier that could not easily be reversed. As Viénot prepared to return to the Foreign Office, de Gaulle again began to rail against the English and Eden's *pleur-nicheries* (whining). Viénot again calmed him down and left to see Eden, who had told the ambassador he would be available all night. Eden turned out to be at Churchill's headquarters, and Viénot found the two men together there.

He explained the misunderstanding about the speech to the French people, but Churchill nevertheless broke out into an "explosion of hatred," a diatribe against de Gaulle, accusing him of treason in the midst of battle, of having no regard for the young English and American soldiers who would die for France: "Their blood has no meaning for you. . . . [D]e Gaulle has always been an element of discord between the three democracies. . . . [He], devoured by personal ambition, is only a ballerina on stage, who thinks only of his own political future." While Viénot interrupted Churchill several times to tell him he would not listen to such accusations, Eden managed to calm things down enough so they could discuss de Gaulle's radio address. Churchill, of course, wanted to review its content, but Viénot replied that the content was strictly up to de Gaulle. When it came to the MMLA, Viénot was startled to learn that Churchill knew little about what its purpose was, and had to be told that its absence, since it was strictly for administrative purposes, would not lead to more Allied bloodshed, as Churchill had just vehemently charged. Said Viénot, there would be none of the existing problem if, as the CFLN had long demanded, there had been a civil affairs accord, and Churchill was aware of it. The prime minister proceeded to accuse Viénot, whom Duff Cooper characterized "as one of the gentlest and the best of men,"[42] of attempting to blackmail him, and Viénot was again forced to say he would not stand to be addressed that way. Churchill could have had an accord, said Viénot. Now he was discovering only too late how serious the matter was. Churchill retorted that it was de Gaulle's pride that had led him to want Roosevelt to address him as a supplicant on his knees.

Viénot, who had had to contain himself during the conversation, abruptly headed for the door but turned to say to an angry but now startled Churchill, who had neither risen nor held out his hand to the departing ambassador: "You have been unjust, said things to me that are false, violent, and that you will regret having said. As for me, on this historic night, what I want to say to you is that in spite of all, France thanks you!" Then, in the next room, he told Eden: "It's extraordinary. Whether I am with de Gaulle or with Churchill, everything in Franco-British relations seems impossible. When I am with you, everything seems simple. We discuss as friends, on the same side of the barricades, not as adversaries."

It was now past three in the morning, but Viénot went to wake de Gaulle and report on his conversation with Churchill. This time a more relaxed de Gaulle listened quietly but remarked that everything turned violent when one wanted to speak to Churchill. Viénot, trying to justify Churchill's belligerence, reminded the general that this was the most important night of the prime minister's existence, that he had a right to be nervous, and that there was reflected in his attitude not only his dismay at de Gaulle's refusal to "let himself be had" but also the love a seventy-year-old man had for France but was nevertheless *incompréhensif*—lacking in understanding. Strangely enough, in the middle of the night, after all the outbursts, a calm de Gaulle now revealed to Viénot his vision of the future of Anglo-French relations. It was important that there be established something more solid than an old-style alliance such as that of 1940, this time on a basis of both economic cooperation and security. He could appreciate, he said, that Great Britain had tried to detach itself from the United States in matters concerning France, because of the particular interest it had in French affairs. A sobered Viénot expressed his regret that de Gaulle had not been able to make views such as these clear to Churchill earlier in the day, and de Gaulle admitted to him that he felt he had perhaps gone too far. It was too late now, so he let the exhausted Viénot go home to sleep.

The night ended, and D-Day dawned. It should be noted that in his diary, on May 22, Eisenhower wrote, "I believe that once the operation is started I can secure from the French the cooperation I need." After D-Day he would at last be left to his own devices.[43] For his part, Boislambert, in a memo for de Gaulle on June 6, indicated that in all likelihood, given the attitudes of Eisenhower and others on the spot, all civil affairs issues would be resolved to the satisfaction of the French.[44] In fact, behind the scenes, on May 25 Eisenhower's headquarters had sent a directive to the British and American army groups that would land in Normandy that stated quite clearly: "Military government will *not* be established in liberated France.... [T]he French themselves will conduct all aspects of civilian administration in their country, even in areas of military operations. . . . [T]he MMLA is to be used as a direct channel to local authorities[,] . . . the latter to be responsible for reestablishing French civil administration and judicial authority."[45]

On June 6, 155,000 Allied troops landed in Normandy, along with their equipment. Among them were a small Free French commando group of some 177 men and a detachment of French paratroopers. Several French naval and air units also participated. (General Leclerc's Second Armored Division would not land until the first of August, but would distinguish itself in battle thereafter.) Eisenhower's message to the French was delivered by air drop and over the airwaves on D-Day, with its directive to the French to obey his orders. Several hours later, at six o'clock in the evening, after some pressure from the Foreign Office and much anxiety over whether he would actually mention the discord within the Allied camp, de Gaulle gave his own address, with its contradictory message that all Frenchmen should obey orders emanating from representatives of the Provisional Government of the French Republic, saying that it was the duty of Frenchmen everywhere to join in what was the battle of and for France. To the consternation of his aide General Ismay, Churchill, listening to de Gaulle's speech in his office at 10 Downing Street, wept tears of emotion, saying to the unbelieving Ismay, "You tub of lard, have you no sensitivity?"[46]

In contrast, back in Vichy, Marshal Pétain and Pierre Laval, now aware of the landings, issued their own orders to the French people. "German and Anglo-Saxon armies war with each other on our soil," proclaimed Pétain. "France has become a battleground.... We are not in the war. Your duty," he told the French, "is to maintain a strict neutrality. I want no fratricidal war. Frenchmen must not rise up against one another." Laval went further, insisting: "You must not take part in combat. Those who ask you to cease work or incite you to revolt are enemies of our nation." He referred to the battle as a "foreign war." The new ultra-rightist minister of the interior, Joseph Darnand, imposed upon Pétain by the Germans, went beyond even Laval, ordering the paramilitary Vichy Milice to combat "saboteurs, traitors, and defeatists," in other words, those who helped the Allies.[47]

Whatever the Vichy authorities might say, however, long-planned orders for action had already been sent from London to the FFI commanders of the twelve military zones corresponding to the regions, and to the fifty-one networks and groups working with the British Special Operations executive. According to a later report, of 1,050 objectives—the blowing up of rail lines, bridges, and telecommunications facilities—950 were attained in the first few hours after Allied troops landed. The 130 trains blocked around the Lille railroad center as a result became a prime objective for Allied bombardments. The Resistance made its valuable contribution. Later it would be FFI forces and French paratroopers who would liberate Brittany. To the south, unfortunately, German forces crushed redoubts set up by Resistance groups, most notably in the Vercors.

In London, two days after D-Day de Gaulle had a lengthy discussion with Anthony Eden, Duff Cooper, and Ambassador Pierre Viénot. Again he insisted that Eisenhower's proclamation essentially introduced AMGOT into France (something of an exaggeration, to say the least) and that the issuance of the "fausse monnaie" made cooperation between French administration and Allied armies impossible (certainly another exaggeration). The exclusion of France from vital matters of interest to itself, such as negotiation of the Italian armistice—and eventually of a German armistice—would rule out any international system founded on cooperation between France and England and the United States. Eden insisted on the willingness of his government to reach an accord, while de Gaulle continued to maintain that his trip had only military and symbolic significance, so political negotiations were out of the question. At a press conference two days later he repeated his charges. Nevertheless, perhaps relieved at the success of the landings, he suddenly changed his stance. Since the English had made a proposal, he was willing to have Ambassador Viénot enter into talks with the Foreign Office to reach an agreement based on the CFLN memorandum of September 1943 and then, if an agreement were reached, to approach Washington.[48]

Progress was slow in France, and controversy persisted in London. Churchill continued to quarrel with Eden and the rest of his cabinet over the issue of France and to condemn de Gaulle. When the prime minister visited the Normandy beachhead, in what appeared to be a deliberate snub to the French leader he took with him Marshal Smuts (provoking another outburst in Parliament by Harold Nicolson, who charged Churchill with doing everything to offend de Gaulle, who should by rights have accompanied him instead. Scathing press criticism and a parliamentary storm also erupted as a consequence).[49]

On June 14 de Gaulle set sail for France on a French destroyer, *La Combattante*, despite a last-minute attempt by the prime minister to prevent him from going, an attempt firmly rejected by the British War Cabinet. As the vessel approached the coast, Ambassador Viénot, standing on the bridge next to de Gaulle, said, "Do you realize, *mon Général*, that it is four years to the day that the Germans entered Paris?" De Gaulle replied, "*Eh bien*, they made a mistake!"[50] In a moment that moved them all, he and his party took their first steps on French soil, which they had left so long ago, near General Bernard Montgomery's headquarters. Montgomery received them graciously. De Gaulle mentioned to him that he had dispatched a member of his party, François Coulet, to Bayeux to take over as regional commissioner from the resident Vichy appointee, who happened to have been very helpful to the newly arrived English, who had let him stay in office. Montgomery's intelligence officials had told him that everywhere they went they had heard from the French the name "de Gaulle," and as a result he paid little attention and had no objection to the commissioner's removal. De Gaulle then began a tour of the beachhead. Few Frenchmen could recognize him: they knew only his voice from BBC broadcasts. But as the word spread, crowds gathered in the streets to cheer him, and when he reached Bayeux, the population crowded the sidewalks as he walked down the main street, stopping to kiss a child, shake hands with an old man, receive a bouquet of flowers from a young girl. Despite Churchill's injunction that de Gaulle could go to France only if he avoided holding public meetings, he addressed the enthusiastic townspeople who had assembled on the place du Château, for whom until then de Gaulle had been just a name. He was greeted in Bayeux by one of the MMLA officers, Colonel Claude Chandon, the man who would later persuade the German officer commanding the garrison on Mont Saint-Michel to surrender so that no harm would come to that most glorious of medieval monuments.[51] He went on to tour the battered town of Isigny, and then returned to sail back to England on the *Combattante*. François Coulet, who accompanied him, noted that in Bayeux, which had hardly been touched by the fighting, the crowds did not exhibit the delirious enthusiasm of the people of Isigny, which had been virtually flattened. There de Gaulle was met with that same wild enthusiasm that had greeted him when he toured Corsica months earlier.[52]

The visit was a success. People responded as de Gaulle had hoped, and numerous reports sent back to England and widely circulated testified to the enthusiasm with which he had been greeted.[53] In addition, in his view he had nipped AMGOT in the bud by installing Coulet as regional commissioner. As he told one of his entourage: "You see, we had to confront the Allies with a fait accompli. Our new authorities are in place. You will see that they won't say anything."[54] As if to bear out his view, between June 8 and 20 the exile governments of Czechoslovakia, Poland, Belgium, Luxemburg, Norway, and Yugoslavia recognized the Gaullist-led GPRF as the government of France. So did a number of Latin American countries. As a further result, as Eden and others noted, de Gaulle became much more relaxed. He was a gracious host when Eden visited him at the Connaught Hotel on the eve of his departure for Algiers on June 16—"He was in a more reasonable mood than I had ever known him," wrote Eden—and thanked Eden for the hospitality and courtesy extended to him during his sojourn in England.[55]

His confidence renewed, de Gaulle left behind instructions to his subordinates to fix matters up as much as possible, and General Koenig soon reached an agreement on the status of French commanders fighting in France: their authority would be equal to that of any other Allied commander. While this left open the issue of appeal to higher authority, Koenig was satisfied and revoked the limitations on MMLA officers, the rest of whom were soon dispatched to military headquarters and liberated communities. In short order Eisenhower observed that they were working effectively with Allied officials.[56] General Koenig also managed to settle provisionally the matter of the "fausse monnaie." Coulet, the regional commissioner in Bayeux, had announced that if Frenchmen received the notes, they would not be accepted in payment of taxes, thus making them valueless. But Koenig, observing that little of the money was circulating and that the matter was being negotiated in Washington, met with other Allied officers, both British and American, as well as with Coulet's aides. They came to an agreement to let the currency be accepted, and to keep the matter secret, but to let the Banque de France ultimately reimburse those who accepted the notes, with the hope that higher authorities would ratify the accord.[57] The irritating issue soon faded into insignificance, in part because Coulet had brought with him substantial sums of French francs, and because local banks were also well equipped with them, so that few of the American bills needed to be used.

. . .

Coulet's appointment as the first regional commissioner raised hackles among some Resistance leaders, who saw in the appointment a unilateral move by London to bypass the Conseil national de la Résistance, which had named another man, Henri Bourdeau de Fontenay, to take charge of Normandy. They were reassured when de Gaulle pointed out to them that this was a temporary appointment, made only two days before the landings. Coulet, de Gaulle told them, had previously served the general in several capacities since the early days; the circumstances of de Gaulle's visit to Normandy and of Coulet's presence in London gave de Gaulle an opportunity not to be missed at a moment when Fontenay was unable to get to the area. Fontenay would take over when he could. In the event, given the slow-moving military operations, it would be three months before he would arrive.

François Coulet was a relatively inexperienced young man of thirty-eight. Conscious that on short notice he had been given the enormous responsibility of being the first person to restore republican authority in a country shackled for four years, he moved rapidly with his six prominent aides to strengthen his position as the GPRF regional commissioner. He faced no opposition from the Vichyite commissioner whom he replaced and who furnished him with much necessary information. He appointed his own administrators and representatives of the Provisional Government and publicly posted a proclamation of the assumption of authority by the GPRF. He found that the Normans passed from one regime to another almost without paying attention: there was no opposition from the Left or from any Vichyite remnants. He was quickly able to get matters moving as he toured the localities within the liberated area where Allied civil affairs officers were working on such matters as relief, medical care, and rehousing. He himself saw to the startup of a local newspaper, reorganization of municipal and prefectural offices, and so on. Coulet was a Protestant, but he persuaded a reluctant bishop of Bayeux to have a Te Deum sung in the undamaged cathedral.

Coulet was also conscious that he would have to deal with Allied authorities with whom no formal agreement had been made as to his competence. On June 16 he held a press conference for some fifty journalists who had come ashore with the Allied forces. While many were old hands from North Africa and elsewhere, there were newcomers from Washington who went on the attack: Wasn't he here without the authorization of the Allied governments? He replied that Montgomery's headquarters had been notified by

de Gaulle that he, Coulet, would remain to take over civil authority. Moreover, why should the Provisional Government ask any authorization of its
allies to govern in France? The government of Marshal Pétain had collaborated thoroughly with the enemy; this legitimate one was fighting alongside
the Allies and was the actual government for now. There would be elections
when they were possible, and in the meantime the Allied armies benefited
from an orderly administration by GPRF officials behind the lines that would
support the military action.[58] When one journalist asked, "What if partisans
of Vichy contested your legality?" Coulet inquired pointedly whether the
journalists had encountered any such "partisans of Vichy." And when asked
what he would do if the Allied governments decided not to support him but
return him to England, he laughed. No Allied government interested in the
future of an orderly Europe would commit such a giant blunder!

In fact such a blunder might well have been made. Later in the year,
following the liberation of Paris, Coulet dined with General Walter Bedell
Smith, who told him that between the sixteenth and nineteenth of June a
small detachment was held in readiness to seize him in Bayeux and send
him back to England on orders from higher up which never came, probably
thanks to Eisenhower. Coulet congratulated him on having avoided a mon-
umental gaffe that could really have upset relations between the United
States and the European countries that remained to be liberated.[59]

On June 19 Coulet received another visit, this time from Brigadier
R. M. H. Lewis, head of the local British civil affairs detachment, with
two other lesser officers. Lewis seems to have been worried about Coulet's
presence and asked that Coulet call on him. When the latter refused and
politely invited Lewis to his office at a time that would suit him, Lewis
appeared abruptly, "with the air of a judge," as Coulet later told Koenig.
Coulet, seated behind his desk with Geoffroy de Courcel and Pierre
Laroque at his side, listened while an apparently angry Lewis harangued
him about the tasks of civil affairs, then told him that the military had no
intention of interfering in such matters, and ended by telling Coulet, "As
for the presence here of you and your associates, we'll accept it provisionally while waiting for instructions from our government." Coulet responded
with some vigor that he had been sent to represent the Provisional Government, to affirm and maintain French sovereignty, and that it didn't matter
whether or not the British accepted his presence; he was here, and no instruction from their government would modify that fact. More soothingly,
he affirmed that they were both there to help the Allied military effort in

every way possible, especially by seeing to civilian order and needs, that their goals were the same, and that he did not see—their domains being limited—why either should conflict with the other. Lewis appears to have left much reassured, and Coulet wrote that after this he got along famously with Lewis's superior, Brigadier Thomas Robbins.[60]

Later, in his 1966 memoirs, Coulet gave considerably more color to the incident. The Allied commanders, he wrote, had been made to look ridiculous by the ease and efficiency with which the French assumed their unquestioned authority in the area, and were angered as a result. In this account, it was four or five staff officers, superior in rank, who came to his office with the unequivocal air of military men demanding accounts from a civilian. He assumed, he wrote, that they came on Montgomery's orders, after Montgomery had been dressed down by Churchill for allowing Coulet to take office, following stories reported in the English papers. An obviously angry Lewis harangued Coulet about the military necessities of the time and how the Allied armies would fulfill their mission toward the civilian populations as they advanced. According to Coulet, after his own conciliatory speech in reply, he then deliberately raised his voice, declared that his presence in no way depended on the Allied governments, and then, pounding the table with his fist so that the inkpot on the table jumped, sending ink everywhere (and reminding him of Luther's ink spot on the wall of the Wartburg), told Lewis: "I have received from the GPRF the mission to administer the liberated territories of Normandy. I will renounce this position only on its orders!"[61] He then stood up, forcing the others to stand also, and shook hands with a stunned Lewis. His aide held the door open for the now silent British visitors, who left.

In the following days, Coulet reported at the time, relations were excellent. Brigadier Generals Lewis and Robbins, who had been in command at the civil affairs school at Wimbledon, "showed the greatest regard with respect to the French administration," and Colonel Damon Gunn, the civil affairs officer in the American sector, also showed the "greatest good will." Robbins told him, said Coulet, how pleased he was "to see us installed officially" and declared that his only goal "was to help us resolve our problems."[62] In Coulet's later memoir he would write that the relations following the initial meeting were "perfectly euphoric."[63]

On the chessboard, while Roosevelt hesitated, de Gaulle had moved his man to "check."

CHAPTER 7

After D-Day

THE ALLIES HAD LANDED AND ESTABLISHED THEIR beachhead, and de Gaulle had left behind him in Normandy his first regional commissioner, to establish the presence of his Provisional Government of the French Republic. But in spite of news from England and France, Roosevelt persisted in refusing to recognize him. On June 14, the very day that de Gaulle had visited the Normandy beachhead, Secretary of War Stimson held a long telephone conversation with the president. Stimson felt that de Gaulle was a troublemaker and, worst of all, was creating a widening gap between the British and the Americans. Still, he reasoned that there was no other French leader in sight, and his Provisional Government should be recognized, for all the reasons others were advancing. But Roosevelt, though now agreeing that it was impossible for the Americans to supervise French elections, proceeded to tell Stimson that de Gaulle "will crumble. . . . [T]he British supporters of de Gaulle will be confounded by the progress of events." Contrary to Stimson's thinking that de Gaulle was gaining strength throughout France, Roosevelt believed that "other parties will spring up as the liberation goes on . . . and de Gaulle will become a very little figure." The president "already knew of some such parties."[1]

If Gaullist officials were aware of these views, they would surely have remained convinced that the president might still be trying to block de Gaulle. They may not have known of them, but they certainly learned what Roosevelt told reporters in his June 23 press conference in Washington: he was not particularly impressed by the action of General Charles de Gaulle in naming prefects and subprefects in the liberated areas of Normandy. More French territory should be liberated, he said, before the problem of civil administration, which involved the question of recognizing de Gaulle's committee as a provisional government, would be considered in Washington. Civil administration, he added, cannot well be set up in a battle zone. "Let us liberate a little more of France before we go into the matter of civil administration."[2] Given what was happening in Normandy, this was a rather strange view. And whatever President Roosevelt may have thought about this particular matter, in Normandy, François Coulet went about establishing his authority and that of the Gaullist Provisional Government, installing new mayors, purging magistrates, reorganizing city councils, seeing to relief, nullifying a long list of Vichy laws, and setting up logistic support for the Allies. He also noted that he lacked French liaison personnel in some areas, with the result that Allied officers were interfering in matters they shouldn't. He called on London to send more men.[3]

At the same time, in occupied France, Marshal Pétain and Pierre Laval, in an effort to forestall installation of the GPRF, tried to make use for themselves of what they knew about Roosevelt's antipathy to de Gaulle, his view that other French leaders might emerge, and his attempts to prevent de Gaulle from "seizing" power. Pétain, in addition, was confident that Roosevelt continued to share Admiral Leahy's warm feelings for him, dating from much earlier. His contacts with the Vichy ambassador in Madrid, and through Jacques Lemaigre-Dubreuil, who had fled North Africa when de Gaulle's supremacy was assured, led him to believe he still had the American president's support.

Pétain's earliest hopes had been dashed in 1943. For several months after the Allied invasion of North Africa, through Darlan and then Giraud, a "Pétainist" regime had been maintained there under the Allies, with numerous Vichy officials participating in it, and Vichy laws on such matters as the treatment of Jews being enforced. Pétain had hoped therefore for a subsequent understanding with the Americans. When de Gaulle arrived in Algiers, however, he brought with him the end of the Vichy regime in North Africa. Still undaunted, Pétain now knew he had to change his strategy. His new idea was that he might secure a rapprochement with de Gaulle, who, respecting the idea of legitimacy—incorporated in the National Assembly's vote of full power to Pétain in 1940 coupled with a renunciation of those full powers now—would come to an agreement with Pétain in order to make his transition to power legitimate. The marshal mused that once the Germans were forced out of France, perhaps de Gaulle could join in a government with him and accept a lesser post, such as minister of war; if he proved himself, de Gaulle could eventually become prime minister and perhaps, in a short time, succeed Pétain in power. In fact, in early 1943 the aged Pétain sent a messenger to Algiers through Resistance elements favorable to him to propose this to de Gaulle, hoping that with the backing of Giraud all three might come together, as he put it, "under the Arc de Triomphe," adding, "Je suis prêt à m'effacer pourvu qu'on ne mette pas en cause ma légitimité" (I am ready to fade away of my own volition, as long as my legitimacy is not put into question).[4] He went on to tell de Gaulle that despite the earlier military tribunal's condemnation of de Gaulle for treason, he himself had never had any intention to have him shot.

The messenger was Paul Dungler, an anti-Gaullist Resistance leader, and when he arrived, both de Gaulle and Giraud rejected Pétain's suggestion. Giraud did so reluctantly, sending Pétain a friendly message, but fearing that an assent would further weaken him in Algiers. Dungler, apparently with the knowledge of Allen Dulles in Bern, then went on to make contact with German army intelligence agents who were in on the plots against Hitler, with the intention, once Hitler was done away with, of aiding the Germans in negotiating an armistice with the Allies that would, in addition, keep Pétain in power. The plot against Hitler, of course, failed, and so did this further effort to block de Gaulle.[5]

The year that followed, one in which the Germans suffered defeat on the Russian front and in North Africa, gave the aged Pétain much to think about. On the one hand, Laval had been reinforced in power by the Germans but was told by Hitler, in an interview Laval himself had sought, that if he didn't toe the line, he would be succeeded by a Gauleiter. On the other hand, Laval had little support anywhere in France. Even the extremist collaborators condemned him for being too lax and plotted to do away with him. Then there were the developments in Italy that brought Pétain to consider trying in some way to emulate Marshal Pietro Badoglio in Rome. The latter, assuming power at the fall of Mussolini on July 25, 1943, had managed to obtain an armistice with the Allies, remained in charge of the government, and then joined the Allies. It apparently suggested to Pétain (and was suggested *to* Pétain) that by reforming his government and ridding himself of the unpopular Laval, he might be able to remain in power and act as a mediator between Hitler and the Allies, securing a compro-

mise peace that would save Europe from the growing threat of a revived
Soviet Union. He was perhaps unaware that Hitler was more interested in
a peace with Russia, which might keep his western European gains intact,
than in one with the West, which might force him to give up those gains.[6]

Still later, in late 1943, Pétain, now trying to deal with a much more
uncertain future, prepared a new constitutional act that would bring back
the republic as his successor, and made ready to go on the air to let the
French know what he was going to do. (Laval asked him ironically, *"Tiens,
you're a republican now?"*)[7] He was, of course, blocked by the Germans,
who in reaction went further than ever with respect to France, essentially
turning it into a protectorate. They sent an emissary, Cecil von Renthe-
Fink, to oversee Pétain and to review and accept or reject all regulations
and personnel appointments, in effect to make policy. At the same time
they forced Pétain to take extreme collaborationists whom he hated into
his cabinet while dismissing other cabinet members they distrusted, and
they also blocked his attempt to retire from any political activity. He was
still too useful to them. The Germans allowed him to go to Paris to attend
a ceremony on April 26, 1944, for civilians killed by American air raids
and then to address a crowd of ten thousand from the balcony of the Hôtel
de Ville and later to visit several other cities. As a result, he mused again
about the possibility of being in Paris to greet the incoming Americans as
the head of the French government, and even told the crowd in Paris that
he would return. He was greeted cordially as he toured the city, though he
partially destroyed the effect of his visit two days later when he delivered a
speech in which he declared that the coming liberation was a mirage, that
anyone who belonged to a resistance group compromised the future of the
country, whose only protection from bolshevism lay in the defense of the
continent by Germany.[8] (It was, it appears, a speech forced on him by the
Germans, with the threat of replacing him with an extreme collaborationist
as head of government.)[9]

He nevertheless sent messages to the American OSS office in Bern to
try to drum up support by assuring the Americans that in case of Allied
landings, he would insist on French neutrality rather than support for the
Germans. He decided to send a personal envoy to Eisenhower to submit to
him a plan for the formation of a government by himself, Pétain, composed
of persons of whom the Americans would approve. It would denounce the
1940 armistice, following which Pétain would renounce his powers and call
into session the National Assembly.[10] It was a daydream, but one in which

he could indulge when, on May 7, the Germans actually moved him to a residence in Voisins, a small town outside Paris. At least one retired general begged him to come back to Paris—where, he assured Pétain, "a great number of Parisians would support you"—to keep "certain plots" from taking place and to greet the Allies. "If you are in Paris, the Americans will approach you."[11] Returned by the Germans to Vichy, in August 1944, following the Allied landings in Normandy, the old marshal tried again. Presumably encouraged by the Vatican, he sent Admiral Gabriel Auphan, who, like General Weygand, had been opposed to close collaboration with the Germans, to Paris to make contact with the Resistance. He was to try to persuade de Gaulle to come to an agreement with him in order to avoid disorder and discontinuity in the government of France and ensure continued legitimacy, using the argument that he had the backing of the Americans, and in particular of President Roosevelt. De Gaulle, by now in Chartres, refused to see the admiral. Auphan next tried to obtain an audience with General Eisenhower, but was rebuffed on the grounds that the general, following instructions from Washington, could not treat with any representative of Vichy.[12]

Then, as the Allies approached Paris, the Germans seized the marshal in Vichy and sent him against his will first to Belfort, in the northeast of France, then to Germany, along with others in the Vichy government. It marked the end of all Pétain's efforts, and the end of his four years of government in Vichy France.

Before this, however, Prime Minister Laval had followed his own path, seeking a way out of what had become an impasse, but acting too slowly. In August 1943, as the outcome of the war seemed more and more inevitable, a former Socialist but moderate supporter of Vichy, Ludovic-Oscar Frossard, suggested to Laval that he convoke the National Assembly, have it revoke the full powers granted to Marshal Pétain, and organize a vast political movement to the left. Laval apparently rejected the scheme.[13] At least one memo from de Gaulle's intelligence service in London to Algiers suggests that an envoy from Laval had arrived in Madrid to make contact with the Americans. "A second Darlan affair may be in the works," the memo reported, referring to the deal that put Admiral Darlan into power in North Africa in 1942. It requested further information.[14] There is no record of any result. Nevertheless, later, on January 5, 1944, Laval's ambassador in Spain, François Piétri, who had been a minister in several French cabinets in the 1930s, wrote to Laval suggesting a similar plan. Vichy, he argued, would not survive an Allied invasion, but as everyone knew, Roosevelt distrusted de Gaulle, who he thought was virtually a creature of the communists and would not be able to prevent bloody disorder. The president did not want to immerse himself in French politics, but Piétri had learned in Madrid—presumably from American sources—that Washington would like to discuss possibilities with an emissary from the French government outside normal diplomatic channels, and pressed Laval to send one through Madrid while preparing the recommended change in the form of government. (This would also suggest that the earlier move reported by Gaullist sources that an envoy from Laval had already arrived in Madrid had not taken place. Rumors of plots seem to have multiplied.)[15]

Laval responded to Piétri not by sending someone to Madrid but only by inviting his ambassador to Paris. Given Allied bombings and unrest in the French countryside, Piétri was unwilling to chance the trip. In March 1944, however, the ambassador reiterated his suggestion, this time repeating that he had learned from yet another source that the American government might well look favorably on the plan. In late January, it appears, Piétri had received a cousin of French politician Camille Chautemps, now in the United States, who was to go to Washington to try to negotiate on behalf of Pétain.[16] A move by Laval to restore the Third Republic, so long suggested, would confront the Algiers committee with a fait accompli that carried with it the stamp of legitimacy, with a reconstituted National Assembly, the Senate, and perhaps the old and respected Radical Socialist leader Édouard Herriot at the head of government.

Laval, perhaps too hemmed in by the Germans, dismissed Piétri's suggestion at the time. Yet Piétri knew that Laval himself had thought along the same lines, and indeed, at the last moment, as the Allies neared Paris in mid-August and the Germans prepared to leave, Laval did finally try to carry out roughly what had been so frequently proposed. Despite their dislike and suspicion of each other, Pétain apparently agreed to try to participate in Laval's endeavor if circumstances allowed him to.[17] Two weeks before the Allied armies reached Paris, on August 12, 1944, with the approval of German ambassador Otto Abetz, Laval brought the old Radical Socialist Herriot to Paris from where he had been living under house arrest, and over the space of a couple of days tried to get him to call the Assembly and the Senate into being.[18] To strengthen the move, Laval sent several emissaries to urge Pétain, still in Vichy, to come to Paris to participate, since they had, in fact, talked about the possibility beforehand. The marshal, however, suspicious of Laval, still hoping that he himself might be able to reach an agreement with Eisenhower, unable to get German guarantees of safety, failed to do so. For a day or so, with last-minute attempts to gather together legislators to carry out the project, Laval nevertheless thought he might succeed. He was much too late. Herriot made his uncertainty known; the attempt to get the last Senate president, Jules Jeannenay, to come to Paris failed; and the maneuver was apparently finally blocked when SS leader Heinrich Himmler, notified of the attempt, ordered Herriot returned to house arrest and, just as he had forced Pétain to leave Vichy, forced a protesting Pierre Laval to leave Paris under Gestapo escort on August 17, first to Belfort and then to Germany.[19]

Both the Committee of Liberation in Algiers and the Conseil national de la Résistance in France were aware of the possibilities entertained by Pétain and Laval. Emmanuel d'Astier, the commissioner of the interior, told the foreign press about them in Algiers, and the Conseil notified former parliamentarians that they must refuse any demand emanating from Vichy for a convocation of the old National Assembly or the demand that they attend one: "Whatever the inconveniences or the threats that they receive, the CNR warns the parliamentarians who might accede to the request that they would have to be responsible for their actions before the liberated nation."[20] It should be realized that the rumors of behind-the-scene maneuvers abounded in the context of German disinformation campaigns in the form of fake newsletters, fake clandestine radio broadcasts, and planted news stories, all designed to divide and confuse both the Resistance within and anti-Vichy forces without. There is no doubt, however, that Laval and his ambassador in Spain, Piétri, contributed by their actions to Gaullist suspicions that Roosevelt was ready to try almost anything to block de Gaulle.

While all of these maneuvers were going on in what remained of occupied France, in Normandy François Coulet, busy substituting de Gaulle's authority for that of Vichy, found the British thoroughly cooperative.[21] He met with General Montgomery, who at first brusquely questioned the commissioner's authority to refuse the Allied-issued currency. Montgomery, however, was the son of an Anglican bishop, and upon being told that Coulet, was a Protestant, not a Catholic like so many other Frenchmen, he changed his tone to one of cordiality and assured Coulet of his full cooperation. Farther afield, in the American zone, Coulet found that French officers had been weak in allowing the Americans to take actions that infringed on French sovereignty: organizing the election of a mayor or making arrests of Frenchmen on the basis of denunciations by supposed resistants. While his own visit to the area improved the situation, he asked Boislambert to send more MMLA officers to affirm French authority. He pleaded for shipments of food, especially infant formula, and for medical personnel and hospital supplies—and for better pay for the MMLA officers, whose salaries were largely being paid in English pounds, deposited in banks in London. Hettier de Boislambert also recalls mayors' complaints that the absence of MMLA officers gave the Americans too much opportunity to interfere. There was occasional confusion about who was to do what. Despite all the preparation in England, there were British officials on the spot who knew nothing about the planned transition from Vichy governance to that of the GPRF.[22]

François Coulet, following the overriding need to support the military effort and to demonstrate to the Allies that the GPRF representatives would do so, ordered French officials to accede to Allied demands linked to military action: that civilians comply with blackout orders, as well as orders not to use cameras and not to circulate in the few automobiles available. The Allies, he noted, had prepared posters about such matters but, respectful of French sovereignty, had asked the French to authorize them.

Cherbourg was finally liberated on July 1. The Germans had blown up the port facilities, and 100,000 houses had been destroyed or damaged by Allied bombing, but Coulet found the population there much more demonstrative than back in Bayeux. The American Colonel Frank Howley, who was very cooperative, was cheered by the crowd when he addressed them alongside French Gaullist authorities. Coulet reported that he received from the civil affairs officers "the warmest and most concrete assurances" that they would not interfere in his domain, and that they would act only through the French administration. General Julius Holmes, who came from Eisenhower's headquarters and whom the French had distrusted as one who favored AMGOT, as well as the First Army civil affairs officer Colonel Gunn, both visited him to reassure him further.

In fact, there and elsewhere the civil affairs officers who had received their training in the United States and England found plenty to do in helping to restore order, utilities, and transport; making available food supplies; taking care of refugees, the homeless, the wounded, and the sick; clearing the streets; and on and on. A good part of their job was accommodating

the needs of the Allied armed forces—for housing, storage, transportation, recreation—and keeping Allied soldiers in order.[23] In all of this they
seem to have cooperated with the French. Coulet, visiting the liberated but
devastated towns of St. Lô and Coutances, found "the greatest understanding among the American civil affairs officers . . . multiplying their signs of
goodwill." In ruined Coutances he obtained from them the commitment
that the few public buildings left standing would not be requisitioned so
that French authorities could use them.

Winston Churchill visited the area again on July 21, but despite some effort
at making contact, left without visiting Coulet. Still intent on establishing
the Provisional Government's authority, Coulet let the Allied authorities
know that the leader of a foreign government visiting French soil should
pay his respects to the local representative of the Provisional Government
of the French Republic. Two weeks later, on August 6, Clement Atlee,
leader of the Labour Party and the second man in the British cabinet, visited the area and sent a message asking Coulet to dine with him. To the
surprise of the British officers delivering the message, Coulet refused and
made his point quite clear: Allied leaders could not make a habit of coming on tourist visits to French soil without presenting their compliments to
the representative of the French government and coming to see him first.
He got what he wanted. Atlee did ask if he could come, and at a dinner
Coulet arranged for him, Atlee was most amiable, congratulating Coulet
on maneuvering along the difficult path de Gaulle had had to follow. The
precedent Coulet had set was important to him: it reinforced the point that
the French government was now well established in France. When Foreign
Secretary Anthony Eden visited (and Coulet learned later that Eden had
deliberately set out to erase as far as possible the bad impression left by
Prime Minister Churchill), he insisted "almost to an embarrassing degree"
that the British government was grateful for the way Coulet had carried out
his role, calming all the apprehensions that the British had entertained at
the moment Coulet had landed. Coulet apparently replied that the praise
was as exaggerated as were the fears of the Allied governments. He pointed
out that his designation as *commissaire* and the taking up of his functions
were to be explained by the concern of the French Provisional Government that French sovereignty over the liberated territories be immediately
affirmed; this was in no way a defiance of the British and American govern-

ments but rather the logical conclusion of the path followed by the CFLN and then the GPRF.

Eden, wrote Coulet, "seemed to get great pleasure that the people recognized him" as he took a walk in the streets of Bayeux. The American ambassador to SHAEF, William Phillips, leaving for the United States, paid a courtesy call and expressed at length the satisfaction the U.S. government had felt at the way Coulet had administered the liberated territories. Coulet wrote later that like Eden and other Allied leaders who had filed through, Phillips was apparently grateful that he had not raised a guillotine on the main square of Bayeux!

A first report from another regional commissioner, in Rennes, on August 13, noted that contact made with diverse American authorities, and in particular civil affairs officers, had resulted in demonstrating to them all clearly that the new French administrators were well prepared to take over their responsibilities.[24] One other matter that had troubled the waters, the issue of military tribunals for civilians within the war zone, simply disappeared: no Allied military government courts were set up; no civil affairs detachments administered justice. French transgressors were all tried by French courts.

The tasks for civil affairs officers and the emerging French administrators were enormous. The heavy, destructive, and often highly inaccurate Allied bombing, Resistance sabotage, German repression, and the actual fighting led to the death and maiming of thousands of civilians and the destruction of hundreds of thousands of homes, as well as factories, railroad lines and equipment, bridges, roads, and hospitals. The Germans, of course, who had stripped France of so much during the occupation, left little behind that was intact or could be used. Homeless refugees were everywhere, necessitating, among other things—such as feeding them and providing medical care—decisions as to whether and when they could return to devastated villages. It required that much be done in the way of immediate relief and rapid reconstruction of communications facilities, all of which entailed problems of finding and hiring untainted, qualified personnel. Land mines were scattered in the cultivated fields and abandoned villages, and the Allied forces could not take care of them all. The issue of war booty plagued negotiators, since under American military law a soldier risked court-martial if he did not turn it over to his superiors, while the

French laid claim to it themselves. The hiring of French workers by American armed forces required compliance with French laws on compensation, social security payments, and family allocations, and the French wanted to be sure they would be hired through French labor offices.[25]

There were always difficulties: pilfering and black marketing, resentment among civilians at not getting enough relief supplies, and claims that conditions were better under the Germans, while for their part civil affairs officers resented the ungracious acceptance of what was provided at the expense of U.K. civilians, who were severely rationed back home. There were also tensions with French authorities who needed workers for clearing streets and repairing facilities but couldn't pay as much. In the south of France, at least, there was anger over the Allies' desire to use German or Italian prisoners of war instead of French labor, as well as over Allied complaints about French black market activities.

Civil affairs had a dual task: relief and restoration of order on the one hand, and the use of indigenous resources and effort in order to provide support for the prosecution of the war on the other. This meant, among other things, monopolization of transportation, the appropriation of coal stocks, requisition of accommodations, and so on. This last task produced unfortunate consequences. British historian F. S. V. Donnison wrote: "The French were to be allowed little or no more say, at first, in the use of their own resources than they had been by the Germans. It was not so difficult to bear such treatment as part of the lot of a vanquished people; it was hard when it followed 'liberation' by its friends. . . . It is probable that the French never tasted the full bitterness of defeat until they had been 'liberated.'"[26] Planned imports of foodstuffs and relief supplies lagged for a long time. Electricity production had been cut by 65 percent and coal production by 85 percent. By early 1945, after the liberation of Paris, 66 percent of freight was military and 34 percent for civilian purposes, and since more than half of freight capacity had been destroyed, this meant that only some 15 percent of normal civilian needs for personal transportation or transportation of goods and supplies were being met. In the south of France, where the Allied troops either never penetrated or soon left, there were basically only minor conflicts between French civilian authorities and the Allies. But in the north there were far more frequent complaints about requisitions of supplies and housing and over the conduct of the troops, far from home and the usual social constraints that operated there, and ignorant of the hardships the French had suffered for years and continued to suffer, and of the horrendous damage their air forces had inflicted on the country and its population. There were also problems over actions by lower officers, not well acquainted with high policy. The liberators were often cheered but were not always popular.

Among all the myriad tasks in the battered countryside that required negotiation between the Allies and the French was that of deciding what to do about postage stamps: the London GPRF office told Regional Commissioner Coulet that for psychological reasons it was impossible to use stamps with the image of Pétain on them; Coulet wanted to imprint them with a cross of Lorraine and add a surcharge. British Brigadier Thomas Robbins had vague objections, but American Colonel Howley told a French representative that to overprint them would be an insult to the "noble vieillard."[27] The issue was, presumably, solved. Other matters were more pressing.

Historian Jean-Louis Crémieux-Brilhac notes that in their memoirs, Boislambert and Coulet congratulate themselves on their victories in the reconquest of French sovereignty. The major factor, however, was that the Allied High Command in the persons of General Eisenhower, his deputy Walter Bedell Smith, and British General Bernard Law Montgomery all wanted nothing more than to have the GPRF assume its role behind the lines, whatever President Roosevelt might want. General Marshall—never a fan of de Gaulle's—visiting London in mid-June, well informed as to the situation, wired Washington on June 16 that he agreed with Eisenhower's views on the need for recognition of the GPRF and recommended a *political* accord with the Provisional Government, on the grounds that the "diplomatic boycott of the French on the one hand and existing military cooperation on the other" were more and more incompatible.[28] Still nothing happened. Secretary of War Stimson recorded that Roosevelt "gave it scant attention."[29] In England, Eden, however, reflected, "Whatever de Gaulle's gifts or failings, he was a godsend to his country at this hour, when France must otherwise have been distracted by controversy or bathed in blood."[30]

The British now began to act on their own. Ambassador Viénot moved rapidly to follow the instructions left behind by a departing de Gaulle. By June 30 he was able to cable Algiers that agreement with the British government had been reached on all points: a de facto recognition of the Provisional Government, a categorical affirmation of French sovereignty, the disappearance of any idea of supervision by the commander in chief even in the military zone, and an affirmation of the complete equality of the Provisional Government with all other Allied governments. He also transmitted Eden's declaration to the effect that the British government would accept no modification of these agreements by the Americans without Gaullist consent.[31] In July Eden and René Massigli, the GPRF commissioner for foreign affairs, initialed an exchange of notes that ratified these accords, essentially constituting a de facto recognition of GPRF authority and laying the groundwork, as de Gaulle's director of economic affairs, Hervé Alphand, declared over the BBC, for the "return of France to its historic place among the nations."[32]

As a result of the Franco-British agreements, in early July the time now seemed ripe to almost everyone on the Allied side—British, French, American—for de Gaulle to visit Washington, though de Gaulle wanted the invitation to come from the president, while Roosevelt wanted the visit to be at the request of de Gaulle. (When de Gaulle hesitated about the timing, Roosevelt told his close aide William Hassett, "He's a nut.")[33] The issue of who would make the request was finessed, and it was determined that formal recognition would be left off the agenda, but de Gaulle was nevertheless greeted like a head of state by a seventeen-gun salute at National Airport on July 6, 1944, for what proved to be essentially a ceremonial visit. He was fêted, wined and dined, and met with not just Roosevelt but two of his other severest critics, Leahy and Hull, both of whom found him less forbidding than they had thought. The indefatigable Leahy nevertheless wrote in his memoirs: "I had a better opinion after talking to him. However, I remained unconvinced that he and his Committee of Liberation necessarily represented the form of government that the people of France wished to have after their nation's liberation from the Nazis."[34] De Gaulle paid his respects to the commander of the American Expeditionary Force in World War I, the aging General John "Black Jack" Pershing. Roosevelt was charming but wrote later that he thought de Gaulle was "essentially selfish," while de Gaulle thought that Roosevelt, who had spoken at length about the United States' role in the postwar world, had a will to power "cloaked in idealism."[35] Even Stimson, who had done so much to try to attenuate Roosevelt's anti-Gaullist policy, considered de Gaulle "a man of twisted pride and out-of-date ideas," while Roosevelt's aide William Hassett wrote in his diary, "Now let's hope the temperamental Gaul keeps his feet on the ground with no delusions about his reincarnation as Joan of Arc or Clemenceau."[36] De Gaulle, outside Blair House where he was lodged like other heads of state, facing enthusiastic crowds waving French flags and shouting "Vive de Gaulle!" emphasized in his own fashion to one of his envoys, Pierre Mendès-France, that the visit had formalized nothing and that the establishment had kept its distance. "I was cheered," he told Mendès-France sarcastically, "by negroes, Jews, cripples, and cuckolds!"[37] On July 11, following the visit, Roosevelt held a press conference in which, while admitting that essentially he had accepted de Gaulle's de facto authority in liberated areas, if Eisenhower ran into conflict between CFLN authorities and other French groups, it would be up to Ike to decide with whom to deal. For President Roosevelt, the "local authorities" doctrine was not yet fully dead.

Yet one thing now seemed clear. Roosevelt, it was true, still refused formal recognition and, like Leahy, maintained his reservations. To most people other than the president, however, the visit signified that de Gaulle had already, basically, won the unequal contest between the two men. Without conceding anything to the president of the most powerful nation in the world, who had tried everything he could to sideline de Gaulle, the general was now recognized by almost everyone else as the leader of a soon-to-be-restored France. To French and Franco-Americans who attended a reception for him at the Waldorf-Astoria, when he moved on to New York, and who wept when he spoke of "La France de l'histoire, la France éternelle," he was the man not just of the Resistance but of the resurrection.[38] He had, in their view, dissipated misunderstandings and restored France to its position in the world. That view was shared by the French press, reporting on the visit.[39]

In Washington, after de Gaulle had left, Roosevelt gave in to a group composed of Secretary of War Stimson, his undersecretary John J. McCloy, and Henry Morgenthau Jr., secretary of the treasury. While trying to get Roosevelt to do at least *something*, they had come up with a formula he finally found acceptable. Roosevelt proclaimed at his press conference on July 11 that he recognized the GPRF as "'the de facto authority' for the civil administration of France during the period of the Liberation" (thus still reserving his stance on what would come after). As noted earlier, Secretary Stimson recorded the conversation he had with the president on June 14, when Roosevelt told him that the British were wrong, he knew support for de Gaulle would crumble, and he still thought that actual recognition would cause a revolution in France.[40] The fact gives some substance to the view of Pétain and Laval that Roosevelt might still be willing to support their moves to block de Gaulle and to de Gaulle's view that Roosevelt actually tried (as I discuss later). The president seems to have been supplied with some knowledge of Pétain's and Laval's activities through American sources in Bern, Geneva, and Madrid.[41] Roosevelt was also told in a memorandum from OSS leader General "Wild Bill" Donovan that despite the supposed unity of the Resistance in France under the Conseil national de la Résistance, and its proclaimed support for de Gaulle, there were resistance groups that were much at odds, that they regarded de Gaulle more as a symbol than as a political leader, and that the president should reiterate his support for de Gaulle as a military leader but not recognize his regime until later, when French opinion could be ascertained. (Donovan had been influenced by tales of scandal in the Gaullist intelligence service under Passy, and in North Africa he had supported Giraud and had his men work with him.)[42] It may be noted that this memo contrasts strongly with the earlier OSS memo of March 27, 1943 (see chapter. 2), which reflected the views of analysts rather than of Donovan himself, to the effect that de Gaulle was everywhere recognized as the leader of French resistance.

Historian Arthur Funk, reflecting on Roosevelt's growing belief that a civil war might well break out in France between rightists grouped around Pétain and Vichy and a leftist, communist-inspired Gaullist resistance, sees events in Greece and Yugoslavia as providing support for Roosevelt's unlikely view. In Greece, freed of the Germans, a civil war was raging between communists and British-supported royalist forces, while in Yugoslavia Tito's communist partisans fought with Draza Mihailovic's royalist Chetniks. Roosevelt's insistence that American occupation forces in Germany have supply routes that did not pass through France was certainly based on his view that France might also well be riven by such a civil war.[43]

It is noteworthy, writes Funk, that virtually no one outside the White House shared Roosevelt's view. Resistance leader and future regional commissioner Raymond Aubrac replied to a Roosevelt press conference during which the president said, "How do we know what the French people want since no one has been in France recently?" Aubrac, in Algiers, responded, "I have—I can attest to the support for the CFLN manifested daily." Downed airmen who had escaped could attest to it too. Contact between France and Algiers was constant, with couriers risking their lives. "Americans should know it, the French will never understand the hesitation. . . . The French people who receive their liberators will show it."[44]

. . .

Events in France finally began to move quickly at the beginning of August 1944. General Philippe Leclerc's Second Armored Division landed in France on August 1, about the same time as the decisive Allied breakout at Avranches that would send the Germans reeling backwards. Both Churchill and Eisenhower had wanted a French division in action on the northern front, and Eisenhower had implicitly promised that it would be the first to enter Paris. It was soon in action. Far more important in numbers was the First French Army, commanded by General Jean de Lattre de Tassigny, which landed on the south coast of France on August 15. His soldiers outnumbered the Americans involved in the landings by seven divisions to three—200,000 men in all—and de Lattre de Tassigny took part in all the planning. The advance in the south was rapid when Hitler, for the first time, ordered a retreat, on August 17, leaving forces only in the major ports of Toulon and Marseilles, both of which were captured by French forces in heavy fighting well in advance of what had been planned. Marseilles, despite German destruction, soon became the most important port in Allied hands in terms of tonnage landed.

Fighting hard, aided by FFI harassment of the retreating Germans, the Franco-American forces moved north. It was happenstance that the first contact between Allied forces from Normandy and those from the south were two French units, from de Lattre de Tassigny's First Army and Leclerc's Second Armored Division. Behind the new line formed by the junction of the Allied armies, Resistance forces took numerous German prisoners and freed the whole southwest of France, putting into place both men who emerged directly from the Resistance and those named by the Gaullist government in Algiers. The southwest nevertheless tested de Gaulle's resolve: he would subsequently, after the liberation of Paris, have to tour the whole region, where in major towns such as Bordeaux, Limoges, Montpellier, and Toulouse the communists had taken over, and where in other places a measure of chaos reigned. It was proof of his authority that he managed in short order to reestablish what he thought of as "republican legality."

Eisenhower had planned to bypass Paris as he forced the Germans northeast, but when the communist Colonel Henri Rol-Tanguy began an insurrection by the Resistance in Paris, Eisenhower was persuaded by de Gaulle to change his mind. Either the German garrison would crush the insurrection or the communist-led FFI in Paris would win, and would be in power when the Allies entered, able to influence the new government more than de Gaulle wanted. As a result, after some hesitation on Eisenhower's part, and after more heavy fighting, Leclerc's Second Armored Division entered Paris on September 25. Little food had come into the city for weeks, public services had been on strike for ten days, and poorly armed FFI had fought the German garrison from windows and from behind hastily erected street barricades. But General Dietrich von Choltitz, who surrendered to Leclerc, kept Paris relatively intact, despite Hitler's earlier hysterical order, relayed through General Günther von Kluge, that it be defended to the last and destroyed in the effort. (German officers meeting in Saint-Germain-en-Laye two days later decided to ignore the orders.) The crowds greeting Leclerc's forces were delirious with joy, even as sporadic fighting continued.

De Gaulle had flown from Algiers to arrive in France on the twentieth, and on the twenty-fifth he followed the Second Division into Paris. There were several conflicts and mishaps over the flight, and typically, de Gaulle thought of them as deliberate American attempts to delay his arrival while last-minute maneuvers by Laval took place.[45] The next day, having reestablished himself in the Ministry of Defense, where he had last held office under the Third Republic in 1940, he led a parade on foot down the Champs-Elysées between rapturous crowds lining the sidewalks, attended Mass in Notre Dame, and addressed a cheering throng from the balcony of the Hôtel de Ville. It was here, where he proclaimed that Paris had been liberated by its own people, with the help of the French armed forces, with the support of all of France, the real France, "la France éternelle," that he refused Georges Bidault's suggestion that he proclaim the restoration of the republic. The republic, he declared, had never ceased to exist. The Vichy regime was merely an illegal interval. With the support of Eisenhower, he had had Leclerc's division march down the Champs-Élysées behind him and an American division parade down a day or so later while he stood on the reviewing stand, both to demonstrate to the still unruly Resistance that the Allied armed forces were behind him. Eisenhower, conscious of political realities, overruled his subordinates, who had wanted the two divisions out of Paris and on the front lines.

In short order the Provisional Government moved from Algiers to Paris, thanks to all the preparatory work done in London in conjunction with the Conseil national de la Résistance and others. Symbolically and practically this was the most important thing it could have done: a French govern-ment existed now, as always, in Paris with all of its ministries established in their own buildings. Decrees were soon issued that, nominally at least, disarmed the Resistance groupings (much to the anger of some of them) and integrating those who wanted to continue the fight into the French army. Eisenhower personally saw to it that enough uniforms would be made available to them. Resistance leaders were brought into the enlarged Provisional Government and the enlarged Consultative Assembly. On No-vember 7 the new Assembly met in the National Assembly building for the first time since June 1940. On November 11 (Armistice Day for the First World War) de Gaulle's crucial early supporter and often enemy Winston Churchill visited him in Paris.

Everything had been done to make the visit a success. The whole first floor of the sumptuous Foreign Office on the Quai d'Orsay was given over to Churchill's party. "The Prime Minister was delighted to find that he had a golden bath, which had been prepared by Goering for his own use, and still more delighted that the Foreign Secretary's bath was only of silver," observed British envoy Duff Cooper. Churchill and de Gaulle toured Paris in an open car in streets lined with such wildly cheering packed crowds, he later recalled, that "the reception had to be seen to be believed. It was greater than anything I have ever known. . . . [T]he cheering was the loud-est, most spontaneous and most genuine."[46] Pastor Marc Boegner, presi-dent of the Protestant National Council, wrote: "We shouted our gratitude to the man who held on and the one who had resisted. We wept with joy in the middle of the crowd."[47] In discussions and dinners that followed, the fulsome expressions of goodwill continued, though they masked some dissension over the future course of events. When Duff Cooper presented his letters of credence a week later, "de Gaulle was very genial and smiling. His staff say that they have never known him so nearly happy."[48] The next day de Gaulle left for Moscow to sign a general treaty of friendship with Stalin's Soviet Union.

In the meantime, on October 23, 1944, Franklin D. Roosevelt, as a result of maneuvering within his administration, finally recognized the Gouver-nement provisoire de la République française as the de facto government of France. (It may be noted, however, that at a press conference three days later he declared that France would not participate immediately in conver-sations on world security.)[49]

When so many governments, officials, and groups within and without the United States had pressed for recognition of the GPRF, it is legitimate to ask whether Roosevelt's well-known views of de Gaulle and his fear of what would happen if de Gaulle tried to "seize" power were the only reasons for the delay. Was it possible that Roosevelt was informed of Pétain's and Laval's attempts to block de Gaulle, and that with the failure of other, earlier possible alternatives—Generals Weygand, Edgard de Larminat, and Giraud, among others—he had actually supported them? Was this why he used the formula on July 22, 1944, that the Allies would accept the GPRF as "'the de facto authority' for the civil administration of France during the period of the Liberation," leaving open the possibility of later change?

De Gaulle certainly appears to have thought so. In his *Mémoires* he writes that Laval had, through contacts with Allen Dulles, "verified that Washington would look gratefully upon a project that would top or put aside de Gaulle." He writes later that General Eisenhower's hesitation about sending Leclerc's Second Armored Division into Paris "made him believe that the military command found itself held up by the political project pursued by Laval, favored by Roosevelt." The transfer of Leclerc from General Patton's to General Hodges's command, and Eisenhower's failure to sign an earlier accord on relations between the Allied armed forces and the French administration while he waited for authorization to do so, all convinced de Gaulle that the matter could be explained only by White House intrigue, in hopes that the Laval-Herriot move would succeed.[50] Historian Jean-Baptiste Duroselle supports this view when he writes that once the Laval-Herriot move had failed, Eisenhower gave "the green light" to move on Paris on August 22.[51] De Gaulle also goes on to explain the well-known premature BBC announcement that Paris had been liberated as having "without a doubt the purpose of getting the Americans to surmount their mental reservations."[52]

Vichy's ambassador in Spain, François Piétri, who had had contacts with various Americans in or passing through Madrid, had certainly tried to convince Laval that he would have American support for his maneuvers. Another former Third Republic minister, Georges Bonnet, who had taken refuge in Geneva, claimed to have heard from the American chargé d'affaires in Madrid, S. Pinckney Tuck, that the Americans hoped to see Édouard Herriot in power in France at the time of victory rather than de Gaulle.[53] Emmanuel d'Astier de la Vigerie, the interior commissioner in the CFLN in Algiers, who would later become a communist deputy, believed that the Americans were in direct contact with Laval.[54] A memo from intelligence services in Algiers to André Phillip, the *commissaire de l'intérieur* in London, dated June 10, 1944, states that Bernard Fäye, friend of and adviser to Pétain and head of the Bibliothèque nationale, had received a letter from Robert Murphy and Admiral Leahy asking Pétain to stay on as head of government and revise the constitution.[55] I have found no trace of such a letter. But Fäye had been a member of a committee of *notables* who were trying to revise Franco-German relations and get rid of Laval, and who, in the same memo, were said to have met with a special American envoy. Members had been in contact with Colonel Georges Groussard, an anti-Nazi resistant who, like Bonnet, had fled to Geneva, and who was himself in contact with British intelligence services and the British consul-general in Geneva, and with Allen Dulles, the OSS chief in Bern. The anti-Gaullist Resistance circles to which Groussard belonged had hoped to get the Americans to support members of the Third Republic National Assembly to move into power before General de Gaulle arrived.

The contentions are all rather vague and speculative. There is no question that there were contacts between elements in Vichy and Americans in Bern and Madrid. Whether they represented an actual political effort on the part of President Franklin D. Roosevelt to forestall de Gaulle is perhaps to some people still an open question, though de Gaulle and several French authors were sure of the answer. Pierre Queille, in his diplomatic history of Vichy, unfortunately undocumented, writes that Roosevelt had, in fact, actually promised Pétain that the Americans would support a government headed by him, and that this helps explain why Pétain thought his approaches to de Gaulle, mentioned earlier in this chapter, might succeed, since de Gaulle would know he had American backing.[56] Those who are skeptical, however, point out that there is no documentation to confirm it, only verbal declarations on the subject, and only speculation based on Roosevelt's known suspicions about de Gaulle and such comments as the one he made to Secretary of War Stimson to the effect that he *knew* that other Frenchmen would arise to take de Gaulle's place. Moreover, as we have seen, in his cable to General Eisenhower on March 15, 1944, he had specifically directed the general not to rely on collaborators in any French administration and instructed him that his relations with the Vichy regime should be only in order to terminate it.

Did OSS chief Allen Dulles in the Swiss capital, Bern, act to help non-Gaullists in France? The record shows that his organization provided communications between the Resistance in France and the Gaullist London and Algiers offices, while at one point, when the Algiers Gaullists wanted the French embassy in Bern to get rid of its pro-Vichy personnel, Dulles wrote that he had talked this over with the Gaullist commissioner for foreign affairs, René Massigli, "a personal friend of mine," said Dulles, whose attitude he understood. In both 1943 and 1944 he cabled Washington about the growth of support in France for de Gaulle and, it may be stressed, the danger of denying recognition to the French Provisional Government. It would hardly seem that he was acting to try to block de Gaulle.

It is true that Dulles's office maintained a channel of communication with Pétain through a friend of former prime minister Herriot, André Enfière, who told Dulles that he supported de Gaulle, was working with Georges Bidault, now head of the National Resistance Council, and wanted to make sure that a democratic solution was found. He believed that bringing back Herriot and members of the National Assembly through cooperation with Pétain would ensure that a democratic transition would take place.[57] Jean-Paul Cointet, in his biography of Laval, writes, "Haunted by an arrival of de Gaulle in the vans of communism, certain American services could have lent themselves to 'operation Herriot,' which does not imply an acceptance of Pierre Laval."[58] Annie Lacroix-Riz of the University of Paris, unlike most other historians, however, had no doubt about what the United States intended when she told the readers of the *Monde Diplomatique* in May 2003: "Laval believed the U.S. pledge that he would play a key role after a separate peace agreement pitting Germany, Britain, and the United States against the Soviets was reached. . . . [T]he separate peace proposal failed to take into account the Red Army's key role in crushing Hitler's Wehrmacht."[59] This Marxist historian cites no sources for her rather convoluted view about an American "pledge" to Laval.

From Bern, Dulles offered to fund the Resistance organization Combat, founded by Henri Frenay, through an emissary who had joined it and who had been, in the 1930s, a member of the royalist paramilitary group the Camelots du Roi. The Gaullist intelligence chief in London, Colonel Passy, was so suspicious that he refused the funding for Combat from Bern at a time when the Resistance organization desperately needed the money. The Service de Travail obligatoire, which obliged young Frenchmen to go to work in Germany, had just been enacted, sending thousands of young men to join the Maquis in order to evade the law. They needed support. But

Passy was convinced that the OSS funding hid a plot to isolate de Gaulle and support Giraud.[60] De Gaulle, in late 1943 in Algiers, voiced his own suspicions about what the Americans might be up to, inferring that on some plea of military expediency they would strike a deal with Vichy. Edwin Wilson, the American envoy who had replaced Robert Murphy, and whose relations with de Gaulle were much friendlier, reported: "I said I was astounded that he should make such an inference. . . . [T[he only dealings we would have with Vichy would be to liquidate it." And when Cordell Hull was informed of this fear he replied: "That is preposterous. The chance of that is zero, simply zero."[61] Nevertheless, de Gaulle's suspicions persisted and led him to make a statement in late March 1944 before the Provisional Assembly: "All attempts to maintain even partially or by camouflage any part of Vichy or any artificial powers foreign to the government will be intolerable and condemned in advance."[62]

Whatever may be the case, in January 1944 the State Department had formally informed René Massigli, the foreign affairs commissioner in Algiers, that it would certainly not support the Vichy regime: "The Allies and the Supreme Allied Commander will have no dealings or relations with the Vichy Regime except for the purpose of abolishing it. No person will be retained or employed in any office by the Allied military authorities who has willfully collaborated with the enemy."[63] In the *Washington Post,* however, French diplomats in Washington were quoted as saying that the State Department statement "did not constitute an answer to General de Gaulle. . . . [T]he Committee would like to know positively with whom the allies are going to deal."[64]

Then in Washington, in response to continued rumors that the administration supported negotiations with Vichy, and in reply to de Gaulle, at a press conference on April 7 Secretary of State Cordell Hull issued a vehement denial followed by another formal statement: "The absurd reports and rumors . . . are false on their face." He went on to state that the earlier relations with Vichy that ended in November 1942 were intended to keep the French fleet and the French empire out of German hands, and indicated no sympathy for that regime. "No loyal supporter of the Allied cause would make the ridiculous charge that the United States government, while sending its military forces and vast military supplies to the most distant battlefields to prosecute the war against the Axis powers would at the same time have any dealings or relations with the Vichy regime except for the purpose of abolishing it." Moreover, he remarked in his memoirs, "neither the State Department nor Eisenhower had any intention of encouraging any rival group that might emerge in France."[65]

Biographer-journalist Don Cook, in *Charles de Gaulle,* argues persuasively that the de Gaulle logic and his suspicions were "badly flawed and totally unfair." Cook continues:

> If he had any reading at all of the American political scene, he would have known that it would have been political suicide for FDR, then embarking on his fourth-term election campaign, suddenly to attempt to make a deal with Laval at the very moment of the liberation of Paris. The furor over the Darlan deal in 1942 would have been nothing to the political storm which any deal with the Vichyites in 1944 would have raised. . . . The Laval plot could not and did not have the slightest effect on either Roosevelt's political decisions or Eisenhower's battle decisions. . . . [T]he affair remains a measure of how far de Gaulle could go in concocting deliberate mistrust of his allies when he chose to do so.[66]

It is notable, also, that the 1944 Republican presidential candidate, Thomas E. Dewey, was in favor of prompt recognition of the de Gaulle government, making it even more unlikely that candidate Roosevelt would have taken the risk of dealing with Vichy representatives.

André Kaspi, in *La Libération de la France,* comes to the same conclusion as Cook with respect to Eisenhower's decision about the move on Paris: it was dictated by military, not political, conditions.[67] And then, conclusively, there is Roosevelt's directive to Eisenhower of March 15: "You will have no talks or relations with the Vichy Regime except for the purpose of terminating its administration in toto."[68] Finally, there was the already noted attempt by Admiral Auphan, Pétain's envoy, to see Eisenhower shortly before the liberation of Paris, when Eisenhower, on direct instruction from Washington that he should have no contact with Vichy representatives, refused to meet with him.

It is hard to find any reason for supporting the Gaullist-instigated suspicions that Roosevelt was ready to deal with either Pétain or Laval.

·   ·   ·

It still took pressure on President Roosevelt to issue his declaration of de facto recognition on October 23. By this time all his own personal, strongly held expectations had been falsified by events. There was no civil war as a result of the Gaullist takeover of power. There was no communist-led revolution; if anything, de Gaulle had acted to curb communist ambitions. And de Gaulle was working with democratic institutions and parties, reinvigorating the Provisional Assembly, certainly not acting as a dictator. None of those rival French leaders Roosevelt believed in had emerged. De Gaulle had been cheered by massive crowds wherever he appeared. On September 13 a message from Eisenhower's headquarters to the State Department stated that recognition would be helpful on all counts, especially in strengthening the French central government so that it could continue to establish its authority behind the battle lines and maintain the order Eisenhower needed. It also stated that the French people could not understand why there was any delay: French newspapers were full of angry speculation about why it was being withheld. British and American newspapers joined in the chorus. Typically, the *Daily Telegraph* declared that recognition was "indispensable" and that the British were astonished at the "inexplicable delay." In Switzerland the *Gazette de Lausanne* called it "intenable"—unbearable—and speculated that it was because of the Americans' desire to keep France out of postwar councils.[69] Selden Chapin, the State Department representative to the French Committee of National Liberation (now known in most quarters as the Provisional Government of the French Republic), chimed in on September 15 and again on September 21 with telegrams to Washington stressing the need for rapid recognition. Cordell Hull, in what author Julian Hurstfield calls "an uncharacteristic burst of activity," sent several memoranda to Roosevelt—one on September 17, another on September 21, and yet another on October 3—underlining all the reasons for immediate recognition and emphasizing that de Gaulle had obviously been acclaimed as a national leader. Withholding recognition now would jeopardize American prestige in France and perhaps weaken the new government.[70]

The president, however, heroically resisted all these pressures and recommendations that he should take into account the realities of the evolving situation. On September 21 (almost a month after de Gaulle's triumphal entry into Paris), Roosevelt, amazingly, told Hull, "It is best to let things go along as they are for the moment." Recognition would be "premature."[71] It may be noted that on that same day, September 21, the State Department had sent an envoy to Paris, Jefferson Cafferey, who found himself in the anomalous position of being an ambassador to a government the United States did not recognize and which therefore had not accredited him.

One month later the president finally yielded, perhaps because now even Admiral Leahy was telling him he should. Winston Churchill had wired him to urge immediate recognition on October 14.[72] Eisenhower, on October 20, had wired General Marshall again that now, with winter coming on and an already difficult supply situation to cope with, any move to sustain de Gaulle's central government would be helpful, especially recognition. On the same day Cafferey, quoting Eisenhower, cabled the president that recognition was an urgent matter

Most accounts report that on October 22 Roosevelt told Churchill he would communicate with him about recognition within the next few days, but that on October 23 the State Department, jumping the gun, issued a statement of recognition, thus surprising an annoyed Churchill, to whom Roosevelt subsequently apologized. In fact, the reality appears a little more complex, perhaps because there was some lack of communication between the highest ranks and their staffs. On October 19 Roosevelt had written Churchill that he preferred that the two of them, rather than the State Department and Foreign Office, handle the matter. But the record shows that despite this preference, there were detailed exchanges between the State Department, the Foreign Office, and the Soviet Department of Foreign Affairs on the timing of a joint recognition, then agreement among them, as well as with the Canadian representative. Then the four representatives proceeded together to the Quai d'Orsay at 5 PM on October 23 to present their letters of recognition to Foreign Affairs Commissioner Georges Bidault, who thanked them warmly and told them they could now be accredited as ambassadors with no further ado.[73] There appears to have been complete coordination among the Allies.

De Gaulle, the victor, as we have seen, did not allow himself to be impressed.

The tasks before de Gaulle and his government were enormous, given that the infrastructure and the productive facilities in France were worn out if not in ruins, that fighting was continuing in the northeast, and that the political ferment de Gaulle was determined to tamp down was still bubbling throughout the country. On his September tour of the southwest, where the wild acclaim he received reinforced his authority, he flattered and praised the Partisan forces, but made them either join de Lattre de Tassigny's First Army or give up their weapons. The Resistance forces, many of whose spokesman had written of the need for a national revolution and a thorough cleansing of the body politic, and many of whom were communist, never coalesced into a single political movement. The Conseil national de la Résistance faded out of the picture, and in the face of Gaullist insistence on a strong state with control from the center, so did the CDLs—the Comités départementaux de Libération—on which many Resistance leaders had pinned their hopes.[74] The result was that old parties reappeared on the political scene: the much-strengthened Communists, the Socialists, and the weakened Radical Socialists, too linked in the public mind with the despised Third Republic. Along with these a new Christian Democratic Party appeared, forged out of several movements. It would play a leading political role with the Socialists and Communists in the new Fourth Republic in the next few years. A further result was that, in the face of the resurgence of the political parties and their disputes, and the strong position of the Communist Party, which campaigned for a constitution providing legislative supremacy, President de Gaulle did what so many of his American wartime opponents had said he would not do: on January 20, 1946, a Sunday when there were no newspapers, he resigned.

In 1946 he left behind an economy whose recovery had virtually ground to a halt owing to the prolongation of the war, two of the coldest winters on record, and summer drought, all of which had greatly increased the sheer difficulties recovery would have faced even without these complicating factors. To his credit he also left Jean Monnet in a position of power over a new economic planning body that would do much for the economy in the future. The empire, on which de Gaulle had based his rise to power and which he hoped to liberalize so that it would serve to return France to its position as a world power, was in a ferment that would eventually lead to its dissolution. The government over which he had presided was still only provisional: no new constitution was in place, and the one being proposed, which he strongly opposed, was defeated in a referendum on May 5, 1946. Not until the election of a new Constituent Assembly in June, somewhat more conservative than the first, was the resulting draft constitution of the Fourth Republic, again opposed by de Gaulle, accepted in a referendum later in the year.

Whether de Gaulle expected to be called back immediately or not after his resignation in 1946 was never clear; it would take twelve years and one false start—the creation of the Rassemblement du Peuple Français under his leadership in 1948, a movement that failed to achieve majority status—before a crisis in the empire, in North Africa, would bring him back to power in 1958. It was only then that he would finally create a Fifth Republic more to his liking, with a strong executive.

But before de Gaulle left in 1946, he had done what Roosevelt was sure would never happen, and against which Roosevelt had for a long time fought: the Frenchman had led France back into world councils. Roosevelt kept him from attending the Yalta Conference, but with American acquiescence France became one of the four permanent members of the United Nations Security Council and a leading member in all the related international organizations. Roosevelt agreed with Churchill at Yalta to let France be one of the four countries occupying Germany and Austria. It became a member of the European Advisory Commission, and Paris became the site of the long-drawn-out negotiations for European peace treaties. It would soon become the leader of the movement for European unity.

France, militarily weak, economically in ruins, in a world that would rapidly become "bipolar," dominated by the United States and the Soviet Union, had nevertheless, led by de Gaulle, again become a key player in world politics.

Conclusion

AMGOT—Myth or Reality?

A FULL SIXTY YEARS AFTER THE LIBERATION OF PARIS, the influential and respected *Monde Diplomatique* could publish on the front page of its May 2005 issue the article by Sorbonne historian Annie Lacroix-Riz cited in the preface to this book. "The United States," she wrote, referring to the wartime period, "intended that France, together with soon-to-be defeated Italy, Germany, and Japan, was to be part of a protectorate run by the Allied Military Government of the Occupied Territories (Amgot). . . . Amgot would have abolished its national sovereignty, including its right to issue currency." And on French television at about the same time, panelists could agree that General de Gaulle had blocked the Americans from instituting a military government in France, while a French-Canadian publication could take the same position.

Much earlier, in 1954, de Gaulle himself had charged the Americans with planning a military government. In subsequent years, numbers of his supporters came up with their own versions. Jurist André Gros wrote, "De Gaulle, between the fourth and fourteenth of June 1944, settled the sinister issue of AMGOT," and de Gaulle's aide Claude Hettier de Boislambert declared that the Allies planned "a total taking in hand of the administration of France down to the smallest detail. . . . [A]ll the infrastructure of the country would be in the hands of those who would not fail to be quickly called 'our new occupiers.'"[1] Lacroix-Riz's version, so many years

later, is perhaps extreme. Other French sources do not talk of the "aboli-
tion of sovereignty" or of abolishing the "right to issue currency," neither of
which has any basis in fact. But that such a sober publication as the *Monde
Diplomatique* could print such a dubious piece, and that others followed
suit, is an indication of the lasting effect of the outpouring of memoirs in
the years following the liberation of France in the form of articles and
books by French participants in those events.

True, President Roosevelt did, in 1943, talk of an Allied military government to both Winston Churchill and Secretary of State Cordell Hull, and
approved the creation of the military government schools. And until the
bitter end he refused all but a limited form of recognition to the French
Provisional Government. But as this account has shown, he was in no way
actually ready to install a military government in France in June 1944, at
the time of liberation, as so many French writers still seem to think. In
fact, in England, both Allied commanders and French officials were ready
to install a French civil administration as soon as possible. Eisenhower and
his staff—with so much else on their hands—counted on it, and so did the
French. Both were well acquainted with each other's views. Well before
June 6, 1944, there was no longer any question of an Allied military government in France.

Why, then, under these circumstances, did members of the French
Committee of National Liberation subsequently write that they actually
expected President Roosevelt to introduce a military government, but that
he was blocked only at the very last moment? If they did not actually believe he would do it—as their writings at the time seem to indicate—why
in later years did they assert that he would, and why was the view that he
intended to do so as widespread as it became?

Admittedly, the American president, after the unexpected and almost in-
comprehensible collapse of France in 1940, gave the French reason enough
for apprehension.

The American military on the spot in North Africa had much to do
with allowing the Vichy regime to continue in existence there, but it was
Roosevelt who insisted on the military having the authority of an occupying power. He told Free French envoys André Philip and Adrien Tixier two
weeks after the North African landings, in November 1942 that "so long as
the United States was the 'occupying power' in North Africa, the final deci-

sions would be reached solely by the occupying power." He also "expressed it as his policy that until all of France were liberated, the sole decision as to what, if any, Frenchmen would administer the liberated territory *was a matter solely for this government to determine.*"² Which in essence meant that it would take on the role of an occupying power. The point, then, was made clear to de Gaulle's envoys and therefore to de Gaulle himself and those surrounding him at the time. As of late 1942 AMGOT in some form appeared to the Gaullists to be very much in the works. They did not even have to know of Roosevelt's May 1943 telegram to Winston Churchill saying that he thought a military government in France was appropriate, since they had already learned it from him directly.

They also were very much aware that Roosevelt had approved the creation of the schools at Charlottesville and elsewhere in the United States, parallel to the English schools that were turning out civil affairs officers trained to act in France, and that there were detailed civil affairs guidebooks prepared for every French community. As one British historian wrote, "it was at first far from clear that the Civil Affairs organization might not find itself committed to a much more direct form of administration than in fact became necessary."³

Roosevelt's attitude toward France constantly reinforced French apprehensions. After all, he discounted any possibility of a revived France playing an important role in the world after the end of the war, and discussed partially dismembering France and dissolving much of the French empire. He maintained diplomatic relations with the Vichy government for almost three years, and his State Department officials refused for most of that time to make any move that might imply diplomatic relations with the emerging Free French movement, while constantly denigrating de Gaulle's status as a leader. All through the war years, once the president's attention turned to France following the Dakar disaster, which he blamed on de Gaulle's failings, and the affair of Saint Pierre and Miquelon, which led him to distrust de Gaulle, he constantly tried to intervene in, and direct, French affairs, demonstrating at the time what the British historian of civil affairs F. S. V. Donnison called "principled, consistent and implacable hostility to de Gaulle."⁴ If the hapless Admiral Darlan ended up, in Roosevelt's words, a "temporary expedient," Roosevelt or his lieutenants tried to promote Generals de Larminat and Giraud as alternatives to de Gaulle, and later in the game suggested a triumvirate of other Frenchmen to Winston Churchill. General Giraud had, in Roosevelt's eyes, the great advantage of having no pretensions as to creating a French government-in-exile. Roosevelt would repeat on several occasions that no such government would be acceptable. This, of course, put him in direct opposition to General de Gaulle, to whom such a government was absolutely necessary for purposes of defending French interests both during and after the war.

Roosevelt consistently saw to it or suggested that de Gaulle be kept out of major decisions that would affect France, and on numerous occasions tried to interfere directly in French affairs. Reacting to de Gaulle's move to curb Giraud's authority in September 1943, Roosevelt proposed to cut off arms to the French North African army, and was only dissuaded by General Marshall, who knew the French troops were needed by his commanders. It was due to General Eisenhower and to Churchill that the president's directive to Eisenhower to *order* the Gaullist regime in North Africa to desist from trying three Vichyite officials was softened to a suggestion to defer the trials until after the war. In August 1943 the president made the quite extraordinary argument that if de Gaulle moved to dismiss the Vichyite governor Pierre Boisson in Dakar, West Africa, he should actually be opposed by force, and wrote that this was the moment when he might actually break with de Gaulle. It was also in late 1943 that the president wrote Churchill that he saw no reason why France should have any part in the temporary governance of defeated Italy: Roosevelt and Churchill could do a better job without French interference.

Following the formation of the French Committee of National Liberation on June 4, 1943, in Algiers, the new committee called for recognition of its legitimate authority by Allied powers—a move supported by the Allied military commanders and their political advisers in North Africa—but both Churchill and Roosevelt dragged their feet, the latter more than the former. Only after three months did they grudgingly issue their statement recognizing the CFLN, not as a government-in-exile but as an authority for areas that accepted it. It was also shortly after this that Roosevelt wrote Churchill that perhaps they should reconstitute the French National Liberation Committee with members approved by the two of them—in other words, that he and Churchill should decide on the makeup of what was now, in effect, the French government-in-exile—though Roosevelt refused to recognize it as such.

The president also tried to see to it that France would not participate in the new European Advisory Commission, the standing body created at the Moscow conference of 1943 to deal with the problems of the reconstruction of Europe. Only later would the French be allowed to join and to have an occupation zone in Germany. Churchill was forced to agree when Roosevelt decided, in early 1945, that de Gaulle should not be invited to what had been planned as a Four Power conference at Yalta, where major decisions on postwar policy were to be made. The president was determined that in the future France should definitely not sit in on world councils.

Charles de Gaulle, stiff, unyielding, demanding, ungenerous, authoritarian in tendency, with his reliance on the French empire and his exalted view of himself as leader of a restored France set to rejoin the powers, did not do much to make Franklin D. Roosevelt less hostile or less disdainful of his pretensions, although the general tried to explain himself and his democratic aims to Roosevelt on several occasions. It was his pretensions as well as his actions in North Africa, the Middle East, and elsewhere that confirmed what Roosevelt's closest advisers told the president: de Gaulle should not be allowed to try to install himself in power in France, where he was surely not as popular as he thought, and where it would be impossible to dislodge him. His attempt to "seize" power might well result in civil war.

The president and his advisers knew, of course, of how little military power the Free French could bring to bear in comparison to the United States, the United Kingdom, the Soviet Union, and even the Polish government-in-exile, and as a result they saw little reason to pay attention to French demands. What they failed to take into account was that de Gaulle, with so little to contribute, nevertheless had a major aim — the restoration of France — and that the discrepancy between his means and his goals explained both his seemingly exaggerated sensitivity to being slighted and his almost aggressive defense of French interests as he saw them.

As the date for the invasion of Europe came closer, with all the extraordinary problems that it entailed, on the scene in England and in Algiers, we have seen that two developments ensured that there would be no AMGOT in France and that Roosevelt's continued attempts to keep de Gaulle out of power would fail. The first was that Eisenhower, Bedell Smith, and others, those who would actually carry out the liberation of France, were already convinced that only de Gaulle could prevent chaos at the time, and that he had the full support of the Resistance forces, on whose important help they counted, and the support of most of the French public. They knew that the French Provisional Government was ready to take over the administration of the country, a move they actively supported as relieving them of unwanted obligations, and they did their best to persuade President Roosevelt to let them act on this conviction. In this they had the full cooperation of the British. As a result of the president's obstinacy, however, and his singular conviction that de Gaulle's entry into France might provoke civil war, there were real difficulties in determining the roles that Allied civil affairs officers and French MMLA officers would play, particularly within the zone of military operations. Nevertheless, in spite of the president, officials in England went ahead on their own to settle the issues: Gaullist officials would be allowed to take over and administer French liberated territories as soon as possible—and they knew it.

The second development was one that would permit the swift Gaullist takeover of power in liberated areas. In Algiers the CFLN had created an embryo administration that could be almost immediately installed within France from top to bottom. Eisenhower knew of this and let the French know he wanted them to carry out their intentions. It is true that when François Coulet began to exercise his authority as the first regional commissioner of the French Provisional Government within Normandy shortly after the landings, Roosevelt, at his press conference on June 23, 1944, ten days after Coulet's installation, told the press it was much too early to do such a thing. It should wait until much larger areas of France were liberated. Presumably he thought that civil affairs officers should be taking over local administration, something the SHAEF offices in London had long ago rejected. The president's statement, however, had no effect: SHAEF officials had communicated their views to the French involved in the matter, including Hettier de Boislambert, head of the Mission militaire de Liaison administrative, and allowed the CFLN officials to take over administration whenever territories were liberated.

There was, in addition, never any intent to follow the AMGOT model used in Sicily, where military government personnel had their own separate line of command, and where they actually took over an administration that had faded away. What is crucial is that, as their numerous memos indicate, French officials in London knew all of this. In January 1944 Pierre Laroque, who was in control of planning for civil affairs in London, wrote to de Gaulle in Algiers that he had come to realize that no AMGOT was intended for France, so there was no need to block it. He and other French officials also knew of the Allies' determination to leave administration to the French as soon as military conditions permitted. It is worth noting that in March 1944 Hettier de Boislambert wrote, "Allied intervention in what concerns French administration and civilian population will be limited as soon as Allied command is convinced that military operation will not be hampered by installation of civilian authority."[5] The main point of contention was over authority within the military zone, but once Boislambert pointed out to Brigadier General Lee that the sections in the "Civil Affairs Handbook" dealing with this were unacceptable, infringing, as he saw them, on French sovereignty, they were immediately amended to satisfy him. The diplomatic flap over Roosevelt's insistence that the word "may" remain in his March 15, 1944, directive to Eisenhower rather than the word "should," as to whether Eisenhower was to empower the CFLN to appoint civilian personnel, had little effect except to annoy people. Bt contrast, Cordell Hull's April 9, 1944, speech to the effect that French civil authority should be established as rapidly as possible, and that the CFLN was the obvious organization to do so, reassured everyone in England. Once the landings had taken place, no one in the Allied camp tried to keep CFLN personnel from taking on the administrative roles assigned to them, even if President Roosevelt declared to the press that their actions were premature.

In the light of all these developments, why the discrepancy between what Gaullist officials wrote in memos, letters, and telegrams about American aims and activities around the time of liberation and what they were to write later in their memoirs? Those memoirs would both create and perpetuate what was essentially a myth that influenced both historians and public officials in their negative views of American policy and contributed to the widespread anti-Americanism that has continued to flourish in France.

The answer, it would seem, lies in the necessity for de Gaulle and his immediate entourage to bring together French citizens with disparate views on what was to be done and how it was to be done, to create among all of them the sense that de Gaulle's committee was the legitimate representative for all Frenchmen, and that among all the clashing personalities and ideologies, salvation for France lay in following General de Gaulle. For the Gaullists, one part of the overall strategy in bringing this about lay in creating an external common enemy—the Allied governments—and in arguing that it was only due to de Gaulle's efforts that France was saved from their machinations. If it was necessary to exaggerate, distort somewhat, or enhance their accounts of what happened, so be it.

In contrast to earlier histories, at least two more recent works by French historians cited in this book now accept this conclusion. One is by Jean-Louis Crémieux-Brilhac, a historian who escaped from a German prison camp in 1941 and joined de Gaulle in London. There he served as secretary to the propaganda committee of the Free French and prepared broadcasts to France. Some fifty years later, in his history of the Free French movement, he concludes, on the basis of much that has been cited in this book, that the menace of an AMGOT "that obsessed us for months" in London and angered de Gaulle was a "collective phantasm," fed by Roosevelt, and blown up out of all proportion by the French because it had the advantage of unifying around the CFLN all the factions in Algiers and in the Resistance. De Gaulle wanted the verbally contested sovereignty of his Provisional Government to appear to have been wrenched from the Allies by an immense struggle.[6]

André Kaspi, a Sorbonne historian and director of the research center on American history, wrote in the first, 1995 edition of *La Libération de la France,* "A shadow of mystery floats over the acronym AMGOT that solid studies may someday dissipate." But he also asserts that "Roosevelt had never really decided on an AMGOT for France, but rather . . . it was an *épouvantail* [a scarecrow] that he waved around when he wanted to show that he had not relaxed his stubbornness and that de Gaulle took up when he wanted to rally French unity behind him."[7]

While there were genuine conflicts with the Allies, Crémieux-Brilhac concludes, the real victory for the Free French was not stopping a planned AMGOT but the conquest of opinion in France and the unification of the disparate Resistance forces, jealous of their autonomy. It started with the initial act of June 18, 1940, and continued through the actions of a handful of audacious volunteers, then the daring act of incorporating the communists, the maturing of a democratic program of reforms, the creation of a "clandestine state," and finally the actual activities at the time of liberation.

In short, the menace of an AMGOT for France, perhaps real in the early years of the war, was in the end mainly a Gaullist myth, built on the foundation of President Roosevelt's unrealistic aim of installing a military government and his very real personal opposition to de Gaulle, used by the Gaullist movement to rally French opinion. But it had its lasting effect by helping to create in the postwar years a negative influence on Franco-

American relations, which after all, across the centuries, have never been smooth.

The France of Louis XVI may have given crucial help to the American Revolution, and France in that period drew fervent admiration from such Americans as Benjamin Franklin and Thomas Jefferson. Yet a few years later the two nations fought an undeclared naval war. The nineteenth century gave rise—despite Tocqueville—to the French image of a surging America as a nation of money-grubbers, while the Americans largely saw the French as a frivolous nation who deserved their loss to the more energetic and industrious Germans in 1870. In the years that followed, however, newly wealthy Americans viewed France as a place of gracious living and artistic merit, while the French sent America the Statue of Liberty, and both came to distrust German bluster and militarism. A resident American community in Paris with all the institutions of an American small town helped bring about, at the outbreak of the Great War of 1914, an outpouring of private American support for France, and eventually, of course, there came an American intervention that probably saved the Allies from defeat.

But frictions developed over postwar policy, over the Treaty of Versailles, and, most important, over the U.S. Senate's rejection of a security treaty signed with a France that feared a German resurgence in the future. American doughboys left France either impressed by what they had seen and eager to come back or bitterly critical of the French, with little realization that the war in the west had been fought primarily on French soil and that the French had suffered ten times the casualties that the Americans had. The "Lost Generation" of the 1920s and thirsty Americans rediscovered a freer France during Prohibition. Then the Great Depression brought France's repudiation of its war debt to the United States, to the anger of Americans—and a French view of an American Shylock insisting on its pound of flesh—and then brought to the French the dismal spectacle of an American retreat into legislated isolation based on a strong sense that Americans had been lured into a conflict that was none of their business and that they must never fight a land war in Europe again. The French could not count on American help in 1939.

For Americans, the collapse of France in June 1940 revealed the inherent weakness of the French. To the French, the lack of American support mirrored the situation in World War I, when the United States waited three years to enter the conflict, which had, of course, already exhausted the French. The antagonism between the Free French and the Roosevelt administration remained mainly at the governmental level, and de Gaulle became generally popular in American media. But there is little question—and numerous historians of the period confirm it—that the wartime conflicts colored de Gaulle's persistent view of the British and Americans. In 1950 he welcomed the North Atlantic Treaty, with its guarantee that an attack on one party to the treaty constituted an attack on all. But he opposed the American attempt to insist on creation of a European army in 1953, and in 1966, to American annoyance, he insisted that NATO headquarters be moved out of France and withdrew from its command structure. Earlier, when he returned to power in 1958, he had been rebuffed by President Eisenhower over his suggestion for tripartite control over nuclear weapons policy, and he therefore moved to create the French nuclear Force de Frappe. He could not depend on an American-controlled nuclear retaliatory force for security. Independence of policy was a necessity. In 1963 he vetoed British entry into the European Common Market: Britain would be a stalking horse for the Anglo-Americans.

In many respects this postwar record mirrored the attitude de Gaulle had developed during the war: he could not trust others to take into account vital French interests. Only an independent France could do so. De Gaulle's actions also reflected widespread popular French views. If the French celebrated liberation by the Allies in 1944, they never forgot the vast damage and innumerable French casualties that American bombing and the fighting had caused.[8] If America had brought Marshall Plan aid, it had also tried to bully the French into accepting a European army in which national armed forces would be merged. Despite strong pressure from the Eisenhower administration, the French parliament rejected the treaty that would have created it. Then, when the French and English attacked Egypt for having nationalized the Suez Canal in 1956, the Americans forced them to withdraw, an act they never forgot. Just as the French had lamented the "Americanization" of their society in the 1920s, they did so again in the 1960s. The behavior of American tourists in the first two postwar decades, with all the money they had to throw around in comparison to the French, still rebuilding from the impoverishment caused by the war, did little to help.

The litany of grievances could continue. It would perhaps conclude with the reasoned refusal of the French to help with the American attack on Iraq in 2003, which caused a media outburst of anti-French bitterness in the United States, where, it would seem in addition, the administration took little account of the historical record on the needs of military government. To the French, the invasion simply looked like another misuse of America's overwhelming force.

In other words, across the years after World War II an atmosphere existed in France in which French claims about American intentions to impose AMGOT on France back in 1944 could and did flourish. Serious historiography has only recently begun to dispel these claims.

Did Roosevelt want a military government for France for six months or a year? Well, yes, maybe, more or less. The main support for the idea that he did is in his somewhat off-the-cuff comments to Churchill and Hull and in the curriculum at the military government training schools. There were also the frequent reiterations that no government created *outside* French territory would be recognized. Did he plan for it? Not really. As newspaper commentators reiterated, there was no way the Americans could organize free elections in France. The French would have to do it. The president could envisage the Allied commander in chief giving orders to French administrators through civil affairs officers, but the "local authorities" doctrine meant that administrators would indeed be French, and he never really thought through what it would mean to have the Allied commander in chief act as military governor. General Eisenhower certainly had no intention of doing so, and the original draft of his June 6, 1944, speech to the French—the one for which the State Department submitted the new draft unacceptable to de Gaulle—clearly indicates this.

The myth of an American military government in liberated France persists in French memories. But my dinner companion of so many years ago who first piqued my interest when he told me he had turned back that boatload of American military government personnel ready to govern France was, in fact, mythologizing. It could not and did not happen that way.

Notes

Introduction

1. President Roosevelt to British Prime Minister (Churchill), in U.S. Department of State, *Foreign Relations of the United States: Diplomatic Papers, 1943, Europe*, vol. 2 (France) (Washington, D.C.: U.S. Government Printing Office, 1964), 111–12; hereafter *FRUS 1943*.
2. Cordell Hull, *The Memoirs of Cordell Hull* (New York: Macmillan, 1948), 1245.
3. Alfred D. Chandler, ed., *The Papers of Dwight David Eisenhower: The War Years*, vol. 3 (Baltimore: Johns Hopkins University Press, 1970), 1913.
4. Ibid., 1908. Some accounts have it that the note was discovered when Eisenhower's shirt was being put in the wash, others that he put it in his billfold and subsequently passed it on.
5. Quoted in André Kaspi, *La Libération de la France* (Paris: Perrin, 2004), 56. Others quote it, but not de Gaulle.
6. Charles de Gaulle, *Mémoires de guerre*, 3 vols. (Paris: Plon, 1956), 2:211–12.
7. Ibid., 297–98.
8. André Gros, "Le Quai d'Orsay," *Espoir*, no. 92 (June 1993): 54.
9. Diane de Bellescize, "L'Interime gouvernemental des secrétaires généraux," in *Le Retablissement de la légalité républicaine, 1944: Actes de Colloque, 6/18/1994* (Paris: Complexe, 1996), 94.
10. Claude Hettier de Boislambert, *Les Fers de l'espoir* (Paris: Plon, 1978), 425–26.
11. Charles-Louis Foulon, "Les États-Unis et la France Combattante," *Espoir*, no. 26 (March 1979): 66.
12. De Gaulle, *Mémoires*, 3:339.
13. François Coulet, *Vertu des temps difficiles* (Paris: Plon, 1967), 117.

1. America and the Fall of France

1. Basil Liddell Hart, "The Military Strategist," in *Churchill Revised: A Critical Assessment*, ed. A. J. P. Taylor (New York: Dial Press, 1969), 206.
2. John Lukacs, *The Duel: 10 May–31 July 1940* (New York: Ticknor & Fields, 1991), 63.

3. On the relative size of air forces, see Jean Monnet, *Mémoires* (Paris: Fayard, 1976), 157, where a balance sheet from early 1940 claims a German bomber superiority over the two Allies of two to one and a fighter superiority of three to two, but says nothing of the quality of the planes. This convinced Monnet of the urgent need for purchases from the United States, but contrasts enormously with the wild estimates of German superiority issued by defeatist French leaders in 1940. Postwar figures revealed in French parliamentary inquiries show an actual superiority of the Allies in numbers of usable aircraft, and an inexplicable failure to use them. See, for example, Orville Bullitt, ed., *For the President: Personal and Secret: Correspondence between Franklin D. Roosevelt and William C. Bullitt* (Boston: Houghton Mifflin, 1972), 421.

4. Will Brownell and Richard N. Billings, *So Close to Greatness: A Biography of William C. Bullitt* (New York: Macmillan, 1987), 231.

5. François Coulet, *Vertu des temps difficiles* (Paris: Plon, 1967), 69, points out also that Russian weaknesses revealed in the Winter War with Finland also helped convince Hitler he could easily beat the Russians.

6. Ernest R. May, *Strange Victory: Hitler's Conquest of France* (New York: Hill and Wang, 2000), 287.

7. Bullitt, *For the President*, 428.

8. Cordell Hull, *Memoirs of Cordell Hull* (New York: Macmillan, 1948), 768.

9. On Reynaud's "ten-to-one" claim, see Bullitt, *For the President*, 419. Debate still continues over the causes of the French defeat and the rapid German victory. French military leaders ascribed it to a lack of modern arms caused in part by worker laziness resulting from 1936 Popular Front legislation curbing working hours and establishing paid vacations. But as early as July 1941, German general Kurt Liebmann, argued in the *Militär Wochenblatt* that French tanks were better protected and more robust than German tanks and could have been used in existing French autonomous mechanized and motorized units. The Allies at the time could field more divisions than the Germans. What was lacking was a faith in the usefulness of French weapons, an unwillingness to use them properly, a disastrous lack of communications, a failure of strategy. In other words, the failure was that of the French High Command. The view is widely shared today. See Hervé Alphand, quoting Liebmann, in *L'Étonnement d'être* (Paris: Fayard, 1977), 89.

10. Quoted in Jean Marc de Foville, *L'Entrée des Allemands à Paris* (Paris: Calman Levy, 1965), 256.

11. Charles de Gaulle, *Mémoires de guerre*, 3 vols. (Paris: Plon, 1956), 2:45.

12. U.S. Department of State, *Foreign Relations of the United States: Diplomatic Papers, 1940, Europe*, vol. 2 (France) (Washington, D.C.: U.S. Government Printing Office, 1957), 462; hereafter *FRUS 1940*. Albert Lebrun, the president, and Marshal Pétain, the new prime minister, told Bullitt that they expected Germany to crush England rapidly. Admiral Darlan, who smiled when Bullitt asked him if he took pleasure in this prospect, also told Bullitt "he felt certain that

Hitler would attack the United States shortly after disposing of England and equally certain that the defenses of the United States would prove as vulnerable as those of England," 465–66. Other members of the French government told Bullitt virtually the same thing.

13. Nerin E. Gun, *Les Secrets des archives américaines: Pétain, Laval, de Gaulle* (Paris: Albin Michel, 1979), 44.

14. Anthony Eden, *The Reckoning: The Memoirs of Anthony Eden* (Boston: Houghton Mifflin, 1965), 133.

15. Duff Cooper, *Old Men Forget* (London: Rupert Hart-Davis, 1953), 284.

16. Harold Macmillan, *The Blast of War* (London: Macmillan, 1967), 81.

17. Eden, *The Reckoning,* 123, 211.

18. See Monnet, *Mémoires,* 180.

19. In March 1940 Arnold, hoping to minimize the shipments to Europe, testified before a predominantly isolationist Congress that supplying England and France would be at the expense of Air Corps growth and development. As a result Arnold had been kept out of vital negotiations by President Roosevelt. See Major General John W. Huston, *American Airpower Comes of Age: General Henry "Hap" Arnold's World War II Diaries* (Maxwell Air Force Base, Ala.: Air University Press, 2002), "Biography," passim.

20. See, for example, the arguments analyzed in Julian G. Hurstfield, *America and the French Nation* (Chapel Hill: University of North Carolina Press, 1986), chap. 2.

21. François Kersaudy, *De Gaulle et Churchill* (Paris: Perrin, 2003), 274. Roosevelt's sometimes casual manner of suggesting unusual moves occasionally concealed a strong opinion but often reflected his sometimes flippant approach to a complicated issue he didn't want to deal with at the moment.

22. Quoted in Mario Rossi, *Roosevelt and the French* (Westport: Praeger, 1993), 79, who also describes in detail Roosevelt's experiences and attitudes toward France and Pétain (1–11, 69–71).

23. There is still discussion as to whether this was even possible, given the lack of any planning, the chaos, and the shortage of shipping and materiel. Pétain argued that such a transfer would so enrage the Germans that they would refuse an armistice. The complete disarray in the government at the time, many have argued, made it impossible for it to act.

24. Claude Hettier de Boislambert, *Les Fers de l'espoir* (Paris: Plon, 1978), 208.

25. Ibid., 178.

26. On the *Times* article, see Jean-Louis Crémieux-Brilhac, *La France Libre* (Paris: Gallimard, 2001), 65–66.

27. Henri Michel, *Paris allemand* (Paris: Albin Michel, 1981), 50.

28. See Boislambert, *Les Fers de l'espoir,* 183–84.

29. Geoffroy de Courcel quoted by General Jean Simon, "Allocution sur la mort de Geoffroy de Courcel," *Espoir,* no. 92 (June 1993): 105.

30. Monnet, *Mémoires,* 151–52.

31. See Crémieux-Brilhac, *La France Libre,* 74–75, who notes that in his *Mémoires de Gaulle* gave short shrift to this premature, failed attempt and did not reprint the text of his broadcast.

32. See Curtis Cate, *Antoine de Saint-Exupéry: His Life and Times* (London: Heineman, 1970), 415.

33. Labarthe, a constant opponent of Vichy, published a review called *La France Libre.* As time went by, it became more and more critical of the general, and Labarthe subsequently joined in moves with others in London to oust him. See Guy Perrier, *Le Colonel Passy et les services secrets de la France Libre* (Paris: Hachette, 1999), 65–66.

34. Alphand, *L'Étonnement d'être,* 106.

35. Crémieux-Brilhac, *La France Libre,* 111, 133.

36. Coulet, *Vertu,* 73.

37. E. Burrin des Roziers, "Hommage à Geoffroy de Courcel," *Espoir,* no. 92 (June 1993): 30.

38. *FRUS 1940,* vol. 2 (France), 452, 456, 458.

39. Christine Levisse-Touzé, *L'Afrique du nord dans la guerre, 1939–1945* (Paris: Albin-Michel, 1998), 128.

40. Jean Bouton, *De Mers-el-Kébir à Londres* (Paris: Plon, 1980), 111.

41. Quoted ibid., 126.

42. Ibid., 111.

43. Cate, *Saint-Exupéry,* 412.

44. *FRUS 1940,* vol. 2 (France), 470; and see also Pierre Queille, *Histoire diplomatique de Vichy* (Paris: Albatros, 1976), who details in chap. 2 the events surrounding Mers-el-Kébir, the violent reactions of some elements at Vichy, the German attempt to gain control of the French empire, and resultant crises.

45. Quoted in an interview in *Espoir,* no. 92 (June 1993): 24.

46. Coulet, *Vertu,* 116.

47. Eden, *The Reckoning,* 431.

48. U.S. Department of State, *Foreign Relations of the United States: Diplomatic Papers, 1941, Europe,* vol. 2 (France) (Washington, D.C.: U.S. Government Printing Office, 1959), 119; hereafter *FRUS 1941.*

49. His view of the disorder in the Gaullist camp is corroborated by many, including Hervé Alphand, a high official in the Third Republic who became a member of the Gaullist hierarchy. Alphand wrote that on his arrival at Gaullist headquarters in London in 1941, "his French friends painted the darkest picture of what he would find: jealousies, personal quarrels, political plots." Alphand, *L'Étonnement d'être,* 88.

50. *FRUS 1943,* vol. 2 (France), 76.

51. William D. Leahy, *I Was There* (New York: McGraw-Hill, 1950), 43.

52. Ibid., 43.

53. Quoted in Jean-Paul Cointet, *Pierre Laval* (Paris: Fayard, 1993), 420.

54. Crémieux-Brilhac, *La France Libre,* 452–53. Among these was a message from

the outstanding French parliamentarian and former minister Georges Mandel, who argued that the American opposition and British hesitation could do nothing but give comfort to the enemy and confuse French opinion.

55. Charles Bohlen, *Witness to History: 1929–1969* (New York: Norton, 1973), 206.

56. Eden, *The Reckoning*, 519.

57. Leahy, *I Was There*, 235.

58. Quoted in Anthony Beevor and Artemis Cooper, *Paris after the Liberation* (London: Penguin, 1995), 122.

59. Harold Ickes, *Diary*, July 28, 1945, quoted in Hurstfield, *America*, 92.

60. For a fuller discussion, see chapter 2.

61. Breckinridge Long, *The War Diaries of Breckinridge Long* (Lincoln: University of Nebraska Press, 1966), 240, 294, 305, 354.

62. Adolf A. Berle, *Navigating the Rapids* (New York: Harcourt, Brace, 1973), 413; *FRUS 1943*, vol. 2 (France), 169–71.

63. Berle, *Navigating the Rapids*, 455.

64. Eden, *The Reckoning*, 394.

65. *FRUS 1941*, vol. 2 (France), 205.

66. Hurstfield, *America*, 113; François Charles-Roux, "Bataille pour des principes," *Espoir*, no. 27 (June 1979): 5.

67. Memorandum, January 20, 1944, H. F. Matthews files, General Records of the Department of State, Bureau of European Affairs, Record Group 59, National Archives, Washington, D.C.

68. Hull, *Memoirs*, 1159, 1160.

69. Hull listed all of the presumed consequences of recognizing de Gaulle in his *Memoirs:* a complete break with Vichy, withdrawal of embassy and consular staffs, leaving the field clear to collaborationists, rupture of fruitful relations with General Weygand in North Africa, and withdrawal of personnel in Morocco, Tunisia, and Algeria. He also made a rather startling remark that it would be contrary to the American principle of noninterference in the internal affairs of another country! Hull, *Memoirs*, 961.

70. Ibid., 961–62; letter quoted in Hurstfield, *America*, 135.

71. Hull, *Memoirs*, 962.

72. Leahy, *I Was There*, 143.

73. Hurstfield, *America*, 112, 107.

74. Both dispatches are quoted in Gun, *Secrets*, 94.

75. Raoul Aglion, "The Free French and the United States from 1940 to 1944," in *De Gaulle and the United States*, ed. Robert O. Paxton and Nicholas Wahl (Oxford: Berg Publishers, 1994), 33.

76. Ibid., 41. See also Hurstfield, *America*, 85; Crémieux-Brilhac, *La France Libre*, 350.

77. Conversation with chargé d'affaires Murphy, July 29, 1940, in *FRUS 1940*, vol. 2 (France), 379.

78. Hurstfield, *America*, chap. 4, passim.

79. René Cassin, *Les Hommes partis de rien* (Paris: Plon, 1975), 210, 289.
80. Crémieux-Brilhac, *La France Libre*, 345.
81. Aglion, "The Free French and the United States," 41, writes of forty thousand refugees. Crémieux-Brilhac, *La France Libre*, 350, cites a much smaller number, eight or nine thousand.
82. Henri de Kerillis to de Gaulle, February 17, 1941, quoted in Hurstfield, *America*, 104.
83. Quoted in Cate, *Saint-Exupéry*, 460.
84. Ibid., 449.
85. Aglion, "The Free French and the United States," 36. See also the biography by Jean-Luc Barré, *Jacques and Raïssa Maritain: Beggars for Heaven* (Notre Dame: University of Notre Dame Press, 2006), in which the author points out that Maritain was nevertheless instrumental in obtaining visas for many intellectuals, including Gaullists.
86. Alphand, *L'Étonnement d'être*, 138.
87. Henri de Kerillis, *Français, voici la vérité!* (New York: Éditions de la Maison Française, 1942), passim.
88. Henri de Kerillis, *De Gaulle dictateur* (Montreal: Librairie Beauchemin, 1945), passim.
89. See Jacques Habert, "Les Journaux de la France Combattante: *Pour la Victoire et France Amérique*," http://bardina.org/journfroo.html.
90. Crémieux-Brilhac, *La France Libre*, 1207.
91. Alphand, *L'Étonnement d'être*, 144.
92. Crémieux Brilhac, *La France Libre*, 364.

2. Positions Defined

1. Charles de Gaulle, *Mémoires de guerre*, 3 vols. (Paris: Plon, 1954), 1:270.
2. See Charles-Roux, "Batailles pour des principes," *Espoir*, no. 27 (June, 1979): 11.
3. *FRUS 1943*, 2:23.
4. Boislambert, who had come ashore undetected and was in Dakar at the time, argues in his memoirs that there were enough anti-Vichyites in the town, several of whom he had rallied, so that with a little more effort Dakar could have been taken, but that the British, in particular, were reluctant participants in the whole effort. Boislambert was captured, imprisoned, and sent to France, where he was condemned to death, but escaped to rejoin de Gaulle in England. Claude Hettier de Boislambert, *Les Fers de l'espoir* (Paris: Plon, 1978), 244–50.
5. Jean-Louis Crémieux-Brilhac, *La France Libre* (Paris: Gallimard, 2001), 157–58; François Kersaudy, *De Gaulle et Churchill* (Paris: Perrin, 2001), 103–4; Christopher S. Thompson, "Prologue to Conflict," in *De Gaulle and the United States*, ed. Robert O. Paxton and Nicholas Wahl (Oxford: Berg Publishers, 1994), 27–28.

6. Thompson, "Prologue to Conflict," 27.

7. Christine Levisse-Touzé, *L'Afrique dans la guerre, 1939–1945* (Paris: Albin Michel, 1990), 128.

8. Robert D. Murphy, *Diplomat among Warriors* (Garden City, N.Y.: Doubleday, 1964), 76.

9. Don Cook, *Charles de Gaulle: A Biography* (New York: G. P. Putnam's Sons, 1983), 113.

10. Gabriel Auphan and Jacques Mordai, *La Marine française dans la seconde guerre mondiale* (Paris: France Empire, 1976), 290.

11. Hettier de Boislambert, *Les Fers de l'espoir*, 255.

12. Crémieux-Brilhac, *La France Libre,* 167, citing both de Gaulle's and Catroux's memoirs. De Gaulle's salutations to Catroux were unusually effusive. See de Gaulle, *Mémoires,* 1:290–92.

13. Text in de Gaulle, *Mémoires,* 1:304. It is cited as Order no. 1.

14. Ibid., 313–17.

15. Crémieux-Brilhac, *La France Libre,* 184. Crémieux-Brilhac also notes, however, that de Gaulle's attempts at what were essentially diplomatic contacts with other countries were reined in by the British government.

16. Arthur Layton Funk, *Charles de Gaulle: The Crucial Years, 1943–1944* (Norman: University of Oklahoma Press, 1959), 10–11.

17. Crémieux-Brilhac, *La France Libre,* 199. The Free French husband of American reporter Dorothy Tartière was shot in the back by Vichy Frenchmen while returning to his own side after he had approached them when they flew a white flag to parley. See Dorothy Tartière with M. R. Werner, *A House near Paris* (New York: Simon & Schuster, 1946), 314–19.

18. Quoted in Anthony Eden, *The Reckoning: The Memoirs of Anthony Eden* (Boston: Houghton Mifflin, 1965), 220.

19. François Coulet, "Indépendance et Libération, 1940–1945," *Espoir,* no. 27 (June 1979): 113.

20. Quoted as having been said to General Paul Legentilhomme, in Crémieux-Brilhac, *La France Libre,* 211.

21. Duff Cooper, *Old Men Forget* (London: Rupert Hart-Davis, 1953), 321–22.

22. Henri Michel, *Darlan* (Paris: Hachette, 1986), 352.

23. Coulet, *Vertu,* 114–15.

24. Kersaudy, *De Gaulle et Churchill,* 147–48.

25. Eden, *The Reckoning,* 290.

26. Hervé Alphand, *L'Étonnement d'être* (Paris: Fayard, 1977), 88, 109.

27. Press clipping, April 28, 1944, 72/AJ/609, Archives nationales, Paris.

28. Quoted in Kersaudy, *De Gaulle,* 174.

29. David Schoenbrun, *The Three Lives of Charles de Gaulle* (New York: Atheneum, 1966), 110.

30. Crémieux-Brilhac, *La France Libre,* 369.

31. *FRUS 1941*, vol. 2 (France), 498–500.

32. Ibid., 562.

33. Ibid., 551.

34. Cordell Hull, *The Memoirs of Cordell Hull* (New York: Macmillan, 1948) 1134.

35. Cook, *Charles de Gaulle*, 143.

36. Crémieux-Brilhac, *La France Libre*, 404. In fact Roosevelt did consider that after the war New Caledonia should harbor an American base.

37. Kersaudy, *De Gaulle*, 193; and see Crémieux-Brilhac, *La France Libre*, 421.

38. Crémieux-Brillac, *La France Libre*, 483.

39. Quoted in Milton Viorst, *Hostile Allies: FDR and de Gaulle* (New York: Macmillan, 1965), 91.

40. The incident is described in Mario Rossi, *Roosevelt and the French* (Westport: Praeger, 1993), 86.

41. Crémieux-Brilhac, *La France Libre*, 546–47, gives a verbatim account of the conversation.

42. De Gaulle's aide Claude Hettier de Boislambert argues that the failure to land in Tunisia led to heavy losses, and that if de Gaulle had been in on the whole operation, which his forces could have supported, losses would have been further minimized. Boislambert, *Les Fers de l'espoir*, 404. The assertion is problematic. Christine Levisse-Touzé, in *L'Afrique dans la guerre, 1939–1945*, 223, writes that the disciplined army of Africa "manifested an unwavering fidelity to the marshal," and the same was true of the navy and the air force, from which only three pilots defected to the resistance. The inability of General Giraud, brought to Africa by the Americans to stop the fighting—because he did not represent Pétain—speaks further to this point of the loyal Pétainism of the officers.

43. Quoted in Funk, *Charles de Gaulle*, 32.

44. William D. Leahy, *I Was There* (New York: McGraw-Hill, 1950), 133.

45. A detailed account of all the maneuvers is in Hal Vaughan, *FDR's Twelve Apostles* (Guilford, Conn.: Lyons Press, 2006), passim.

46. Nerin E. Gun, *Les Secrets des archives américaines: Pétain, Laval, de Gaulle* (Paris: Albin Michel, 1979), 326.

47. Kersaudy, *De Gaulle*, 222.

48. See, for example, Jean-Baptiste Duroselle, *Politique étrangère de la France: L'abîme, 1939–1944* (Paris: Imprimerie Nationale, 1986), 421–22, 459–60.

49. Gun, *Les Secrets*, 338.

50. Ibid., 318.

51. See G. Ward Price, *Giraud and the African Scene* (New York: Macmillan, 1944), 260.

52. Historian Jean-Baptiste Duroselle states flatly, "Nothing serious had been done to avoid French resistance." Duroselle, *Politique étrangère*, 484. Pinning hopes on Giraud was a mirage. This is hardly fair to Murphy's strenuous efforts. See Vaughan, *FDR's Twelve Apostles*, passim.

53. See Michel, *Darlan,* passim; and Alphand, *L'Étonnement d'être,* 78.

54. U.S. Department of State, *Foreign Relations of the United States: Diplomatic Papers, 1942; Europe,* vol. 2 (France) (Washington, D.C.: U.S. Government Printing Office, 1962), 404; hereafter *FRUS 1942.*

55. Dwight D. Eisenhower, *Crusade in Europe* (New York: Doubleday, Permabooks Edition, 1952), 133. It may be noted that shortly after the American landings, men around Pétain tried to get him to take the opportunity to fly to North Africa—a plane was held in readiness for him—where he could take command of French forces on the Allied side. He refused. See Jean Paul Cointet, *Pierre Laval* (Paris: Fayard, 1993), 413.

56. *FRUS 1942,* vol. 2 (France), 447. Marshall also suggested that interned Free French and Jews and others not be released precipitously, since they might disturb operations. Eisenhower would see to alleviating their situation later.

57. See Michel, *Darlin,* 352, who goes on to say that "only he [Darlan] could resolve the crisis of conscience that paralyzed the military of North Africa."

58. Ibid., 361.

59. Alphand, *L'Étonnement d'être,* 129–30.

60. Telegram to London, December 15, 1942, F/1a/3715, Archives nationales, Paris.

61. Alphand, *L'Étonnement d'être,* 129.

62. Régine Torrent, *La France américaine: Controverses de la libération* (Brussels: Éditions Racine, 2004), 118.

63. Kersaudy, *De Gaulle,* 229.

64. Quoted in Julian G. Hurstfield, *America and the French Nation* (Chapel Hill: University of North Carolina Press, 1986), 167.

65. *FRUS 1942,* vol. 2 (France), 446–47.

66. Torrent, *La France américaine,* 119.

67. *FRUS 1942,* vol. 2 (France), 482.

68. Annie Lacroix-Riz, "How to Manage the Peace: When the U.S. Wanted to Take Over France," *Monde Diplomatique* (May 2003): 1.

69. Harold Macmillan, *The Blast of War* (London: Macmillan, 1967), 428.

70. Hull, *Memoirs,* 1202.

71. Quoted in Kersaudy, *De Gaulle,* 224.

72. The text is in de Gaulle, *Mémoires,* 1:672.

73. Alphand, now in London as aide-de-camp to de Gaulle, kept a diary of these events; see Hervé Alphand, "Bataille pour des principes," *Espoir,* no. 27 (June 1979): 4–18.

74. Crémieux-Brillac, *France Libre,* 573–75.

75. F/1a/3715, Archives nationales, Paris.

76. Rossi, *Roosevelt and the French,* 102–4.

77. Telegram, December 18, 1942, F/1a/3715, Archives nationales, Paris.

78. Pierre Queille, *Histoire diplomatique de Vichy* (Paris: Albatros, 1976), 227, n. 5.

79. Leahy, *I Was There,* 142; F/1a/3836, folder 112, Archives nationales, Paris.

80. See Queuille, *Histoire diplomatique de Vichy*, 286–87.
81. Funk, *Charles de Gaulle*, 48–50; Vaughan, *Twelve Apostles*, passim.
82. René Massigli, *Une Comédie des erreurs, 1943–1956*, (Paris: Plon, 1978), 23; Macmillan, *The Blast of War*, passim.

3. Giraud, de Gaulle, and the Committee of French National Liberation

1. François Kersaudy, *De Gaulle et Churchill* (Paris: Perrin, 2003), 246, quoting Robert Murphy.
2. *FRUS 1943*, vol. 2 (France), 24.
3. *FRUS 1942*, vol. 2 (France), 500–501; emphasis added.
4. On the extent of Vichy influence in North Africa under Giraud, see Henry Queuille, *Histoire diplomatique de Vichy* (Paris: Albatros, 1976), 286–87.
5. Jean-Louis Crémieux-Brilhac, *La France Libre* (Paris: Gallimard, 2001), 600.
6. Elliott Roosevelt, *As He Saw It* (New York: Duell, Sloan, Pierce, 1946), 91.
7. Jean-Baptiste Duroselle, *Politique étrangère de la France: L'abîme 1939–1944* (Paris: Imprimerie Nationale, 1982), 476.
8. See Charles-Louis Foulon, "Les États Unis et la France Combattante," *Espoir*, no. 26 (March, 1979): 64, which compiles a list of Roosevelt's views that led to French distrust. In January 1944 Roosevelt repeated his view that Indochina must pass under international trusteeship. U.S. Department of State, *Foreign Relations of the United States: Diplomatic Papers, 1944, Europe*, vol. 3 (France) (Washington, D.C.: U.S. Government Printing Office, 1966), 773; hereafter *FRUS 1944*.
9. Nerin E. Gun, *Les Secrets des archives américaines: Pétain, Laval, de Gaulle* (Paris: Albin Michel, 1979), 337–38.
10. Harold Macmillan, *The Blast of War* (London: Macmillan, 1967), 250–51.
11. Crémieux-Brilhac, *La France Libre*, 599.
12. François Charles-Roux, "Batailles pour des principes," *Espoir*, no. 27 (June 1979): 11–12. Typically, Cordell Hull in his *Memoirs* refers to de Gaulle's "almost frantic efforts to fly to Algeria for a conference with General Giraud." Cordell Hull, *The Memoirs of Cordell Hull* (New York: Macmillan, 1948), 1216.
13. William D. Hassett, *Off the Record with F.D.R.: 1942–1945* (New Brunswick: Rutgers University Press, 1958), 153.
14. Hull, *Memoirs*, 1208. At least one historian, Milton Viorst, disputes the whole story, citing Harry Hopkins to the effect that Roosevelt actually made it up, and that when de Gaulle heard it, it increased his animosity. See Milton Viorst, *Hostile Allies: FDR and de Gaulle* (New York: Macmillan, 1965), 146–47. Hull, as his *Memoirs* show, certainly believed it.
15. Claude Hettier de Boislambert, *Les Fers de l'espoir* (Paris: Plon, 1978), 383.
16. See Gun, *Les Secrets*, 338, who also says that Roosevelt rejected three other possibilities: Jean Monnet, General Catroux, and one whom Hull favored, Roger

Cambon, a French diplomat who had resigned at the time of the French armistice in June 1940 to remain in London as a private citizen.

17. According to FDR adviser Samuel Rosenman, quoted in Arthur Layton Funk, *Charles de Gaulle: The Crucial Years, 1943–1944* (Norman: University of Oklahoma Press, 1959), 83.

18. Kersaudy, *De Gaulle et Churchill,* 269.

19. Boislambert, *Les Fers de l'espoir,* 386.

20. François Coulet, "Indépendance et Libération, 1940–1945," *Espoir,* no. 27 (June 1979): 20.

21. See Jean Monnet, *Mémoires* (Paris: Fayard, 1976), 222–24.

22. *FRUS 1943,* vol. 2 (France), 74.

23. Telegram, March 24, 1943, F/1a/3715, Archives nationales, Paris.

24. Charles de Gaulle, *Mémoires de guerre,* 3 vols. (Paris: Plon, 1956), 2:381–85.

25. *FRUS 1942,* vol. 2 (France), 541–42.

26. Introduction to "Lettre du Général de Gaulle à Franklin Roosevelt, le 26 Octobre, 1942," *Espoir,* no. 19 (June 1999): 57.

27. *FRUS 1942,* vol. 2 (France), 547.

28. Crémieux-Brilhac, *La France Libre,* 578–80; Funk, *Charles de Gaulle,* 45–46.

29. See Colonel Passy, *Mémoires du chef des services secrets de la France Libre* (Paris: Odile Jacob, 2000), passim; and Guy Perrier, *Le colonel Passy et les services secrets de la France Libre* (Paris: Hachette, 1999), passim. When the OSS leader "Wild Bill" Donovan brought Passy to Washington in 1944 to be decorated (he had already been decorated by the British, the Dutch, the Norwegians, and the Belgians), the State Department, Justice Department, and FBI director J. Edgar Hoover intervened to prevent it. Hoover called him "De Gaulle's Himmler."

30. See William D. Leahy, *I Was There* (New York: McGraw-Hill, 1950), 146, who remarks that since the British had provided passage as far as Trinidad for the Gaullist official, "the British government seemed at this time determined to exploit de Gaulle at our expense."

31. Quoted in Julian G. Hurstfield, *America and the French Nation* (Chapel Hill: University of North Carolina Press, 1986), 194.

32. Anthony Eden, *The Reckoning: The Memoirs of Anthony Eden* (Boston: Houghton Mifflin, 1965), 448–49. Kersaudy, *De Gaulle et Churchill,* 283, reports all the reasoning and also notes that Churchill passes over the incident very briefly in his memoirs.

33. See, for example, *FRUS 1943,* vol. 2 (France), 60, 61–63.

34. For details, see Crémieux-Brilhac, *La France Libre,* chap. 17, "Le gaullisme politique," 499.

35. Quoted ibid., 553, 805.

36. Folder OSS, Secret 22/4/43, F/1a/3729, Archives nationales, Paris; emphasis added. I have not seen this memorandum, which directly contradicts Leahy, Hull, and Roosevelt, cited anywhere. Donovan himself, later, was less positive in talking to the president about de Gaulle.

37. De Gaulle, *Mémoires,* 2:101. For a succinct account of the enormous difficulties in bringing together the resistance groups, see Duroselle, *Politique étrangère de la France,* chap. 15; and Crémieux-Brilhac, *La France Libre,* chap. 22.

38. *FRUS 1943,* vol. 2 (France), 111–12; emphasis added.

39. Funk, *Charles de Gaulle,* 121; Crémieux-Brilhac, *La France Libre,* passim.

40. De Gaulle, *Mémoires,* 2:446.

41. Cited in François Charles-Roux, "Bataille pour des principes," *Espoir,* no. 27 (June 1979): 13.

42. One problem was that de Gaulle's forces were supplied with British uniforms and equipment, while those of Giraud had been armed with American equipment. It was a relatively minor but complicated issue with which to deal.

43. On the negotiations, see, among others, Macmillan, *The Blast of War,* 327.

44. Eden, *The Reckoning,* 450; Macmillan, *The Blast of War,* 328.

45. The documents establishing the committee are reproduced in de Gaulle, *Mémoires,* 2:488–90.

46. Don Cook, *De Gaulle: A Biography* (New York: G. B. Putnam's, 1983), 188.

47. Funk, *Charles de Gaulle,* 148.

48. Macmillan, *The Blast of War,* 356.

49. See Funk, *Charles de Gaulle,* 148–49; and on the whole question, Macmillan, *The Blast of War,* 359–61.

50. Macmillan, *The Blast of War,* 357.

51. See Hurstfield, *America and the French Nation,* 192–94.

52. FDR to Glassford, May 17, 1943, in *FRUS 1943,* vol. 2 (France), 118.

53. See memos in *FRUS 1943,* vol. 2 (France), 192.

54. Eden, *The Reckoning,* 457.

55. Quoted in Funk, *Charles de Gaulle,* 162.

56. Macmillan, *The Blast of War,* 361.

57. Monnet, *Mémoires,* 241.

58. Macmillan, *The Blast of War,* 326.

59. *FRUS 1943,* vol. 2 (France), 111–13 May 13 and May 18). Cordell Hull's *Memoirs* are riddled with references to "vicious" or "poisonous" Gaullist propaganda.

60. Funk, *Charles de Gaulle,* 184–91.

61. Macmillan, *The Blast of War,* 346.

62. Harry Coles and Albert Weinberg, *Civil Affairs: Soldiers Become Governors,* U.S. Army in World War II (Special Series) (Washington, D.C.: Office of the Chief of Military History, Department of the Army, 1964), 144.

63. F/1a/3729, Archives nationales, Paris.

64. *FRUS 1943,* vol. 2 (France), 67–70.

65. The report, available at the Hoover Institute, is cited in Richard Vinen, *The Unfree French: Life under the Occupation* (London: Allen Lane, 2006), 208.

66. Crémieux-Brilhac, *La France Libre,* 603.

67. André Kaspi, *La Libération de la France* (Paris: Perrin, 2004), 137.

68. F/1a/3815, Archives nationales, Paris.

69. François Charles-Roux, "Bataille pour des principes," *Espoir,* no. 27 (June 1979): 14.

70. For details, see Macmillan, *The Blast of War,* 439–43. Roosevelt's telegram is on page 441.

71. Harold Macmillan's account of the complexity of the negotiations for the Italian surrender explains much about the lack of coordination with the CFLN. See ibid., chap. 15.

72. Quoted in Anthony Cave-Brown, *The Last Hero: Wild Bill Donovan* (New York: Vintage, 1982), 471.

73. Coulet, "Indépendance et Libération, 1940–1945," 20.

74. Quoted in Crémieux-Brilhac, *La France Libre,* 891.

75. Cook, *De Gaulle,* 188.

76. Monnet, *Mémoires,* 240.

77. For an analysis of why there was so much dissension in the newly constituted body, see René Massigli, *Une Comédie des erreurs, 1943–1956* (Paris: Plon, 1978), 42–43.

78. De Gaulle, *Mémoires,* 2:212.

79. Viorst, *Hostile Allies,* 182.

80. Walter Lippmann, "Today and Tomorrow," *New York Herald Tribune,* November 11, 1943.

81. Macmillan, *The Blast of War,* 410.

82. Quoted in Hull, *Memoirs,* 1245.

83. Quoted ibid., 1245.

84. Crémieux-Brillac, *La France Libre,* 1025.

4. Allied Preparations for Civil Affairs in France

1. Article 43, section 3, of the Annex to the Hague Convention of 1907, in *Treaties and Other International Agreements of the Unites States of America, 1776–1949,* vol. 1, *Multilateral, 1776–1917,* Department of State Publication 8407 (Washington, D.C.: U.S. Government Printing Office, 1968).

2. Harry Coles and Albert Weinberg, *U.S. Army in World War II,* Special Series, *Civil Affairs: Soldiers Become Governors* (Washington, D.C.: Office of the Chief of Military History, Department of the Army, 1964), 6–7.

3. Ibid., chap. 1; see also Earle F. Ziemke, "Civil Affairs Reaches 30," *Military Affairs* 36, no. 4 (December 1972): 130–33.

4. Sir Frederick Morgan, *Overture to Overlord* (Garden City, N.Y.: Doubleday & Co., 1950), 227.

5. Ibid., 235. De Gaulle's aide Hettier de Boislambert considered Morgan a friend who played an important role in helping France avoid AMGOT. See Claude Hettier de Boislambert, *Les Fers de l'espoir* (Paris: Plon, 1978), 135.

6. On all this, see Morgan, *Overture to Overlord,* 235–36; and the introduction to Coles and Weinberg, *Civil Affairs,* passim.

7. F. S. V. Donnison, *History of the Second World War*, U.K. Military Series, *Civil Affairs and Military Government: Central Organization and Planning* (London: Her Majesty's Stationery Office, 1966), 296–98. Among other matters, the need for local currency that developed in the liberated Italian colonial territories prompted planners to make arrangements for the future printing of such currencies—which would raise a terrific row with the French in 1944. See chapter 6.

8. For details on all of these, see F. S. V. Donnison, *History of the Second World War*, U.K. Military Series, *Civil Affairs and Military Government: Northwest Europe* (London: Her Majesty's Stationery Office, 1961), 32–45.

9. For all this and subsequent problems, see Coles and Weinberg, *Civil Affairs*, 6–13.

10. Ibid., 15.

11. Ziemke, "Civil Affairs," 132.

12. Donnison, *Northwest Europe*, 28.

13. Coles and Weinberg, *Civil Affairs*, 95.

14. Ziemke, "Civil Affairs," 133.

15. Coles and Weinberg, *Civil Affairs*, 197.

16. Ibid., 188.

17. Ibid., 158.

18. Ibid., 306–13, 320.

19. Ibid., 73–78.

20. Ibid., 108–13.

21. Donnison, *Northwest Europe*, 34.

22. Ibid., 42.

23. Coles and Weinberg, *Civil Affairs*, 677. Hettier de Boislambert, in his memoirs, refers to Eisenhower's overcoming "the obstacles created by the ill will of Holmes and his staff" (*Les Fers de l'espoir*, 433).

24. Indicative of the problems is that when a decision was reached to set up a Combined Civil Affairs Committee, it took arduous negotiations to determine whether it would be located in London—near the prospective invasion and probably subject to greater British influence at a time when there were different conceptions about what was to be done and what the Allied interests were—or in Washington, near the Combined Chiefs of Staff, and in the country from which most of the resources would come. It all ended, as is so often the case, in a compromise: the committee would be set up in Washington but with a subsidiary committee in London. Coles and Weinberg, *Civil Affairs*, 114–19.

25. Donnison, *Northwest Europe*, 26–27; see also Morgan, *Overture to Overlord*, 229.

26. F/1a/3836, folder 3, Archives nationales, Paris.

27. A copy of one of these guidebooks is in the Archives nationales. It was not just the French who amused themselves at the expense of the handbooks. The English authors of *Paris after the Liberation* described the Paris handbook, inaccurately,

as essentially a guide to Parisian brothels. Antony Beever and Artemis Cooper, *Paris after the Liberation: 1944–1949* (London: Penguin Books, 1995), 140.

28. One such author, Charles Louis Foulon, makes a major error to support his argument of a "concrete menace." He writes that according to the "General Handbook," during the liberation, men of Vichy were not to be used at the national level, but at the local level anyone could be used—a point directly contradicted in American directives that excluded the use of collaborators. Charles-Louis Foulon, *Le Pouvoir en province à la libération* (Paris: Armand Colin, 1975), 32.

29. Donnison, *Northwest Europe*, 303.

30. Press clipping from *Times,* F/1a/ 3836, Archives nationales, Paris.

31. Coles and Weinberg, *Civil Affairs*, 660–62.

32. For the complete text, see ibid., 662, but significantly it is also in F/1a/ 3836, no. 121, Archives nationales, Paris, and summarized in Cordell Hull, *The Memoirs of Cordell Hull* (New York: Macmillan, 1948), 1244.

33. Anthony Eden, *The Reckoning: The Memoirs of Anthony Eden* (Boston: Houghton Mifflin, 1965), 520.

34. Henry L. Stimson and McGeorge Bundy, *On Active Service in Peace and War* (New York: Harper and Brothers, 1947), 547–49. Stimson was angered by de Gaulle's stance on the American-issued currency, but he returned to the position he had reluctantly reached earlier: "America cannot supervise the elections of a great country like France." De Gaulle and his party "are apparently the only available representatives of the French people at the present time."

35. The exchanges between the English and the Americans, and between Cordell Hull and the president, are all in Coles and Weinberg, *Civil Affairs*, 661–65.

36. Macmillan, *The Blast of War* (London: Macmillan, 1967), 415.

37. Coles and Weinberg, *Civil Affairs,* 144.

38. Jean-Louis Crémieux-Brilhac, *La France Libre* (Paris: Gallimard, 2001), 974–76; Charles de Gaulle, *Mémoires de guerre*, 3 vols. (Paris: Plon, 1956), 2:213–14; Stephen Ambrose, *Eisenhower: Soldier and President* (New York: Simon & Schuster, 1990), 121.

39. Coles and Weinberg, *Civil Affairs*, 665.

40. *FRUS 1944*, vol. 3 (France), 649–50.

41. Hervé Alphand, *L'Étonnement d'être* (Paris: Fayard, 1977), 174.

42. *FRUS 1944,* vol. 3 (France), 683.

43. Crémieux-Brilhac, *La France Libre*, 1029–31.

44. F/1a/3836, Archives nationales, Paris.

45. F/1a/3815, Archives nationales, Paris.

46. There were numerous separate sections to deal with such matters as police, justice, food and agriculture, public works, and so on. F/1a/3836, Archives nationales, Paris.

47. F/1a/3836, folder 112, Archives nationales, Paris.

48. F/1a/3836, folder 3, Archives nationales, Paris.

49. October 12, 1943, report, reprinted in Boislambert, *Les Fers de l'espoir*, 419.

50. F/1a/3840, Archives nationales, Paris, which contains his memo, Lee's report to his superiors, and undated memos registering the changes to paragraphs 19, 26, 39, and 46. See also Foulon, *Le Pouvoir en province*, 68.

51. Boislambert, *Les Fers de l'espoir,* 430.

52. Ibid., 425–26.

53. It may be noted that Hull had seen de Gaulle in Algiers on his way to the Moscow conference in October 1943. De Gaulle, he wrote, "was more friendly than I thought would be the case." Hull, *Memoirs,* 1275.

54. Ibid., 1429.

55. De Gaulle, *Mémoires,* 2:631.

56. F/1a/3840 and 3815, Archives nationales, Paris.

57. *FRUS 1944,* vol. 3 (France), 681.

58. Hull, *Memoirs,* 1430.

5. *French Preparations for Liberation*

1. Both quoted in Charles-Louis Foulon, *Le Pouvoir en province à la libération* (Paris: Armand Colin, 1975), 43. On the earlier period, see Guy Perrier, *Le Colonel Passy et les services secrets de la France Libre* (Paris: Hachette, 1999), chap. 8.

2. For a balanced discussion of all of these, see Jean-Louis Crémieux-Brilhac, *La France Libre* (Paris: Gallimard, 2001), chap. 17, "Le Gaullisme Politique."

3. See Perrier, *Le Colonel Passy,* chap. 15. One specific instance is recounted in Guy Penaud, *Histoire de la résistance en Périgord* (Périgeux: Pierre Fanlac, 1985), 283–84.

4. Foulon, *Le Pouvoir en province,* 63.

5. Quoted ibid., 71.

6. "Liberation and the Seizure of Power" (undated report, spring 1943), quoted ibid., 49.

7. Manuel Baudot, *Libération de la Normandie* (Paris: Hachette, 1974), 216.

8. Moulin's legendary status may be explained in part by the fact that he had managed to get seventeen different representatives of resistance movements, political parties, and trade unions together in one place—Paris—at one time, all of whom were either wanted by or being tracked by the Gestapo.

9. See the lengthy discussion on this matter in Crémieux-Brilhac, *La France Libre,* 540.

10. See Arthur Layton Funk, *Charles de Gaulle: The Crucial Years, 1943–1944* (Norman: University of Oklahoma Press, 1959), 191; and Crémieux-Brilhac, *La France Libre,* 900.

11. Crémieux-Brilhac, *La France Libre,* 907, 909.

12. Saint-John Perse (Alexis Saint-Léger), *Oeuvres complètes* (Paris: Gallimard, 1972), 619–27.

13. Crémieux-Brilhac, *La France Libre,* 910–11.

14. *FRUS 1944*, vol. 4 (France), 689–90, 700.

15. Ibid., 73.

16. Foulon, *Le Pouvoir en province*, 64–65.

17. Ibid., 64. Jean Moulin was replaced by Georges Bidault as head of the CNR.

18. F. S. V. Donnison, *Civil Affairs and Military Government: Northwest Europe* (London: Her Majesty's Stationery Office, 1961), 80–81.

19. Foulon, *Le Pouvoir en province*, 48 and passim.

20. Within the Vichy regime there was always a conflict between the conservative idealists, who saw creation of the regions as a return to the more decentralized, genuine France of the ancien régime, and the fact that regional prefects, in the end, were mere transmission belts for commands from the authoritarian Vichy government.

21. Foulon, *Le Pouvoir en province*, 98.

22. Quoted ibid., 89.

23. F/1a/ 3840, Archives nationales, Paris.

24. Claude Hettier de Boislambert, *Les Fers de l'espoir* (Paris: Plon, 1978), 415.

25. F/1a/3836, Archives nationales, Paris.

26. F/1a/3840, Archives nationales, Paris.

27. For details, see the undated memo "Protection du patrimoine culturel français" F/1a/3840, Archives nationales, Paris.

28. On all these matters, see reports by Boislambert, F/1a/3836, Archives nationales, Paris.

29. F/1a/3840, Archives nationales, Paris.

30. De Gaulle, *Mémoires*, 2:636.

6. D-Day

1. André Kaspi, *La Libération de la France: Juin 1944–janvier 1946* (Paris: Perrin, 2004), 43. Other sources give somewhat different but equally formidable numbers.

2. Sir Frederick Morgan, *Overture to Overlord* (Garden City, N.Y.: Doubleday & Co., 1950), 279.

3. François Kersaudy, *De Gaulle et Churchill* (Paris: Perrin, 2003), 339.

4. Harry Coles and Albert Weinberg, *U.S. Army in World War II*, Special Series, *Civil Affairs: Soldiers Become Governors* (Washington, D.C.: Office of the Chief of Military History, Department of the Army, 1964), 665.

5. Ibid., 665–66.

6. Ibid., 667.

7. Jean-Louis Crémieux-Brilhac, *La France Libre* (Paris: Gallimard, 2001), 1227.

8. Duff Cooper, *Old Men Forget* (London: Rupert Hart-Davis, 1953), 324.

9. All quotations from the memorandum are from Coles and Weinberg, *Civil Affairs*, 667–68; emphasis added.

10. F. S. V. Donnison, *Civil Affairs and Military Government: Northwest Europe* (London: Her Majesty's Stationery Office, 1961), 50–51.

11. Cordell Hull, *The Memoirs of Cordell Hull* (New York: Macmillan, 1948), 1430.

12. All of the quotes that follow are found in press clippings in 72/AJ/609, Archives nationales, Paris.

13. Hervé Alphand, *L'Étonnement d'être* (Paris: Fayard, 1977), 161.

14. Hull, *Memoirs*, 1431.

15. Kersaudy, *De Gaulle et Churchill*, 339.

16. Coles and Weinberg, *Civil Affairs*, 669.

17. Protestant Pastor Marc Boegner wrote of opinion turning against the Americans, of the "hideous human and material consequences of the massive bombardments against France," adding, "Military efficacy does not always seem to justify such massacres." *Carnets du Pasteur Boegner, 1940–1945* (Paris: Fayard, 1992), 238, 260.

18. Coles and Weinberg, *Civil Affairs*, 669.

19. Charles de Gaulle, *Mémoires de guerre*, 3 vols. (Paris: Plon, 1956), 2:245.

20. Julian G. Hurstfield, *America and the French Nation* (Chapel Hill: University of North Carolina Press, 1986), 209.

21. Harold Nicolson, *The War Years: Diaries and Letters, 1939–45*, 2 vols. (New York: Atheneum, 1967), 2:373.

22. Press clippings in 72/AJ/609, Archives nationales, Paris.

23. *FRUS 1944*, vol. 3 (France), 694.

24. Breckinridge Long, *The War Diaries of Breckinridge Long* (Lincoln: University of Nebraska Press, 1966), 354.

25. Earlier, in October 1943, Laroque in London had asked Algiers why it had made no decision to print French money for use by Allied troops, as the Belgian and Dutch governments had done. Civil affairs instructors at Wimbledon wondered why the French authorities hadn't done the same thing. F/1a/3836, Archives nationales,Paris. The answer was the lack of a civil affairs agreement. *FRUS 1944*, vol. 3 (France), 702.

26. Cooper, *Old Men Forget*, 329.

27. On all the maneuvers, see telegrams recounting them in *FRUS 1944*, vol. 3 (France), 692–95.

28. Kersaudy, *De Gaulle et Churchill*, 353.

29. For the account that follows, see ibid, 360.

30. De Gaulle, *Mémoires*, 2:226.

31. Milton Viorst, *Hostile Allies: FDR and de Gaulle* (New York: Macmillan, 1965), 201.

32. Cooper, *Old Men Forget*, 330.

33. See Crémieux-Brilhac, *La France Libre*, 1225, who quotes the original draft from the U.S. National Archives, Washington, D.C.

34. On the whole incident, see Kersaudy, *De Gaulle et Churchill*, 360; Cooper, *Old Men Forget*, 330; Anthony Eden, *The Reckoning: The Memoirs of Anthony Eden* (Boston: Houghton Mifflin, 1965), 526.

35. Nicolson, *The War Years*, 2:385. Nicolson thinks that Churchill was highly moved by the whole occasion and that de Gaulle's recalcitrance was unfortunate.

36. Arthur Bryant, *The Turn of the Tide* (Garden City, N.Y.: Doubleday), 206.

37. Cooper, *Old Men Forget*, 332; Claude Hettier de Boislambert, *Les Fers de l'espoir* (Paris: Plon, 1978), 436–37.

38. Cooper, *Old Men Forget*, 332; Eden, *The Reckoning*, 529.

39. Jean Planchais, "La nuit la plus longue," introduction to Pierre Viénot's account, published thirty years later by his widow in *Le Monde*, June 6, 1974, 1. The account that follows is drawn largely from this source.

40. Crémieux-Brilhac, *La France Libre*, 1228.

41. Quoted in Kersaudy, *De Gaulle et Churchill*, 362.

42. Cooper, *Old Men Forget*, 331.

43. From Eisenhower's papers, quoted in Hurstfield, *America and the French Nation*, 213.

44. Boislambert, *Les Fers de l'espoir*, 437–39.

45. F. S. V. Donnison, *History of the Second World War*, UK Military Series, *Civil Affairs and Military Government: Central Organization and Planning* (London: Her Majesty's Stationery Office, 1966), 69.

46. Quoted in Crémieux-Brilhac, *La France Libre*, 1231.

47. Kaspi, *La Libération de la France*, 60–62.

48. See telegram to Queuille and Massigli, June 9, 1945, in de Gaulle, *Mémoires*, 2:642.

49. Nicolson, *The War Years*, 2:379.

50. Kersaudy, *De Gaulle et Churchill*, 371.

51. Boislambert, *Les Fers de l'espoir*, 444.

52. François Coulet, *Vertu des temps difficiles* (Paris: Plon, 1967), 230.

53. See as an example a report by the British Intelligence Corps cited in Kersaudy, *De Gaulle et Churchill*, 372; and a Second Army report in Dennison, *Central Organization and Planning*, 79.

54. Kersaudy, *De Gaulle et Churchill*, 373.

55. Eden, *The Reckoning*, 531.

56. Viorst, *Hostile Allies*, 206.

57. F/1a/4005, folders 79 and 83, Archives nationales, Paris.

58. Pierre Laroque, the French official who had dealt with civil affairs officers in England and accompanied Coulet, "practiced a policy of tacit accords which the Americans tolerated," writes Foulon. As Laroque later told him, "the military, fundamentally, wanted just that." Charles-Louis Foulon, *Le Pouvoir en province à la libération* (Paris: Armand Colin, 1975), 103.

59. François Coulet, "Indépendance et Libération, 1940–1945," *Espoir*, no. 27 (June 1975): 19–28.

60. François Coulet to General Koenig, F/1a/4007, Archives nationales, Paris.

61. Coulet, *Vertu des temps difficiles*, 247–48.

62. François Coulet, reports, F/1a/4005 Archives nationales, Paris.

63. Coulet, *Vertu des temps difficiles*, 247–48.

7. After D-Day

1. Henry L. Stimson and McGeorge Bundy, *On Active Service in Peace and War* (New York: Harper and Brothers, 1947), 550–51.

2. "President Favors Delay on Algiers: Says Too Little Area Is Free to Consider the de Gaullist Appointees at Present," *New York Times*, June 24, 1944.

3. F/1a/4005, no. 78, Archives nationales, Paris.

4. Quoted in J. R. Tournoux, *Pétain et de Gaulle* (Paris: Plon, 1964), 319. See also the detailed undocumented accounts in Pierre Queille, *Histoire diplomatique de Vichy* (Paris: Albatros, 1976), chap. 7.

5. On the Dungler affair, see R. Harris Smith, *OSS: The Secret History of America's First Central Intelligence Agency* (Berkeley: University of California Press, 1972), 181.

6. See Queille, *Histoire diplomatique de Vichy*, 309.

7. Jean Paul Cointet, *Pierre Laval* (Paris: Fayard, 1993), 440, quoting from notes made by Laval's daughter, Josée de Chambrun.

8. Ibid., 472.

9. Queille, *Histoire diplomatique de Vichy*, 316.

10. Jean-Paul Cointet, *Histoire de Vichy* (Paris: Perrin, 2003), 317.

11. General Charles Brécard, Grand Chancellor of the Legion of Honor, quoted in Pierre Bourget, *Paris, Year 44* (Paris: Plon, 1984), 52–53.

12. Admiral Gabriel Auphan and Jacques Mordal, *La Marine française dans la seconde guerre mondiale* (Paris: France Empire, 1976), 592–94.

13. Georges Boris to André Phillip, F/1a/3715, Archives nationales, Paris.

14. F/1a/3715, Archives nationales, Paris.

15. On all these moves, see François Piétri, *Mes Années d'Espagne* (Paris: Plon, 1954), passim; and telegrams, 1943–44, F/1a/3816, Archives nationales, Paris.

16. CFLN telegram, April 14, 1944, F/1a/3816, Archives nationales, Paris.

17. Cointet, *Pierre Laval*, 484–85.

18. Onlookers wrote that, with Laval's world collapsing around him, at meals together the two old men reminisced about their better days of influence in peacetime during the Third Republic in the 1920s and 1930s.

19. Herriot, it may be noted, declared that he had come to Paris at Laval's request because while he could understand Laval, an old parliamentarian, he believed that Pétain was an enemy of the republic. "I have no more confidence in him than I have in de Gaulle," he remarked; "they are both ambitious, and that's the reason I came." Cointet, *Laval*, 497.

20. Charles-Louis Foulon, "Les États-Unis et la France Combattante," *Espoir*, no. 26 (March 1979): 96 (quoting a notice from the CNR, n.d.). The Algiers press conference statement is found in 72/A1/609, Archives nationales, Paris.

21. On his experiences both in and outside Bayeux, recounted in the following paragraphs, see his several reports in F/1a/4005, Archives nationales, Paris.

22. See Claude Hettier de Boislambert, *Les Fers de l'espoir* (Paris: Plon, 1978), 447; and F. S. V. Donnison, *Civil Affairs and Military Government: Northwest Europe* (London: Her Majesty's Stationery Office, 1961), 80, for an example.

23. For a detailed personal account of a civil affairs officer's activities, see Major General John J. Maginnis, *Military Government Journal: Normandy to Berlin* (Amherst: University of Massachusetts Press, 1971), passim.

24. F/1a/1069, Archives nationales, Paris.

25. A mixed Allied commission presided over by the English Brigadier-General Robbins, and including Pierre Laroque and other French representatives, resolved these issues. See Marcel Bandat, *Libération de la Normandie* (Paris: Hachette, 1974) 219.

26. F. S. V. Donnison, *History of the Second World War*, U.K. Military Series, *Civil Affairs and Military Government: Central Organization and Planning* (London: Her Majesty's Stationery Office, 1966), 100–101.

27. F/1a/4005, no. 524, Archives nationales, Paris.

28. Jean-Louis Crémieux-Brilhac, *La France Libre* (Paris: Gallimard, 2001), 1141–42.

29. Stimson and Bundy, *On Active Service*, 550.

30. Eden, *The Reckoning*, 531.

31. On July 20 a worn-out Viénot, a badly wounded veteran of World War I, an escapee from Vichy's prisons, the artisan of these agreements, died of a heart attack. Decorated in the First World War, he was posthumously made a "Compagnon de la Libération."

32. For the text, see Charles-Louis Foulon, *Le Pouvoir en province à la libération* (Paris: Armand Colin, 1975), 111–15.

33. William D. Hassett, *Off the Record with F.D.R.: 1942–1945* (New Brunswick: Rutgers University Press, 1958), 257.

34. William D. Leahy, *I Was There* (New York: McGraw-Hill, 1950), 244.

35. De Gaulle, Mémoirs, 2, 238: Roosevelt is quoted in Julian G. Hurstfield, *America and the French Nation* (Chapel Hill: University of North Carolina Press, 1986), 215. See also Milton Viorst, *Hostile Allies: FDR and de Gaulle* (New York: Macmillan, 1965), 207; Duff Cooper, *Old Men Forget* (London: Rupert Hart-Davis, 1953), 334; Crémieux-Brilhac, *La France Libre*, 1245–48.

36. Stimson and Bundy, *On Active Service*, 552; Hassett, *Off the Record*, 261.

37. Crémieux-Brilhac, *La France Libre*, 1246.

38. Ibid., 1246.

39. 72/AJ/609, Archives nationales, Paris.

40. Quoted in Hurstfield, *America and the French Nation*, 219.

41. See Hubert Cole, *Laval* (New York: G. B. Putnam's Sons, 1963), 262, who writes that André Enfière, a friend of Herriot's, told Laval that Roosevelt would support a government headed by Herriot.

42. See Anthony Cave Brown, *The Last Hero: Wild Bill Donovan* (New York: Vintage, 1982), 319–40, and OSS memorandum, Donovan to Roosevelt, declassified 1973 (1–5).

43. Arthur Layton Funk, *Charles de Gaulle: The Crucial Years, 1943–1944* (Norman: University of Oklahoma Press, 1959), 265–66.

44. F/1a/72/A1/609, Archives nationales, Paris.

45. See Cole, *Laval*, 264, who also, along with other authors, details the last-minute maneuvers by Laval.

46. Cooper, *Old Men Forget*, 340.

47. Marc Boegner, *Carnets du Pasteur Boegner, 1940–1945* (Paris: Fayard, 1992), 379.

48. Cooper, *Old Men Forget*, 342.

49. Press clipping, 72/AJ/1893, Archives nationales, Paris.

50. Charles de Gaulle, *Mémoires de guerre*, vol. 2 (Paris: Plon, 1956), 290–91, 297.

51. Jean-Baptiste Duroselle, *Politique étrangère de la France: L'abîme, 1939–1944* (Paris: Imprimerie Nationale, 1986), 660.

52. De Gaulle, *Mémoires*, 2:303.

53. Cointet, *Pierre Laval*, 315.

54. Papiers d'Emmanuel d'Astier de la Vigerie, Archives nationales, Paris, passim.

55. F/1a/3815, Archives nationales, Paris; see also F/1a/3715.

56. Queuille, *Histoire diplomatique de Vichy*, 312.

57. Neal H. Petersen, ed., *From Hitler's Doorstep: The Wartime Intelligence Reports of Allen Dulles, 1942–45* (University Park: Pennsylvania State University Press, 1966), Document 4-17, 334.

58. Cointet, *Pierre Laval*, 491.

59. Annie Lacroix-Riz, "How to Manage the Peace: When America Wanted to Take Over France," *Monde Diplomatique* (May 2003): 1.

60. Fabrizio Calvi, *OSS: La Guerre secrète en France* (Paris: Hachette, 1990), 134. See also Petersen, *From Hitler's Doorstep*, 67, 69, 159; and Smith, *OSS*, 170, 180, who notes that the OSS officer in charge in Algiers, Henry Hyde, was, like his chief, Donovan, an anti-Gaullist who supported the Giraudists and around whom a number of them had rallied.

61. Wilson memo, November 10, 1944, in *FRUS 1943*, vol. 2 (France), 190. For Hull, see ibid.

62. De Gaulle, *Mémoires*, 2:565, in a long declaration to the Provisional Assembly on the future of France, March 18, 1944.

63. *FRUS 1944*, vol. 3 (France), 642.

64. "Destruction of Regime Pledged in Reply to de Gaulle" *Washington Post*, March 22, 1944, 3.

65. *FRUS 1944*, vol. 3 (France), 659; Cordell Hull, *The Memoirs of Cordell Hull* (New York: Macmillan, 1948), 1428.

66. Don Cook, *De Gaulle: A Biography* (New York: G. B. Putnam's, 1983), 237.

67. André Kaspi, *La Libération de la France: Juin 1944–janvier 1946* (Paris: Perrin, 2004), 125.

68. Harry Coles and Albert Weinberg, *U.S. Army in World War II*, Special Series, *Civil Affairs: Soldiers Become Governors* (Washington, D.C.: Office of the Chief of Military History, Department of the Army, 1964), 668.

69. See files in 72 AJ/1893, Archives nationals, Paris, which are full of press clippings on the matter.

70. For all these messages, see *FRUS 1944*, vol. 3 (France), 735–37.

71. On all these maneuvers, see Hurstfield, *America and the French Nation*, 220–21; and Hull, *Memoirs*, 735–39.

72. *FRUS 1944*, vol. 3 (France), 739.

73. All these exchanges as well as the Churchill-Roosevelt exchange are in *FRUS 1944*, vol. 3 (France), 741–47.

74. See Kaspi, *La Libération de la France*, chap. 14, passim.

Conclusion

1. André Gros, "Le Quai d'Orsay," *Espoir*, no. 92 (June 1993): 54, Claude Hettier de Boislambert, *Les Fers de l'espoir* (Paris: Plon, 1978), 425–26.

2. *FRUS 1942*, vol. 2 (France), 547.

3. F. S. V. Donnison, *Civil Affairs and Military Government: Northwest Europe* (London: Her Majesty's Stationery Office, 1961), 81. The American writer David Schoenbrun, in *The Three Lives of Charles de Gaulle* (London: H. Hamilton, 1966), 157, states that the fundamental flaw in Roosevelt's view was that de Gaulle had dictatorial ambitions, when in fact his sole consideration was "France."

4. Julian G. Hurstfield, *America and the French Nation* (Chapel Hill: University of North Carolina Press, 1986), 195.

5. F/1a/3836, Archives nationales, Paris.

6. Jean-Louis Crémieux-Brilhac, *La France Libre* (Paris: Gallimard, 2001), 48–49.

7. André Kaspi, *La Libération de la France: Juin 1944–Janvier 1946* (Paris: Perrin, 1995), 51, 52–53.

8. When Eisenhower became the first commander of NATO in October 1950 and subsequently suggested that NATO strategy might be to withdraw to Brittany and then counterattack, the French would have none of it: they could endure no more occupation and liberation. The line of defense had to be in Germany, and Eisenhower publicly accepted this.

Index

Aglion, Raoul, 30
Allied Control Commission for Italy: creation of, 97; Roosevelt and French participation in, 97
Alphand, Hervé, 20, 35, 148, 174; on Darlan deal, 63; on de Gaulle's nature, 48; on French refugees, 32; on Roosevelt negotiation with CFLN, 114
America First Committee, 14
AMGOT (Allied Military Government of Occupied Territories), 4–7, 92, 104, 107, 189, 191; de Gaulle's view of, 4, 150, 156, 158; envisioned for France, 102, 169; French certainty of, 96, 108, 110–11; French reassured about, 115–16, 135; and Italy, 105; persistence in postwar opinion, 199; view of recent historians, 196; why never established, 193–94
Anfa (Casablanca) meeting of Roosevelt, Churchill, de Gaulle, and Giraud, 70–75, 101; de Gaulle and invitation to, 73; and French future, 71–75; Giraud receives U.S. support, 72–73
ANVIL (Allied invasion of southern France), 138, 145, 177
Army Field Manuals on Military Government, 100
Arnold, General Henry "Hap," 13, 203n19
Atherton, Ray, 78
Atlee, Clement, 170

Aubrac, Raymond, 176
Auphan, Admiral Gabriel: on Allied security at Dakar, 41; and negotiation with de Gaulle and Allies, 166, 184
Auriol, Vincent, 126

Badoglio, General Pietro: forms new Italian government, 93, 164
Bellescize, Diane de, 5
Berle, Adolf, 27
Bevin, Ernest, 149
Bidault, Georges: and Allied ambassadors, 186; named head of CNR, 182
Biddle, Anthony, 11
Billotte, Colonel Pierre, 65
Blum, Leon, 81, 115
Boegner, Étienne, 27–28
Boegner, Marc (pastor), 27, 218n17; and liberation of Paris, 179
Bogomolov, Alexander (Russian ambassador), 54
Bohlen, Charles, 25
Boislambert, Claude Hettier de, 5, 39, 51, 118–20, 154, 169, 173, 194; and AMGOT, 5, 189; and Anfa, 74–75; and Dakar, 40–42; and Brigadier Lee on "Civil Affairs Handbook," 117, 195; and MMLA, 117, 134–35, 151
Boisson, General Pierre: and Dakar fiasco, 39–40; and Darlan, 62; Roosevelt support for, 87, 89, 91–92, 192; rejects de Gaulle, 18

Hague Peace Conference of 1907: conventions and rights in military zone, 116; on rights and duties of occupying power, 99

Halifax, Earl of (E. F. L. Wood): and Free French, 27–29, 55; and French defeat, 11–12

Hassett, William D., 174

Henry-Haye, Gaston (Vichy ambassador), 29–30

Herriot, Édouard, 182; and Laval, 167–68, 180; supports de Gaulle, 80–81

Hilldring, Major General John, 105

Himmler, SS General Heinrich, 168

Holmes, General Julius, 108; and Coulet in Normandy, 169, 214n23

Hopkins, Harry, 76

Howley, Colonel Frank, 169

Hull, Cordell (U.S. Secretary of State), 68, 71, 80, 82, 85, 92, 96; and "Darlan deal," 64, 66; on dealings with Vichy, 182; on de Gaulle, 28–29, 74, 89; and Dunn-Wright agreement, 111; on the French fleet, 21; and Giraud, 76–77; and Saint Pierre and Miquelon, 50–52; support for CFLN, 118, 120, 142, 185

Hunt, Colonel Irwin L., 99

Italy, 5, 38, 70; AMGOT in, 105–7; and ANVIL, 138; and Pétain maneuvers, 164; surrenders, 92–93

Japanese attack on Pearl Harbor, 49

Jeanneney, Jules: and Laval maneuvers, 168; support for de Gaulle, 81

Journal Officiel de la France Libre, 42

Juin, General Alphonse, 92

Kaspi, André, 184, 196

Kennedy, Joseph, 21

Kerillis, Henri de, 19; on French refugees, 31; views of de Gaulle, 33–34

King, Admiral Ernest J., 55

King George VI, 75

Knox, Frank (U.S. Secretary of the Navy), 29, 67

Koenig, General Marie-Pierre: and Bir Hakeim, 54; at liberation, 119, 138–40; relations with SHAEF, 145, 158

Labarthe, André, 20

Laborde, Admiral Jean de, 62

Lacroix-Riz, Annie, 141; and Clark-Darlan agreement, 64, 189–90; and U.S. "pledge" to Laval, 182

Larminat, General Edgard de, 84

Laroque, Pierre, 160, 194; on Allied intentions, 115–17; establishes SMEA in London, 115

Laval, Pierre, 30, 31, 128, 164–5; and D-Day proclamation, 155; on French support for de Gaulle, 25; maneuvers to forestall de Gaulle, 4, 7, 166–68, 176, 180–82, 220n19; and possible Roosevelt support for, 182, 184

Leahy, Admiral William D., 35, 79; ambassador to Vichy, 24–25; and assassination of Darlan, 67; on de Gaulle, 25–26, 57; and Pétain, 25, 53, 128, 174; on Pétain and French at liberation, 25, 145; on recognition of GPRF, 186

Lebrun, Albert, 74

Leclerc, General Phillipe François, 39, 145; arrives in France, 177; enters Paris, 178

Lee, Brigadier General S. Swinton: cooperates with Boislambert, 117–19, 195; and "French House" in U.K., 115. See also Boislambert, Claude Hettier de

Lemaigre-Dubreuil, Jacques, 77; and "Group of Five" 59; supports Giraud, 59, 72; on possible Roosevelt support for Pétain, 163

Lend-Lease, 55

Levant (Syria, Lebanon, Iraq), conflict over, 12, 44–48, 56, 207n17

Lewis, Brigadier General R. M. H., 160–61